Contents

Specification coverage

Some of the content in this book is relevant to A Level only, and this is flagged throughout the book using the following symbol: **A Level only**
The following table also identifies this coverage. The rest of the book is relevant to both AS and A Level.

Specification item	Chapter
Concurrent processing	2
Benefits and drawbacks of concurrent processing	2
Merge sort	5
Quicksort	5
Comparison of complexity	5
Suitability of algorithms/time and space	5
Big-O	5
Constant complexity	5
Linear complexity	5
Polynomial complexity	5
Exponential complexity	5
Logarithmic complexity	5
Dijkstra SPA	5
A*	5
Memory addressing modes	6
Object-oriented programming	6
Attributes	6
Methods	6
Classes	6
Objects	6
Inheritance	6
Polymorphism	6
Encapsulation	6
Lexical analysis	8
Syntax analysis	8
Code generation	8
Optimisation	8
Libraries	8
Linkers and loaders	8
Pipelining and GPUs	10
Floating point arithmetic	12
Bitwise manipulations and masks	12
Logical shift	12
Masking with AND, OR, NOT	12
Linked list	13
Add data to linked list	13
Trees	13
Binary search tree	13
Graphs	13
Graphs depth first traversal	13
Graphs breadth first traversal	13
Hash table	13
De Morgan	14

OCR
A LEVEL

COMPUTER SCIENCE

FOR A LEVEL

Includes AS Level

Windsor and Maidenhead

38060000001610

HODDER
EDUCATION

OCR
A LEVEL

George Rouse
Jason Pitt
Sean O'Byrne

COMPUTER SCIENCE

FOR A LEVEL

Includes AS Level

HODDER
EDUCATION
AN HACHETTE UK COMPANY

The Publishers would like to thank the following for permission to reproduce copyright material:

Photo credits see back of book

Every effort has been made to trace all copyright holders, but if any have been inadvertently overlooked the Publishers will be pleased to make the necessary arrangements at the first opportunity.

Although every effort has been made to ensure that website addresses are correct at time of going to press, Hodder Education cannot be held responsible for the content of any website mentioned in this book. It is sometimes possible to find a relocated web page by typing in the address of the home page for a website in the URL window of your browser.

Hachette UK's policy is to use papers that are natural, renewable and recyclable products and made from wood grown in sustainable forests. The logging and manufacturing processes are expected to conform to the environmental regulations of the country of origin.

Orders: please contact Bookpoint Ltd, 130 Milton Park, Abingdon, Oxon OX14 4SB.

Telephone: +44 (0)1235 827720. Fax: +44 (0)1235 400454. Lines are open 9.00a.m.–5.00p.m., Monday to Saturday, with a 24-hour message answering service. Visit our website at www.hoddereducation.co.uk.

First published in 2015 by

Hodder Education

An Hachette UK Company

338 Euston Road

London NW1 3BH

Impression number 10 9 8 7 6 5 4 3 2 1

Year   2019 2018 2017 2016 2015

Cover photo © jim – Fotolia

Illustrations by Aptara

Typeset in Bliss Light 10.75/13.5 by Aptara, Inc.

Printed in Italy

A catalogue record for this title is available from the British Library.

ISBN 978 1 471 83976 4

Specification item	Chapter
Distributive law	14
Associative law	14
Commutative law	14
Half adder	14
Full adder	14
D Type flip flop	14
Redundancy	15
Normalisation to 3NF	15
Referential integrity	15
ACID	15
Locking	15
Structured query language	15
Network hardware	16
Network security	16
Pagerank algorithm	17
Search engine ranking	17
Client side script	17
Server side script	17
Run-length encoding	17
Encryption	17
Use of hashing	17
Identify features of problem	19
Amenable to computer solution	19
Stakeholders	19
Research similar problems	19
Justify approaches	19
Describe features	19
Limitations	19
Requirements	19
Success criteria	19
Decompose	20
Structure of a solution	20
Algorithms	20
Usability features	20
Variables	20
Data structures	20
Test data development	20
Test data post development	20
Annotated evidence	21
Prototype	21
Test evidence from the iterative process	21
Remedial actions	21
Test evidence from post development	22
Robustness	22
Usability testing	22
Evaluation against success criteria	22
Evidence of usability features	22
Maintenance	22
Further development	22

Introduction to computing

If you are going to study a subject called 'computing' or 'computer science', it is probably a good idea if you start out with an idea about what is involved. You don't need all the detail, but it is best to have an overview so that what follows is not too unexpected. You want to be sure that you get into something that you will enjoy and be good at.

University courses

Already we have a problem. Courses in this area are often called 'computing' but they are sometimes called 'computer science' – and indeed many other things. Universities offer a wide range of courses in the general area of 'computing' and the number of names for these courses can be bewildering. One UK university, taken more or less at random, offers courses in:

- Big Data Analytics
- Computer Science
- Database Professional
- Games Software Development
- Business Information Systems
- Business and ICT
- Web and Cloud Computing
- Enterprise Systems

Another university offers:

- Artificial Intelligence
- Software Engineering

Question

Find out roughly what each of these courses covers.

This list could easily be expanded by looking at the prospectuses of several different universities, and also, don't forget that universities do not have a monopoly on computing learning and development. Some, if not most, of the exciting and innovative work is occurring in companies large and small, from Google and Amazon right through to small outfits developing embedded systems in Bristol or London. Much is also happening through the work of individuals, working alone or in worldwide virtual communities. Computing is one of the most democratic undertakings yet devised by mankind.

So why are there so many courses that are in some way related to 'computing'? And how are so many start-ups, as well as mega-corporations, making a living from computing? You won't see so many different manifestations of Law or Medicine or even English. The fact is that computing is, in human history terms, quite a young discipline. This means that its ramifications are still being explored and new uses for it are being developed all the time.

There has never been a more exciting time to be involved in computer-related activities. Computers continue to make big changes to the way we live, conduct our business and personal relationships and even the way we think. This means that there are lots of ways to earn a living from computing. In recent years, this truth has become widely appreciated and big changes are happening in computing education right now.

Until only a few years ago, computing was hardly studied at all in most UK schools and the same was true of many (but not all) other countries. Although schools have been offering simple courses in computer use since the 1980s, actually studying how to solve hard problems by developing and writing your own code has mostly been ignored. For various reasons, not least initiatives by the UK government, computing has now been made a compulsory part of every child's education in the UK. A few other countries have also taken that route. This has led to an increasing number of school students coming to realise that computing is a lot of fun as well as leading to lucrative careers. *The Sunday Times* reported on 5 October 2014 that new graduates of computer science from one of the top UK universities have the highest starting salaries of any degree holders. Universities are of course aware of this and have increased their offerings to capitalise on this increased awareness and demand.

What's computing all about?

We can make all sorts of subtle distinctions between the multitude of courses and subject headings, but a few overarching facts are in order at this point.

Key term

Algorithm A step-by-step procedure for performing a calculation.

Questions

1. If you are interested in making a living as a programmer, what course should you take at university?
2. Which programming languages are currently the most fashionable?
3. Does it matter which university you go to in order to learn computer science? If so, how do you choose?
4. To make a career in computing, does it even matter whether you *do* go to university?

Algorithms

Computing is an activity that involves using or creating **algorithms**. This is most usually but not necessarily carried out through the use of computers.

Clearly this definition misses out a lot of detail. Computing activities are often categorised in the following way:

- designing and building hardware
- designing and writing software
- managing information
- developing whole systems to manage information, help us communicate or simply to entertain us.

Commonly used headings for relevant activities include:

- computer engineering
- software engineering
- computer science
- information systems
- information technology.

A recent report into computer education in the UK also adds in 'digital literacy', although that is more concerned with the use of computers rather than the creation of something new.

At the heart of computing then, is the development and implementation of algorithms. We need to understand what an algorithm is right at the outset.

Careers in computing

Making a career in computing can be very intellectually rewarding, as well as lucrative. There are so many routes that your career path might take. So who makes a good computer scientist or practitioner? There are certain crucial personal characteristics that are likely to lead to a successful career. A successful computer professional:

- keeps up to date – computing is a fast-moving field
- understands the basics – learning new facts and techniques is easier if you have a grasp of what is at the back of it all
- is a good communicator – some programmers succeed in a team without developing their social skills, but they have to be very very good and need the support of others to communicate their ideas
- must be numerate but does not necessarily have to be a traditional 'mathematician' – in fact, being literate is often more important than having advanced maths skills; computers do most of the 'heavy lifting' in calculations, so devising an algorithm becomes more important than doing calculations yourself
- must be able to understand the business that is using a particular computer system – people buy systems and expertise for real-world reasons, which often means sustaining and growing a business; creative computer people need to be able to see opportunities and devise systems and programs to make use of them.

A little history

Example

Example

Suppose a farmer wants the shoemaker to make him some shoes. The farmer could pay the shoemaker with a sheep. This is fine if the shoemaker wants a sheep at that time but maybe he has enough sheep. He could exchange the sheep with the baker for some bread, but again it can be a pain carrying around a sheep in your pocket when you go out for a small sliced white, and who says how many loaves of bread a sheep is worth? So, humans invented money to get around all these problems.

Computing has existed in human history for millennia. When humans changed from hunter-gatherers to inventing trade and, most importantly, money, the need for complex calculations arose. The invention of money is particularly interesting because with money we have one of the earliest uses of an abstraction, and computers work mostly with abstractions.

And to this day, money really does make the world go round – in a figurative sense. We actually pay the shoemaker (see the example to the left) with something that doesn't really exist except in our minds. The shoemaker is fine with that because he knows that most people play by the same rules. Money works because we have learned to trust that debts will be repaid and we can exchange money for any number of goods and services. That is why it was such a big deal when the banking crisis hit a few years ago. People starting getting worried that debts might not be repaid, and that really could undermine civilisation. With the coming of money, it becomes important to keep records and to establish the relative worth of things. Money is an abstraction and it is an abstraction that made commerce and most of human progress possible. Computers are especially important in this story because they can work on things that are abstractions and the more we learn to formulate and deal with abstractions, the more value we can get from our computer systems.

Record-keeping devices

Various devices have been used down the centuries to assist with record keeping and calculations. An internet search will quickly reveal some of the main stages of development.

The Sumerians were a people who used the abacus from about 2400BC as a means to help them perform calculations.

The Antikythera mechanism dates from about 100BC and is thought to be an early mechanical means of calculating astronomical phenomena.

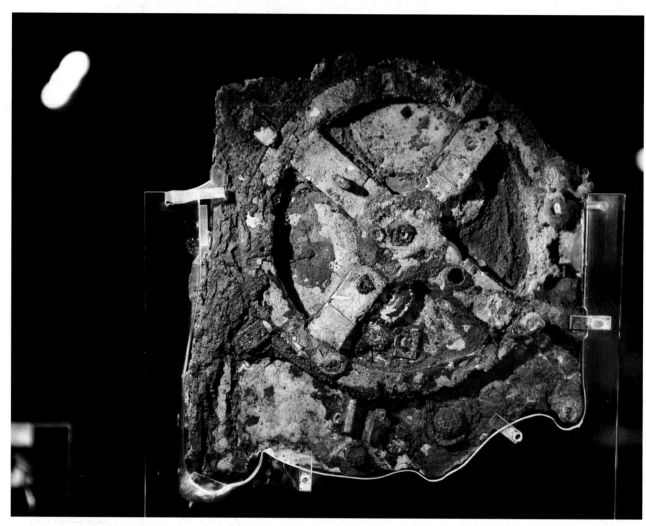

The Antikythera mechanism

Many other devices were invented to assist with calculations, including possibly some programmable machines in the medieval Muslim world. The notion of programmability is an important one in the history of computing and this aspect comes into its own in the inventions of Charles Babbage in the nineteenth century. He developed a mechanical device – the 'difference engine' – in order to mechanise the process of calculation and thereby reduce errors that occur when humans perform calculations.

The difference engine was designed to automate the production of mathematical and astronomical tables, thereby reducing the impact of human error. Babbage went on to design better multi-purpose machines, although they were never fully completed. They did, however, introduce the idea that a machine could be programmed to carry out different jobs. Ada Lovelace, the daughter of Lord Byron, did some work on this machine, devising an algorithm for it to carry out. Sometimes she is credited with being the first programmer on the strength of this.

Introduction to computing

Computing people

Alan Turing

Alan Turing was a mathematician who is now one of the most famous and revered figures in the history of computing, but that was not always so. Because of his work on decrypting enemy communications in the Second World War, his contributions were shrouded in official secrecy for many years.

He is particularly important in the history of computing because of a paper that he published in 1936: On Computable Numbers, With an Application to the Entscheidungsproblem. The Entscheidungsproblem (decision problem) is a challenge to produce an algorithm that can decide if a given statement of logic is provable. Turing proved that this is impossible, with the aid of a hypothetical computing machine that he described, now known as a Turing machine. None of course existed at the time. He showed that some things are not capable of computational solutions. His imagined machine was a remarkably prescient model and led to the subsequent development of real computers, starting with Colossus, several years later.

The difference engine

The Second World War and later

The big strides towards what we would recognise as modern computers occurred during the Second World War. It has now become a well-known story that thanks to the code-breaking efforts at Bletchley Park, notably making use of theoretical work by Alan Turing and electronic expertise from Tommy Flowers, an electronic machine was developed that could very quickly process encrypted data from enemy communications. This allowed the decoding of messages in a realistic time frame and did much to shorten the war. The machine in question was called Colossus and it was made from thousands of electronic valves that received data input from a paper tape.

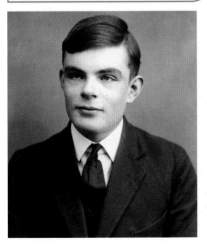

Alan Turing, Tommy Flowers and Colossus

Computing people

Tommy Flowers

Tommy Flowers (1905–98) is less known than other key figures from the Bletchley Park codebreakers of the Second World War but his contribution to the development of computers is immense. Born in London, he started his working life as an apprentice engineer, later joining the GPO. This was the General Post Office, which for many years was responsible not only for mail deliveries but also Britain's telephone system. His particular interest was electronic switching, which was needed to connect telephones automatically rather than to rely on telephone operators plugging cables into a switchboard. Brought in to Bletchley Park to help improve Turing's Bombe devices (these were mechanical machines that used brute-force techniques to break German coded messages), he realised that electronic switching using thermionic valves would be a faster way to process the messages. He built Colossus, which became the world's first programmable electronic computer and it was a fast machine, even by today's standards. This application of switching circuits was an important milestone in the development of all computing and electronic devices.

Although we can rightly credit Colossus as the first electronic computer, it was in fact a single-purpose machine. The first multi-purpose electronic computer came a little later in the US and was called ENIAC (Electronic Numerical Integrator And Computer).

The first multi-purpose electronic computer, ENIAC

ENIAC was received with great excitement because here was a machine that could perform different operations depending on the result of other operations. IF ... THEN had been born, at least in concept. Interestingly, the sort of problems that could be solved by these early programmable machines do not differ in essence from the ones computers solve today; it is just that we have devised many more ways to make use of these capabilities to apply to real-life situations.

ENIAC was developed in order to calculate artillery firing tables and was later used to investigate the feasibility of the hydrogen bomb, showing again how some of the most important and useful human developments have sprung from warfare.

Claude Shannon, working at the Bell Laboratories in New Jersey, developed the study of information theory that led to our realisation that any information at all can be digitised and reduced to binary bit patterns that can then be processed.

So by the 1950s, the usefulness of computers was becoming widely accepted and led to the development of commercial computers that make normal life easier, rather than only machines to help the military win wars and for academics to play with (although both of these remain true today). The first commercial computer in the UK was built for the Lyons Tea Company and was called LEO (Lyons Electronic Office). It was used for clerical problems such as scheduling the delivery of cakes to their tea shops. From hydrogen bombs to cakes – now that is real progress!

The first commercial computer in the UK, LEO

Computing people

Claude Elwood Shannon

Claude Elwood Shannon (1916–2001) was an American mathematician, electronic engineer and cryptographer known as 'the father of information theory'. He excelled in many different fields, to an extent unusual today. He studied both mathematics and electrical engineering at the University of Michigan and MIT, although he often showed more interest in inventing and making things than wrestling with pure mathematical problems.

He made machines that used strings of relays (switches) that represented AND and OR operations by being open or closed. He realised that complex problems could be solved using these relays by applying what was then an obscure branch of mathematics: Boolean algebra.

Perhaps his most significant achievement was his realisation that all information, words, numbers, images and anything else, can be encoded in 0s and 1s and transmitted along a telephone wire. This seems obvious to us today, but in 1948 when he published his paper *A Mathematical Theory of Communication*, it was revolutionary. He laid the foundations of information theory – a synthesis of mathematics, electrical engineering and computer science. This has fundamental importance in the development of all computer systems, having relevance in many fields, such as data compression, natural-language processing, cryptography, linguistics, pattern recognition and data analysis.

He had a wide variety of interests, such as playing the clarinet, juggling and chess. He was one of many talented people who worked at the Bell Laboratories in New Jersey.

Like many computing characters, he was a quirky figure, often seen riding his unicycle around the Bell Laboratories building, sometimes juggling at the same time. He invented what he called the ultimate machine, a featureless box with a switch. When the switch is flipped, a hand comes out and flips it off again: see www.youtube.com/watch?v=Z86V_ICUCD4.

Questions

1. Look up some of the computing history timelines online. Which stages do you think are the most significant?
2. What were the main motivations behind the development of each of Fortran, COBOL and ALGOL?

Programming languages were developing at the same time because it was becoming apparent that physically setting up every single processor step was not the most effective way to get programs developed. Other approaches were possible that could take much of the labour and error out of producing programs. High-level languages were developed that could be changed into machine code by compiler software. So we have computers helping to develop software for computers. This is still an exciting use of processing power.

The first compiler was developed in 1951–52 by Grace Hopper, which allowed users to control a computer with English-like words instead of machine instructions. Fortran followed soon after, and then COBOL and ALGOL.

Computer generations

The major milestones of computer hardware development are often referred to as the five generations of computers.

First generation

These are the first electronic devices that could only work on one problem at a time and had to be programmed in machine code. ENIAC is an example.

Second generation

This was the age of the transistor. This allowed circuits to be built using much smaller components and crucially using less power.

Assembly language was developed to replace raw machine code and the first high-level languages appeared.

A transistor

Third generation

In 1964, the first computers were built using integrated circuits. This was also the era when operating systems were developed and keyboards were used instead of punched cards to input data.

Fourth generation

This is where we are today – the era of microprocessors. It has been evolving into the age of networks, GUIs, the mouse and hand-held devices.

Fifth generation

This is where many people think we are heading next. This could be the era of natural-language processing and artificial intelligence. But the exciting thing is, we don't really know and any number of directions could still become apparent.

A microprocessor

Key points

- Computing encompasses many things
- There are huge numbers of branches of study
- Algorithms are at the heart of computing
- Computing can be a vibrant and well-paid career
- Important developments are happening in many places; both companies and individuals are driving much of the progress
- Computing has developed fast – mostly since the 1940s
- Computing has changed the way we look at life
- No one knows exactly where the developments will lead

Practice questions

1. What is an algorithm?
2. Why are abstractions important in computer science?
3. Discuss the importance of choosing a particular programming language in which to learn how to program.

Study hints

You need to decide why you chose to study Computer Science. This could be for a lot of reasons. Perhaps you think it will be a passport to a good course at university or a good career. Perhaps it is a 'filler' to make up your A/AS Level portfolio. These are perfectly good reasons but the reason most likely to lead to success is that, at some level, you find the subject interesting and you expect to have fun doing it. Computer Science really is interesting at so many levels. Maybe there is a lot of interest in it that you have not yet discovered.

Computer Science is, of course, challenging. At its heart, it requires you to solve problems. Not just mental puzzles like Sudoku or the Tower of Hanoi, but big human problems too. Computer Science is a special subject. It crosses subject boundaries like no other subject. It is a humanities subject as well as a science and a branch of mathematics. Behind the **algorithms** are the technology and also a fascinating story of human achievement. This has its heroes and stories, triumphs and blind alleys and failures. Looking at all these aspects gives the study of the subject depth and context, which makes it a lot easier to understand.

Don't make the mistake of looking for a checklist of things that you need to learn to ensure that you get a good grade. There certainly is such a list – in a way. It is called the *specification*. But, to do really well, you need to have what we call a 'secure' understanding of the material; that is, you need to look beyond the specification. This is really important. The ability to solve the algorithms and to recall the key facts is certainly required, but this will all make so much more sense and become fun to learn if you are able to fit it all into the bigger picture.

Read beyond the book. This book is intended to cover all the material that is required for the specification, but you really need to get more than one perspective on things; for example you may struggle with some of the algorithms. If so, go online and look at other examples and explanations. If one of them makes no sense to you, try another. Eventually, it will click. Don't give up at the first difficulty. Looking at a problem from all angles often produces an 'aha!' moment.

Write lots of code. For any algorithm or problem that you see in the book or that you encounter from your teacher or that simply occurs to you, try to code it up. If you labour to write some practical code to traverse a tree, for example, you will have learned the theory behind it very well indeed. You are lucky in doing Computer Science. Writing programs gives you 'instant gratification', which means that you will get immediate feedback on whether you are doing it right or not.

Try more than one programming language. At the very least, you should become conversant in basic assembly language, as provided with the Little Man Computer, plus a high-level language. If you can add in a second high-level language, even at a superficial level, this also helps a lot in broadening your understanding.

Do set up and interrogate a relational database of at least three linked tables. You would be surprised at how many students never do this and thereby rule out significant numbers of marks. You will gain a lot of background understanding from doing this. Try using SQL to manipulate and interrogate your database.

Go beyond the specification. Your brain is not a finite container where learning one fact displaces another. Making connections helps. If you find something quirky or amusing as you work through the course, by all means follow it up. It will stop you getting bogged down and you will remember what you were working on by association.

Take a look at brief biographies of some of the movers and shakers in the computing world. There are several scattered throughout the book. Many of them are quirky characters who said interesting or crazy things that help you connect more with the subject.

You will need to produce a practical programmed project as part of your assessment. Have that at the back of your mind from an early stage. You may get a good idea along the way for something new and original that will catch your imagination. Don't just write another game that probably will be like a thousand others. There is still a vast world of problems to solve or new takes on old problems.

Keep notes. Of course you will use a computer to do this! Organise them as you go so that it all builds into something that makes sense for you. Use the cloud for this. There is no longer any excuse for saying things like 'my file got corrupted' or 'I accidentally deleted it'.

And of course ... have fun!

Topic 1 Computational thinking

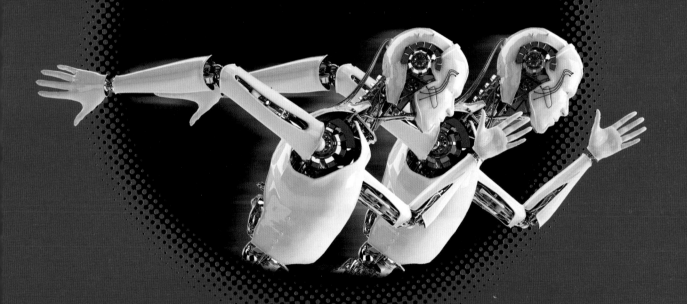

Chapter 1

Computational thinking

Introduction

The expression 'computational thinking' is talked about a lot in computing and educational circles these days. It is not a new concept; the term was first coined in 1996 by Seymour Papert.

Computing people

Seymour Papert

Seymour Papert is a computer scientist who, among other things, helped to develop Logo – a programming language that aimed to help students think 'computationally'.

Figure 1.1 Seymour Papert

Extra info

Logo is a programming language designed by Seymour Papert (among others), and is intended to help children learn programming as well as mathematical concepts. It is very easy to learn and its most well-known feature is *turtle graphics*, where a screen object called a 'turtle' is driven around the screen under programmatic or direct command. Logo is still useful today in demonstrating computational thinking topics such as abstraction and decomposition.

An implementation of turtle graphics is available for Python® and its commands are accessible once the 'turtle' library is loaded into the Python programming environment.

Here is a demonstration program that draws a succession of concentric circles.

```
# turtle graphics
import turtle
a, n = 1, 100
turtle.home()
newpos=0
while a < n:
    turtle.pendown()
    turtle.circle (a,360)
    a+=10
    turtle.penup()
    newpos=newpos-10
    turtle.sety(newpos)
turtle.mainloop()
```

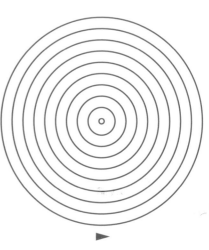

Figure 1.2 The output from the example program; note the turtle (the small triangle) in its finishing position

Computer systems are notoriously difficult to produce. Non-trivial systems soon become complex and, because of this, various methodologies and strategies have been developed to make development easier and to keep large projects under control (see Chapter 9).

The discipline of *software engineering* is concerned with this aspect of systems development and certain practices have become standard and have stood the test of time. New ideas continue to evolve to refine the process yet further.

As well as the development of systems, the greater use of computers has helped to change the way we think about things and understand the world and the universe. One good example is the realisation that we ourselves are the product of digital information in the form of our own DNA.

The realisation that the complexities of life and the world around us are explainable in terms of information systems and often very simple processes, has allowed us to look at the world and ourselves in a new and powerful way.

Understanding how things work in terms of natural information systems also allows us to produce new inventions based on the changed perspectives that computers bring us; for example neural networks borrow understanding from animal nervous systems in order to process large numbers of inputs and predict outcomes that are otherwise uncertain. Some success continues to result from research into artificial intelligence, again, using systems that mimic human behaviour.

In recent years, the nature of **computational thinking** has been developed and given much publicity and impetus by Jeannette Wing in the US.

> **Key term**
>
> **Computational thinking**
> A problem-solving approach that borrows techniques from computer science, notably abstraction, problem decomposition and the development of algorithms. Computational thinking is applied to a wide variety of problem domains and not just to the development of computer systems.

Computing people

Jeannette Wing

At the time of writing, Jeannette Wing is Corporate Vice President of Microsoft Research. In this role she oversees Microsoft's various research laboratories around the world.

Jeannette Wing has had a distinguished career. Prior to joining Microsoft, she worked at the University of Southern California and then Carnegie Mellon University in Pittsburgh, where she was President's Professor of Computer Science.

While at Carnegie Mellon, she devoted much energy to the promotion of computational thinking and how it is a powerful approach to solving a wide variety of problems, not necessarily involving computers. She sees it as a vital skill that should be taught to all children, as important as the 3Rs.

Carnegie Mellon still has a 'Center for Computational Thinking', where computational thinking applications are explored and new ways to apply it are devised.

Figure 1.3 Jeannette Wing

How computers help us think

The widespread use of computers has changed the way in which we solve problems. Here are some examples.

1. We can get the technology to do all the hard work for us. Problems that in the past involved just too much work or time can now be tackled extremely quickly; this means we have to formulate them in such a way as to harness the raw speed and power of a computer. We have to approach problems differently in order to get the best out of the computer's power.

2. Formulating a problem for computer solution in itself clarifies our understanding of the problem. We might not otherwise realise that a problem can be broken down into simpler parts.

3. Understanding how computers store and process data provides us with powerful analogies for understanding how the world works.

Some examples of computational thinking

We can start with something simple. Not that many years ago, anyone who was engaged in some form of creative writing would have to use a pen or maybe a typewriter. The writer of a factual book would need to make copious notes and keep them organised so that a coherent product could be made. Such writing necessarily involved numerous revisions, lots of crossing out and the throwing away of much paper, together with the endless labour of rewriting.

Of course we don't have to do that any more – we have word processors. But the thing is, not only have word processors liberated us from much drudgery, they have also liberated our minds. We are no longer afraid to commit ideas to paper or screen because we can amend what we say so easily. The creative process has been transformed by the technology. We think differently.

On a larger scale, the Human Genome Project used computer technology to process vast amounts of data and also lend insights into how our own biological information processing systems function.

Here are some more examples of how computational thinking can help us, as suggested by Jeannette Wing.

We can:

- look at a problem and assess how difficult it is
- use recursion to apply a simple solution repetitiously
- reformulate a problem into something familiar that we know how to solve
- model a problem so that we can create a program that can be run on a computer
- look at a proposed solution and assess it for elegance and efficiency
- build in processes to our solutions that limit damage and recover from errors
- scale our solutions to cope with bigger similar problems.

Example

Shotgun sequencing

Humans, and all life on Earth, are products of information contained in our nucleic acids – in most cases, this is DNA (deoxyribonucleic acid). This is a long molecule made from repeating units called nucleotides, of which there are only four different types. The sequence of these largely determines our characteristics – our similarities and differences, at least at a physical level.

Shotgun sequencing is a method of breaking up long sequences of DNA into small pieces. These segments can be analysed rapidly to determine the sequences of nucleotides. Computer processing is used to recognise where the short segments overlap and so can be used to determine the overall sequence of the whole molecule. This is much faster and easier to carry out than trying to read a single intact piece of DNA.

In this example, computer programs processed the vast amount of data involved, but also the project was made possible by our understanding that even complicated organs and whole bodies are basically constructed by recursively following a plan.

Question

Think of some other techniques from computer science that translate into real-world problem solving.

When looking at solving a problem with the help of computational thinking, we have to decide first what parts of the problem (if any) are best suited to a computer solution. This links back to the age-old question that predates modern computers: whether a particular problem is computable; that is, is there an **algorithm** that will always give the correct output for a valid input? It has been demonstrated that in some cases, this question is undecidable, so we often have to use our practical experience to make a judgement. We have to decide which parts of a problem are best suited to a human resolution. Computational thinking encourages us to decide what computers are best at and what humans are best at. Good solutions to messy real-world problems need to find good answers to this question.

Breaking down problems

Key term

Decomposition The breaking down of a problem into smaller parts that are easier to solve. The smaller parts can sometimes be solved recursively; that is, they can be run again and again until that part of the problem is solved.

One of the most powerful benefits of thinking in computational terms is that it encourages us not to be frightened of large and complex problems. Over the years, computer scientists and analysts have developed approaches that attempt to break down a large problem into its component parts. This is called **decomposition**. The aim is that the smaller parts are then easier to understand and solve.

This approach, popularised in the 1970s, was called 'top-down design'. Top-down design led to the widespread use of modular programming, where the additional benefits are that different parts of the overall finished program can be assigned to different programmers, lightening the load on each and also making the best use of their individual skills. It is also much easier to debug a program if it is constructed from smaller component parts rather than a big sprawling single entity.

Once an overall design has been decided upon, effectively a menu is produced that leads to the writing of the separate modules. This can be hierarchical, where each sub-problem leads to smaller components in a tree-like structure.

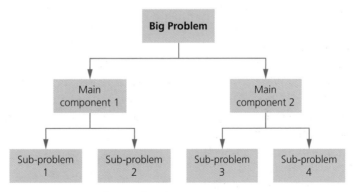

Figure 1.4 A tree hierarchical structure

A drawback of the top-down approach is that it assumes that the whole solution to the problem is knowable in advance. Increasingly, this is not the case, and plans and ideas change as a project develops. Nonetheless, as a starting point, it is useful if a problem can be split up even to some extent.

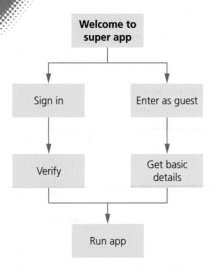

Figure 1.5 Decomposition with alternative pathways

Also, this hierarchical approach is less useful with many more modern applications. With the widespread adoption of event-driven programming, such a neat top-down structure is not always appropriate. However, it is a computational tool that still has its uses.

Decomposition does not have to be hierarchical. It can take into account parallel processes, where alternative paths are possible. It is still a help in breaking down the problem.

Decomposition can be applied at various levels in computing scenarios. As we have seen, we can break down a problem into different functional components that lead to modules or program procedures. We can also break a problem down into processes, data stores and data flows. This approach, again developed in the 1970s, leads to a data-flow diagram. The advantage of this approach is that the major components and activities in a system are laid out before any effort is expended on the finer details of algorithm development.

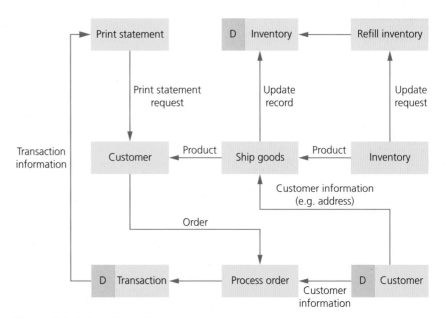

Figure 1.6 A data-flow diagram

Structured programming

Early programs were commonly developed on an ad hoc basis, with no particular rules as to how to lay them out. In particular, programmers often used the now infamous GOTO statement that transferred control unconditionally to some other point in a program.

```
IF condition THEN goto label
```

or worse

```
IF condition THEN goto 230
```

This made programs very hard to read and maintain and was vigorously opposed by the computer scientist Edsger Dijkstra, notably in a letter entitled *Go To Statement Considered Harmful*, where Dijkstra argued for banning the construct from all languages, and over time it did indeed drop from favour, being replaced by structured programming. In structured programming, functions (or procedures) were packaged off and designed to perform just one or a limited set of jobs. This improved readability and you should still make sure that your programs are packaged up into fairly simple modules.

Structured programming gained favour also because it was shown by Böhm and Jacopini in 1966 that any computable function can be carried out by using no more than three different types of programming construct, thereby eliminating the need for GOTO.

These constructs are:

1. **sequence:** executing one statement or subprogram after another
2. **selection:** branching to a different place in a program according to the value of a Boolean expression
3. **iteration:** repeating a section of code until a Boolean expression is true.

So, structured programming is another common method of decomposition routinely used by computer professionals and we can learn from it when tackling many everyday problems – solve one problem at a time!

Objects

Object-oriented programming is a common way of breaking down problems and functionality at the same time. An object, which is based on a class, is a container of attributes (data) and methods (code). This is popular because each object can be isolated from others, which minimises errors due to interference, and it also facilitates the reuse of objects for similar problems. For a full coverage of objects, see pages 91–96.

Decomposition in real life

We decompose problems routinely in real life. What computational thinking gives to us is the realisation that this is what we are doing and the encouragement to break problems down consciously rather than intuitively.

Example

A friend is travelling to visit you at your home. You need to explain how to get there. Consider the following approaches:

1. Get the train to Central Station, then get a taxi to 24 Acacia Avenue.
2. Get the train to Central Station, then get the number 23 bus. Get off the bus after six stops, walk down Back Street, take the second right into Acacia Avenue. Number 24 is 100 metres along on the right.

Clearly, the level of decomposition can be tailored to the need of the moment.

Key points

– Computer scientists have long learned the power of decomposition to solve problems.

– Many ways of decomposition have been developed.
– We can use this key concept to solve many everyday problems.

The power of algorithms

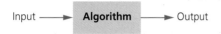

Figure 1.7 An algorithm is a well-defined series of steps that acts on some value or set of values as input and produces another value or set of values as output

An algorithm is, to put it another way, a procedure – in the widest sense of the word. A chef gets the ingredients for a meal as input, carries out various processes (procedures) on them as an algorithm or method and outputs a delicious meal. Organisations have algorithms or procedures for appointing new members of staff, banks have procedures for deciding whether to grant someone a mortgage and schools and colleges have procedures for determining entry to some courses or for disciplining recalcitrant students.

Devising algorithms is another crucial and long-standing part of computational thinking. Although humans have been creating and following algorithms for millennia, it is the development of computers that has highlighted the crucial importance and centrality of algorithms in all problem solving. As with decomposition, becoming adept at formulating algorithms, learning from computer science, has many useful spin-off benefits in the wider world.

Formulating algorithms is notoriously hard to do. For most non-trivial problems, there can be a whole range of possible ways to go about it. Even after a system has been implemented, it is usually the case that better algorithms can be devised that would make the system more robust, easier to use and crucially run faster or use fewer resources. It can often also be the case that the algorithm does not always return the correct result.

The power of algorithms often comes from the short cuts that have been designed into them. This in turn often comes from a proper decomposition of the problem in the first place. Some of the most effective algorithms are based on recursively applying a simple process.

Example

Consider searching an ordered list of numbers in a file for a particular number. This has many practical applications in everyday situations, such as looking up someone's bank account by account number.

You could write an algorithm to start at the beginning and continue until the account is found, or the end of the file is reached.

```
file_item_found= false
input number_required
go to first_record
repeat
read file_item
if file_item == number_required then output record(file_
item)
file_item_found=true
else
move to next record
until file_item_found == true OR end of file
```

This would work. The list might be enormous and could take up significant processor time.

If the list of numbers is in order, better methods exist that could find an item much faster. A well-known example is the *binary search algorithm*. The whole point of this algorithm is to examine the middle item. If this is the item required then the search is complete. If the item is less than the number required, the middle of the left side of the list is examined, otherwise the middle of the right side. Each time an item is checked, the number of remaining items that need to be looked at is halved.

Here is an implementation of the binary search algorithm:

```
search(list[0..N-1], value, low, high) {
        if (high < low)
        return error_message
  mid = (low + high) / 2
  if (list[mid] > value)
        return search(list, value, low, mid-1)
  else if (list[mid] < value)
        return search(list, value, mid+1, high)
  else
        return mid
}
```

This is a recursive algorithm called 'search'. Recursive means that when written as a function, it calls itself from within itself. Notice the lines that start with 'return search'. The beauty of writing this recursively is that very little code is needed to produce an iterative search that will occur as often as needed.

Algorithms cannot work on their own. They are designed to 'do something' 'to' or 'with' something else. The something else is data. If the data has been structured, as in an ordered list, this makes devising an efficient algorithm that much easier. This is another lesson to learn when applying computational thinking to real-world problems.

Designers of algorithms need to bear certain things in mind when producing an algorithmic solution.

Algorithms must exactly describe what they are supposed to do. Any ambiguity will make them unreliable when implemented. Computers don't understand vagueness (unless programmed to do so in an unambiguous way!).

Algorithms must end. No end means no result. This is something to watch for in recursive algorithms. It is easy to miss out an end condition.

Algorithms must be correct. There is no point in running an algorithm if the end result is incorrect.

Algorithms must work with any instance of the same problem. The whole point of presenting algorithms to a computer is that they can be applied to different sets of similar data.

Question

What is the end condition in the binary search implementation given on this page?

- Algorithms are an integral part of the decomposition process.
- Small problems extracted from big problems should be solvable by an algorithm.
- Recursive algorithms are particularly useful in solving simple repetitive problems that may have any number of iterations.

Once an algorithm has been designed, next comes the easy bit — coding it into a programming language. A programmer who knows the syntax of a given language should be able to translate a well-designed algorithm into code.

Practice questions

1. Define the term 'recursion'.
2. GNU is an operating system. Explain why the name GNU is recursive.
3. A library accepts new members and stores data about them. It issues them with a card. It also updates membership details when necessary. When the member leaves, the record for that member is deleted.
   Express this library system as a data-flow diagram.

Chapter 2

Elements of computational thinking

Features that make a problem solvable by computational methods

Example

Here are two closely related problems.

'How can we speed up the throughput to a set of six lifts in a tall building?'

For this, we need to gather data about usage, lift speeds, typical stopping frequencies, strategies for calling lifts, and so on. It should be solvable by fairly standard analytical and algorithmic methods.

But suppose the problem is 'How do we reduce the number of complaints about waiting for lifts in this hotel?'

We could apply the solution to the first problem and hope that satisfies the users. Another approach that has worked is to install mirrors by the lifts. That way, the users have something else to look at when waiting and are less likely to get bored and frustrated.

This is an example of an increasingly common situation where there is a mixture of human reactions and computable problems, showing that humans and computers working together can be a good way to tackle real problems. It also highlights the importance of really understanding what the problem is.

This is an area that has long been studied by computer scientists. In 1936, Alan Turing devised a theoretical computer based on an unlimited memory made from paper tape. Symbols are printed on the tape and at any given moment the machine can manipulate the symbol according to a set of rules. A Turing machine can be used to simulate a computer **algorithm**. One way of deciding if a problem is computable is to test it against the capabilities of a Turing machine.

Computability is whether or not a problem can be solved using an algorithm. It is worth noting that any problem that can be solved by a computer today can also be solved by a Turing machine. Indeed all computers ever made are capable of solving exactly the same set of problems, *given enough time and memory*.

The speed computers run at and the memory that they can access are the limiting factors to the problems we can solve with computers. We increasingly have access to exponentially larger amounts of computing power; we have the internet, data centres, supercomputers, nanocomputers, server farms and more developments are always appearing. This means the range of problems we can practically tackle using computers is increasing.

As we learn more about computers and indeed how to think, solving problems is now a more wide-ranging question than it was. We also have to realise that solving problems is now a joint enterprise between these computing agents and the humans that work with them, so a solvable problem might mean something rather more than just a computable problem.

It can be proved that there are some problems that we will never be able to solve by computer.

Problem recognition

The example given above shows that, given a situation that needs attention, it is important to determine exactly what the problem is: it may not always be what you think.

Some problems are obvious: A traffic queue at a road junction is clearly a problem – it wastes time and causes stress. By using computational and intuitive methods, it may be possible to come up with a solution, if only a partial one.

Backtracking

Backtracking is an algorithmic approach to a problem where partial solutions to a large problem are incrementally built up as a pathway to follow, and then, if the pathway fails at some point, the partial solutions are abandoned and the search begins again at the last potentially successful point. This is a well-known strategy for solving logic problems and is nicely demonstrated by looking at a set of rules in the programming language Prolog.

Question

Your mobile phone is normally fine. It doesn't work today. Explain how you could use backtracking to find what the problem is.

Example

Prolog is a logic-declarative language where rules and relationships are constructed, and from these logical inferences can be made.

Here is a set of rules:

```
give_pay_rise(X):-
works_hard(X),
is_relative(X).

works_hard(alberich).
works_hard(wotan).
works_hard(siegfried).

is_relative(tristan).
is_relative(isolde).
is_relative(siegfried).
```

This set of facts shows us that Alberich works hard and so do Wotan and Siegfried. It also tells us who is a relative.

If we now pose the query:

```
?- give_pay_rise(Who).
```

this asks Prolog to bind to the variable (Who) anyone who fits the rules for give_pay_rise.

Prolog first looks at Alberich. He works hard, but he isn't a relative. So Prolog backtracks and tries again with Wotan. That fails too. Prolog backtracks again and this time, when trying to match all the rules with Siegfried, it succeeds and will output Siegfried.

Key points

– Problem solving can be a disciplined process.
– Some problems are not solvable.
– Some problems are best solved by humans, some by computers and some by a partnership of both.
– Backtracking can be an effective way of solving sequential problems.

Data mining

Data mining is a process for trawling through lots of data that probably comes from many sources. It is a useful way to search for relationships and facts that are probably not immediately obvious to a casual observer. It is also used when the data comes from data sets that are not structured in the same way. So, for example, a supermarket may have data from its loyalty card scheme that shows a few personal details plus purchases made. This is a huge collection of data for a typical large supermarket.

If you perform searches that attempt to find patterns, some of the best algorithms will show whether certain products tend to be bought together, or by the same customer, or by the same demographic group. If you include weather data into the mining operation, you might get correlations showing up between hot weather and ice cream sales, which would be expected, but maybe not what one supermarket found out: that when hurricanes are forecast, people buy more fruit tarts.

Algorithms that help with data mining are known by such terms as 'pattern matching' and 'anomaly detection'. Data mining has become possible because of:

- big databases
- fast processing.

Data mining is useful for many purposes, such as business modelling and planning, as well as disease prediction. Certain groups can be shown to be prone to certain diseases and data mining can sometimes show links with lifestyle factors. This is an aspect of computability that would not have been foreseen in 1936.

Performance modelling

We often want to know how well a system will perform in real life before we have implemented it. It is not feasible to test all possibilities for reasons such as:

- safety
- time
- expense.

You would not test every single configuration of a car body for crash resistance by crashing a real prototype. You would not try re-routing trains on the London Underground by experimenting in the rush hour. You wouldn't try out a new computer system on live exam data in the middle of the exam season.

In all these cases, the sensible thing to do is to build models or simulations in order to best predict the outcomes. Producing computer models is one of the most important uses of computers and is a part of **computational thinking**.

Key point

Why not consider creating a computer model as your programming coursework?

Performance modelling is only as useful as the accuracy of the model and the data that will be fed into it. Various mathematical considerations will form part of a suitable model such as:

- **statistics:** if there is existing relevant data, then it should be taken into account in the model
- **randomisation:** many real-life situations are improperly understood so a random function is often the best we can do to model uncertainty.

Pipelining

Key term

Instruction set The collection of opcodes a processor is able to decode and execute.

Pipelining in computing is a situation where the output of one process is the input to another.

It is useful in RISC (reduced **instruction set**) processors where the stages of the fetch–decode–execute cycle can be separated and thus instructions can be queued up, thereby speeding up the overall process of running a program. While one instruction is being executed, another is being decoded and yet another is being fetched. This is further explained in Chapter 10. It has drawbacks though because if an instruction causes a jump, then the queued instructions will not be the correct ones and the pipelining has to be reset.

The Unix® pipe is a system that connects processes to the outside world (printers, keyboards and the like) by standard input and output streams, thereby relieving the programmer of having to write code to connect to a physical device. This is yet another useful application of abstraction – a virtual concept substitutes for a physical one.

In the Unix command line, you can use a pipe to pass the output of one program to another.

For example the ls (list) command sends a list of the contents of the current working directory to the default output device, usually the console.

Here is some example output from an ls command:

```
sean@zoostorm-ubuntu:~$ ls
Desktop                                                    list
Documents                                                  list.
Downloads                                                  Music
Dropbox                                                    pics backup
examples.desktop                                           Pictures
kompozer_0.8~b3.dfsg.1-0.1ubuntu2_amd64.deb                Public
kompozer-data_0.8~b3.dfsg.1-0.1ubuntu2_all.deb             Templates
kompozer-data_0.8~b3.dfsg.1-0.1ubuntu2_all.deb.1           Videos
```

Figure 2.1 Output from an ls command

Here is the output from ls | head -3. The ls output is piped to the 'head' program with the parameter 3. In other words, output the first three items.

```
sean@zoostorm-ubuntu:~$ ls | head -3
Desktop
Documents
Downloads
```

Figure 2.2 Output from ls | head -3

Just the first three items have been output by the head program.

Question

Itemise some of the inputs, outputs and processes involved in building a house.

Pipelining is a useful technique to use in everyday problems too. Notice that some jobs may be done in parallel if you have the resources (people or processors) to do that. Consider any production line or job, such as making an iced cake:

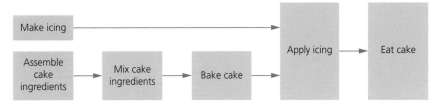

Figure 2.3 Pipeline model

Visualisation to solve problems

Visualisation is a common computing technique to present data in an easy-to-grasp form. At its simplest, it is a matter of presenting tabular data as a graph. More complex visualisations are possible using computer processes, which allow a more sophisticated view of a complex situation. Visualisations can make facts and trends apparent that were never noticed before.

Here is a visualisation of Oyster card use on the London Underground. An Oyster card is a payment card that registers a person's journey by them touching it against a reader when entering or leaving a station. On a map of London on a typical morning, the red circles show where people 'touch in' – in other words, where they board a train – and the green circles show 'touching out' – in other words, where people leave a station. The diameters of the circles show numbers involved.

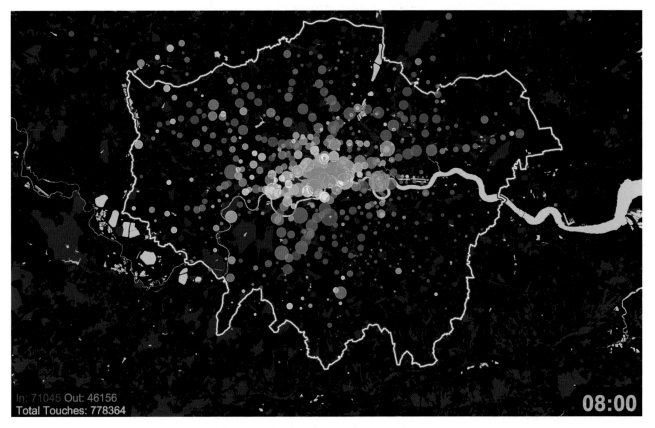

Figure 2.4 Visualisation of Oyster card use on the London Underground

Here is a visualisation of some text from this chapter using software available on wordle.net:

Figure 2.5 A visualisation of the text in this chapter from wordle.net

This example is useful in showing visually the frequency of use of the words in the text. It can help to improve your writing style!

Questions

1. Suggest ways to use computing techniques to visualise data about:
   (a) the age of people living in different parts of a city
   (b) the means of transport used to get from the suburbs into a city centre.
2. In each case, suggest what data would be needed, how it could be collected and whether there is existing software to do the visualisation.

Key points

– Data mining can show patterns and relationships that are not immediately obvious. Computer systems have enabled huge data stores to be examined for pattern matching.

– Pipelining is a common computing technique that can be applied to everyday problems.

– Sometimes complex situations can be best explained by visualisations.

– Computer systems have enabled the production of strikingly effective visualisations.

Thinking abstractly

Example

Fred has lost his mobile phone. It is a Samsung Galaxy, running the latest version of the Android operating system. It is normally in a white case and has a police siren ring tone. Fred last saw it (he thinks) on the window ledge in the bathroom. He can't remember if it is charged up or even switched on. But possibly, he left it in the taxi after coming home last night. It cost a lot of money and has sentimental value because his girlfriend bought it as a birthday present.

An abstraction is a concept of reality. It commonly makes use of symbols to represent components of a problem so that the human mind or a computing agent can process the problem. Abstraction is also about teasing out what does and what does not matter in a scenario.

Questions

Read the example scenario to the left.
1. Itemise information from this description that would be of use in finding the missing phone.
2. Suggest a strategy for finding the phone.
3. Suggest a sequence of steps that would be helpful in finding the phone.

Most problems that we face in everyday life are like in the example. They are messy. All sorts of things may possibly be important in solving a problem but probably are not.

Abstraction helps us maximise our chances of solving a problem by letting us separate out the component parts and decide which are worth investigating. But don't forget, in real life, sometimes information that looks irrelevant can trigger an 'aha!' moment, which is unlikely to be the case in any current computer system.

Abstraction and real-world issues

Abstraction is extremely important in computing, to an extent that using computers to solve real-world problems would be impossible without it.

Every program worth thinking about uses variables. Variables are an abstraction. They represent real-world values or intermediate values in a calculation.

At a higher level, objects are a clear abstraction of real-world things as well as being used to represent other abstractions. We all know what a chair is. It is a real-world object that has a surface to sit on and usually four legs. It is a concept. A real chair will normally comply with these abstractions and can be regarded as one instance of the class 'chair'.

Levels of abstraction

Computer systems make considerable use of another abstraction idea – levels of abstraction. In a complex system, it is often useful to construct an abstraction to represent a large problem and to create lower-level abstractions to deal with component parts.

The power of this approach is that the details in each layer of abstraction can be hidden from the others. This frees up the solution process to concentrate on just one issue at a time, or maybe send the different sub-problems to different staff or different companies to work on.

This idea of levels of abstraction is easily seen in the idea of layering. Layering is found widely, such as in the construction of operating systems, database systems (see Chapter 15), networks (see Chapter 16) and indeed any large system.

Layers are a way of dividing the functionality of a big system into separate areas of interest; for example an operating system will not normally contain code for communicating with any number of peripherals – it will devolve that responsibility to drivers, retaining to itself only the necessary interfaces that connect to the drivers.

The same principle applies to a physical item such as a car. A car designer might be interested in the combustion properties of a new fuel, but that issue is treated separately from the design of the dashboard. Real progress can sometimes be made when creativity is applied across layers, but this is the exception rather than the rule. Specialisation leads to reliability and cost benefits.

Questions

1. Explain how a map is an example of an abstraction.
2. Identify examples of levels of abstraction on a map of your choice.
3. Explain how levels of abstraction assist the map-maker.
4. Explain how levels of abstraction assist the map user.

Thinking ahead

Thinking ahead has always been standard good advice for all sorts of aspects of life. The better you anticipate what needs to be done in any situation, the easier it is to do the job when it happens.

For example, if you plan to decorate your house, you don't get on a ladder and get to work, you first determine how much paint you need, what colour you want, what type of paint you want for a given location, what you need to do to prepare the surface, and then you need to calculate how much paint you need to buy. Once you have all the data you need, you can go to the DIY superstore and buy all the things you need. If you get this wrong, you may find yourself making multiple extra trips only to discover that your colour has now sold out.

Of course, the same disciplines apply to producing computer solutions, but analysts have long formalised how best to do this. Awareness of how the professionals plan ahead can help us with everyday problems.

Inputs and outputs

When planning a computer system, one of the first things an analyst needs to do is to determine what outputs are needed. After all, that is why we have computer systems: to produce outputs.

Suppose an online vendor wants to produce a picking list for customers. This is the list that is sent to a warehouse where the staff use it to collect the items that the customers want when fulfilling the order. The list might look like this:

Picking List			
Order Number	2001	Date	25/01/15
Ordered by	3846		
Item Code	Item Quantity	Location	Quantity
564	10	Shelf A1.1	
755	15	Shelf B3.2	

To get an output like this, the designer of the system needs to ensure that at some stage there are inputs for all the data items on the list. Of course this is part of a larger system, but a similar design process needs to be used.

Caching

Caching is a good example of how 'thinking ahead' can be related to computing processes. In caching, data that is input might be stored in RAM 'in case' it is needed again before the process is shut down. If it is required, it does not need to be read in again from disk, thereby giving a faster response time.

Prefetching is another related computer operation, where an instruction is requested from memory by the CPU before it is required, to speed up instruction throughput. There are algorithms that can predict likely future instructions needed so that they are ready in the cache as soon as they are in fact needed.

In real life, this can be compared with getting your Oyster card (used for payment on public transport) out when you arrive in London and having it in your pocket ready to use instead of having to fish it out of your wallet each time you take a bus or tube.

Question

Explain in detail how prefetching is useful when:
(a) baking a cake
(b) cleaning a car.

Caching brings various other advantages to a computer system, such as reducing the load on a web server because data required by an application can be anticipated, thereby reducing the number of separate access actions.

Caching isn't all good news. It can be very complicated to implement effectively. Also, if the wrong data is cached, then it can be difficult to re-establish the correct sequence of data items or instructions.

Preconditions and reusability

We have already seen that by dividing up a planned system into various component parts, it makes it a lot easier to devise solutions. An added advantage is that separate program modules of any other items such as data stores can be reused in future projects.

One good example of reusing modules in action is the Windows® DLL libraries. A DLL is a Dynamic Link Library. This is a package of program code that can be called at runtime to provide certain functionality to a program. Particularly useful modules are accessed again and again by many programs, for example if you write Windows-based programs, you do not need to write code to make a dialogue box. A DLL can be linked to your code to produce a familiar and standard dialogue box format.

Note that some DLLs are provided with Windows but you can easily write your own if you think that you might need to reuse code. Adding new ones can lead to various difficult problems, as you can see in the section on DLL Hell in Chapter 8.

Code libraries are widespread. Many programming languages have extra collections of commands for use in certain situations. We have already seen how Python has a Logo library and indeed it has many others. They all are examples of reusing code modules, such as the incorporation of the Logo library as mentioned on page 12.

Python uses the command 'import' to bring in these libraries. C and C++ have the preprocessor directive '#include' to bring in 'header files', for example #include <stdio.h> inserts the header file stdio.h into the code being written. This header file is necessary to provide standard input and output functions.

Figure 2.6 Dialogue box

Thinking procedurally

When producing a complete computer system or a single program, we have seen how useful it is to decompose the problem. This makes its solution more manageable. Once a problem has been decomposed, it usually lends itself to the production of program modules that correspond with each sub-problem.

For example, an online ordering system will have sub-problems and hence program modules that deal with customer records, order processing, invoice production, bank account access and stock control at the least. Trying to create a single system to deal with all these separate issues would be highly unlikely to succeed. Also, it is likely that modules to do these jobs already exist and can be customised to fit in with the scenario.

Order order

When planning solutions to a problem, the order may or may not be important. In the case of event-driven solutions, the order of events may

In each of these scenarios, is the order of solution important? For each case, list some of the main sub-problems in a sensible order. Are there any steps where the order does not matter?

1. Building a house.
2. Buying a train ticket online.
3. Buying a drink in a coffee shop.

be unpredictable. You cannot anticipate whether a customer on your website will browse books, kitchen equipment or anything else in some predetermined order. Also, the placing of orders can be unpredictable. Therefore, the modules dealing with display, searching and purchase need to be accessible in any order.

However, a system that processes exam results cannot produce grades until the marks are recorded. It cannot produce certificates until after that. Order can be important. Establishing whether it is important and if so what the order should be is something that is part of computational thinking and can usefully be applied to real life as well.

Thinking logically

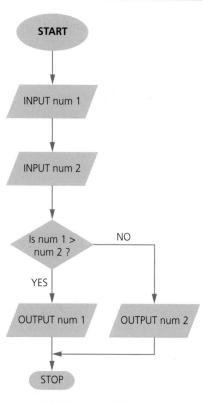

Figure 2.7 Decision flowchart

We have seen (page 7) that in any non-trivial program, there will be points at which decisions need to be made. These will either lead to a branching point (if..then) or a repetition in a loop (for example repeat.. until or do..while).

We have seen that these decisions are based on Boolean expressions. For example in this shell script, an output is produced that depends on the Boolean expression "$character" = "1".

```
echo -n "Enter a number between 1 and 3 inclusive > "
read character
if [ "$character" = "1" ]; then
    echo "You entered one."
```

When planning a program, identifying the decision points is a crucial part of the program design. We can plan these using pseudocode, structured statements or flowcharts; for example the flowchart to the left indicates where a decision will be made about outputting the larger of two different numbers.

The Boolean expression that controls this is 'num1>num2', which of course is either true or false.

A similar process using flowcharts has long been used to plan human activity, for example a disaster recovery plan could be based on the following decision-making process:

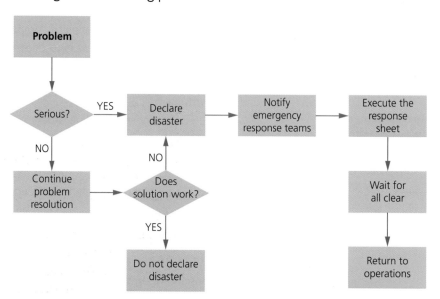

Figure 2.8 Disaster recovery plan

Thinking concurrently

Often, as we have seen, it is possible for different parts of a problem to be tackled at the same time. This is beneficial because it saves time, although it might mean that mistakes are fed into later stages of a project.

Parallel processors enable different parts of a program to be executed simultaneously. Multi-core processors are now common, which have more than one processor mounted on a chip. There are potentially great advantages to having multiple processors. Not only are programs executed faster, but savings are also made on energy and computers can run cooler.

Programs have to be written specially to take advantage of parallel processing and this can make them longer and more complex. Also, the savings in a given program may not be that great if a substantial part of the program must be executed in sequence.

Planning human activities can also benefit from parallel processing. Projects such as building a house or creating a computer system can be planned out using a variety of tools to achieve the greatest efficiency.

Gantt charts are commonly used to plan who does what and make other plans for a project and the bars are used as a visual representation of when tasks occur. Tasks planned to be concurrent are easily shown.

Figure 2.9 A Gantt chart

Key point

There are standard computing practices that have stood the test of time and can be applied to many non-computing scenarios.

Practice questions

1. Devise a visual representation of how your computing project could be planned over a designated time period.
2. You have lost your wallet on the way to school or college. Explain how backtracking can help you find it.
3. Draw a flowchart to show how an email address could be validated as being in the correct format.
4. (a) Explain what pipelining is.
   (b) Show how pipelining can be used to improve the efficiency of a self-service cafeteria.

Topic 2 Problem solving

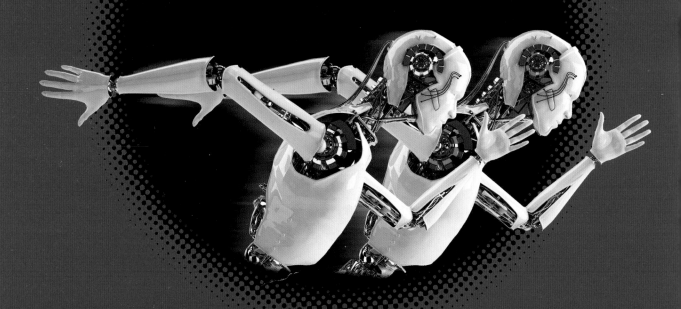

Chapter 3

Problem solving

Introduction

Life makes us solve problems. We encounter problems every day and often solve them without thinking or maybe put them to the back of our mind and ignore them. We do all this pretty much instinctively.

Sometimes our instincts work well for us. A lot may depend on past experience. If we use past experience then we are saving effort because we have solved a similar problem before.

Problem 1

I want to pave my patio. It is 11.5 m by 5.5 m. The paving slabs I want are square with a side length of 50 cm. I need to find out how many to buy.

Solution:

- Divide the patio side length by the slab side length.
- Repeat for the breadth.
- Multiply the two results.

That's a nice simple process. I could code that if I wanted, or even do it in my head or on paper. I would have confidence that the answer is correct – as long as I chose the right steps.

Problem 2

I have an urgent appointment – I have to be at the airport in two hours but before I can go, I have to take the cat to the boarding cattery. It is unthinkable that I can go away for two weeks and leave her alone in the house. But disaster strikes – she is nowhere to be found. Maybe I will have to cancel my trip.

What can I do?

Solution 1: Panic

This sometimes works. I can rush around the house calling 'here cat . . . come on'. But she's wise to this. She knows she's going to be put in a box and taken away from her comfy hidey-hole. So I shake a bag of treats – that usually works. But she knows what's going on and values being left alone more than she values the treats, so no good.

I then rush from room to room. I check the usual places, on the window ledges, under the beds. No good. What about the cupboard under the stairs? She never goes there but you never know. Maybe she snuck out the front door when I packed the car.

During all this time, my blood pressure rises and the cat is calmly licking herself behind the one curtain that I didn't check. There must be a better way.

Questions

1. Is Solution 2 a good one? Might there be a better one?
2. Is this problem solvable by using computational methods?

Question

A salesman lives in Birmingham. He has a week to visit clients in London, Zurich, Amsterdam and Manchester. How can he achieve this?

1. What data does he need?
2. How does he make a decision?
3. Is there a right or even a best answer?

Question

Getting divorced is one of the most stressful and, often, expensive processes anyone can go through. If you do marry, what strategies can be applied to marry someone who is as suitable as possible?

Hint: there actually is a mathematical approach to this!

Key term

Heuristic An approach to problem solving that makes use of experience. It is not guaranteed to produce the best solution but it generally will produce a 'good enough' result. Heuristic methods are sometimes referred to as a 'rule of thumb'.

It is important to realise when 'good enough is good enough' and when it isn't.

Solution 2: Plan ahead

Next time I'll get the cat sorted the day before. So, when it is time to go to the airport, that is one problem less to worry about and I'll be calmer and more likely to make my flight. That's the benefit of thinking ahead.

Problem 3

I have to write a chapter on solving problems and the deadline is fast approaching. What can I do?

Solution 1: Put it off and hope the problem will go away

The trouble is, this rarely happens. Sometimes at work, your boss asks for a report and you know that if you stall, he'll probably forget about it. Now, that is a rational approach to saving effort. Some problems aren't worth bothering with. But the book deadline? It might not be a good idea to try with that one. Who knows, maybe someone will buy the book and it will be a success.

Solution 2: Plan ahead

Before you can write a decent chapter, you need to marshal your ideas. This involves a lot of reading and research. These ideas need to be sifted – some ideas turn out to be interesting, others, on reflection, look less good. Organise them, write them down or, better, use a computer to record them.

Decide what's important and what is not. This is how we solve computational problems too.

The world is full of problems for us to solve. Some are easy to solve and some are impossible. We use various strategies and approaches to solve them. Sometimes these strategies are obvious; sometimes they are completely obscure. Sometimes we can be confident of our solutions, other times we remain in doubt even after applying them. Some problems simply have no solutions. Some problems might be partly solvable by systematic and logical methods backed up by hunches. Which problems are which?

Problem solving does not always have to be the hit-and-miss business that we often make it. Needless to say, many great minds have been applied to the problem-solving approach and one particularly notable investigator was the Hungarian mathematician George Pólya. He wrote widely about problem solving, often making use of **heuristic** approaches.

Example

You want to cross a busy road. There is no official crossing point. How do you make the decision about when to go for it?

This is a classic problem for heuristics. You don't have the time or the equipment to measure the speeds of oncoming vehicles (unless you are operating a speed trap) and even then you don't know if a car will stop or speed up or if that cyclist turning right has seen you. You take in as many items of information as you can about rough speeds, locations and even driving behaviour (is that lorry driver talking on his phone?). Your brain processes this at lightning speed, matches the inputs (roughly) with previous attempts to cross roads and you choose your moment.

George Pólya listed four stages that you should go through when solving a problem (if you have time, that is).

1. Understand the problem

- What do we know about the problem?
- Can you restate the problem in your own words?
- What are the unknowns?
- What data do we have?
- What data do we need but don't have?
- What data do we have but don't need for solving the problem?
- Is it possible to come to a solution?
- Is it possible to partially solve the problem?
- Can the problem be divided into separate sub-problems? This is called 'problem **decomposition**' and is one of the essential aspects of **computational thinking**.
- Can we represent the problem abstractly, with a diagram or variables?

2. Devise a plan

Think about whether you have seen this problem or a similar one before. You might be able to recycle ideas.

- Start breaking the problem into solvable sub-problems.
- Make a list of things you need to do.
- Look for patterns.
- Be creative – think 'outside the box'. Use intuition. Remember – anyone can be creative. Be brave enough to question received wisdom. But also remember that you have a particular problem to solve – solving others is not the point.
- Is there a formula or equation that can help?
- Try solving a similar problem if the real one is looking a bit too difficult at the moment.

3. Carry out your plan

Do this carefully, checking as you go.

Are you sure that each stage is in fact correct?

If your plan isn't working out then don't be afraid to abandon it and start again. If you are in a hole you don't keep digging.

4. Look back over what you have done

Once you have a solution, it is tempting to tick the box that says 'done' and forget about it. Often a solution can be improved. A question computer scientists should ask when they have devised an **algorithm** is 'could this be done better?' We are used to having better and faster computer systems all the time. Not all of the progress is down to better and faster hardware. Much of the improvement is due to better algorithms.

1. You might have got so involved in the detail that you have overlooked the big picture.
2. Could you have done this differently?
3. Have you learned something that you can apply to future problems?

Example

'There are known knowns. These are things we know that we know. There are known unknowns. That is to say, there are things that we know we don't know. But there are also unknown unknowns. There are things we don't know we don't know.'

Donald Rumsfeld, speaking to a US Department of Defense news briefing in February 2002

Question

Can you think of any decisions or strategies made by governments or the management of your own institution that have been obviously bad but were persisted with?

While you are thinking about this, look up 'NHS IT System'. This is one of the most notorious IT failures ever and Chapter 9 also looks at this.

Key points

- Problems come in all shapes and sizes.
- Some problems are unsolvable.
- Problems can often be solved adequately by heuristics.
- There are well-defined processes that help to solve problems.

1. How could you use a laptop to determine the height of a building? Think of as many answers as you can.
2. Town A has 100 school-age children living in it. Town B has 50. There are plans to build a new school to serve them all. How would you go about finding a location for the school that minimises the total distance travelled by all the children?
3. To what extent are heuristic methods of problem solving appropriate for the following scenarios:
   (a) scanning a hard drive for virus signatures
   (b) using light reflectivity on dirty washing to determine which wash cycle to use
   (c) setting the grade boundaries in A level exams (the mark where A becomes B, and so on)
   (d) setting a safe altitude for an aircraft when flying over mountainous terrain?

Chapter 4

Programming techniques

Basic program constructs

Despite all the major advances in computer technology and **algorithms** over the years, the basic approaches to programming and the building blocks involved have remained much the same, with only slow changes occurring from time to time.

As we saw in Chapter 1, Böhm and Jacopini showed in 1966 that any program can be written in a structured manner involving just three constructs: sequence, selection and iteration. This still holds true today, even though these constructs might not always be clear in some programs.

Sequence

A sequence is the execution of statements or functions one after another. This usually forms the bulk of the code in any program.

Selection

Selection is where the flow through a program is interrupted and control is passed to another point in the program. The decision is based on a Boolean expression.

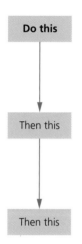

Figure 4.1 A sequence

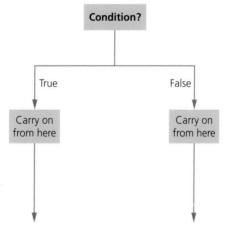

Figure 4.2 A decision with a Boolean expression

In assembly language such as that simulated by the Little Man Computer, branching is achieved by branching commands such as **BRA** and **BRP**.

Branch instructions send program control to a label in the code, so BRP TWOBIG means branch if the accumulator holds a positive value, to the program instruction labelled TWOBIG. BRA PROGEND means if this point is reached go to the label PROGEND and continue from there, which is an instruction to halt the program.

Key terms

BRA Branch always. This is a jump instruction that is always executed.
BRP Branch if the value in the accumulator is positive.

Here is some sample code that shows two branch instructions.

```
INP
STA ONE
INP
STA TWO
SUB ONE
BRP TWOBIG
LDA TWO
OUT
LDA ONE
OUT
BRA PROGEND
TWOBIG LDA ONE
OUT
LDA TWO
OUT
PROGEND HLT
ONE DAT
TWO DAT
```

Most programming languages have facilities to allow branching in various ways although the syntax and structure differs between languages.

For example, selection can be done by using an `if..then` structure. This normally has a fallback option available, usually written as `'else'`. To take the simple case of a menu, it could be written as a series of `if..then` constructs, one within another.

Most languages allow the use of `elseif` condition, which is executed when the `if` condition is false but its own condition is true.

Multiple `elseifs` can be used within one `if` structure. In the example below, the Python® code uses `ifs` and `elseifs` as a way of making choices from a menu. (This would be written as `elif` in Python.)

The following example shows different functions being activated according to the user response to the menu.

```
print("Demo program\n")
print("What do you want to do?\n\n")
print("Add new data\n")
print("Read the file\n")
print("Find record\n")
print("Quit")

while True:
    answer=(input("Press A, R, F or Q: "))
if answer in("A", "a"):
        write_file()
    elif answer in ("R", "r"):
        read_file()
```

```
elif answer in ("F", "f"):
    find_rec()
elif answer in ("Q", "q"):
    break
else:
    print("Invalid response")
```

When `if` is within `if`, they are called nested `if`s. As you can see, they quickly become messy and unreadable, so most languages have a 'case', 'switch' or 'select' statement, which allows multiple options to be written more neatly.

Iteration

Again, controlled by the state of a Boolean expression, a section of code is repeated.

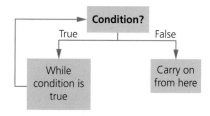

Figure 4.3 Using a Boolean expression to repeat code

Iteration can be implemented with branch instructions in assembly language. High-level languages have various constructs to implement iteration and they basically fall into three categories.

Repeat..until

This tests for a condition at the end of a section of code. A Boolean expression is used just as with the branching decisions. The section is repeated (loops) until the condition is fulfilled. A `repeat..until` is always executed at least once.

While..do or while..endwhile

The syntax of this varies, for example in Python the repeated code is indicated by indentation. The main feature of this construct is that the condition for maintaining or terminating the loop is checked before entry on to the loop. A `while..do` loop may or may not be executed at all.

For..do

Again, this varies in terms of syntax in different languages, but the essential characteristic of this structure is that the loop executes a fixed number of times, controlled by a variable.

Recursion

Recursion is where a procedure or function calls itself. It is a computing strategy where a problem is broken down into small component parts of the same type then solved in a simple way. The results of the solution are then combined together to give the full solution. The strategy is sometimes called 'divide and conquer' and we have seen an example of this in the binary search algorithm on page 19. In that case, a list is successively divided at its midpoint to produce sub-lists until a searched-for item is found.

When writing recursive procedures, it is important to make sure that there is in fact an end point, in order to avoid an endless loop – that is endless until a stack overflow occurs.

Global and local variables

All programs make use of variables to store the values of data items and allow them to be changed. Each variable is of a particular data type, which in some languages has to be explicitly declared in a statement, such as the following examples in the programming language C.

```
int count;
char letter;
char lastname[30];
```

In these examples, `count` is declared as an integer, `letter` as a character – that is just one letter or other character and `lastname` is declared as a sequence of up to 30 characters – a data type that is called *string* in many other languages.

Some languages do not require the programmer explicitly to declare a variable type but they assign the correct type to a variable when a value is passed to it. So, in Python for example, the following statements assign the data types as shown:

```
counter = 100          # integer
temperature = 36.9     # floating point
name     = "Waltraute" # string
```

Because most programs are written as modules, it is important to know whether a certain variable is visible from a part of the code. This is a particular issue if the program is big and potentially many programmers are working on different modules. There is a danger that they may choose the same name for different data items that, if not uncovered by the compiler, could cause conflicts and unexpected effects.

The extent of a program in which a variable is visible is called the variable's scope. This can be global or local.

A global variable is typically declared or initialised outside any subprograms; that is, functions or procedures. It then becomes accessible to code written anywhere in the program. This can be useful if the programmer needs to be able to update a value from various subprograms, perhaps a running total of the results of various types of transaction.

A local variable is declared inside a subprogram. This results in it only being accessible from within that subprogram. It is normally considered good practice to use mostly local variables because then they are less likely to be accidentally altered by other modules. If a local variable has the same name as a global variable it is used instead of the global variable when in scope.

Here is an example of Python code showing the declaration of a global and a local variable.

```
global_variable = 'Hodder'
def example_function():
    local_variable = 'books'
    print (global_variable)
    print (local_variable)
example_function()
print (global_variable)
print (local_variable)
```

Question

Predict the outcome of running the code to the right. (Hint: there will be an error.)

Key points

- Variables can be altered during the running of a program.
- Variables have a data type that is usually (but not always) fixed for the duration of the program.
- Variables are declared in advance in some languages, but not in others.
- Variables can be global or local.
- It is usually safer to use local variables where possible to avoid conflicts.

Functions and procedures

We have seen that all but the smallest programs are built up from subprograms or modules. There are two principal types of subprogram – functions and procedures – although objects are another way of modularising code.

Functions

A function is – mathematically – an algorithm that takes an input and produces an output for each input. In programming, it is strictly speaking the same thing – a section of code that produces an output by processing an input. Some functions have multiple inputs and outputs.

Functions can be regarded as 'black boxes' in as much as once we have them and know what they do, we don't care how they do it – we just know that they will produce the desired result. Once a function exists to do a particular job, it can be reused or called whenever that job is needed.

The usual sequence of events is like this:

- The program comes to a line of code containing a 'function call'.
- Program control passes to the function.
- The instructions inside of the function are executed from the beginning to the end (unless there is code to break this sequence).
- Control passes back to the line containing the function call.
- Any data computed and returned by the function is used in place of the function in the original line of code.

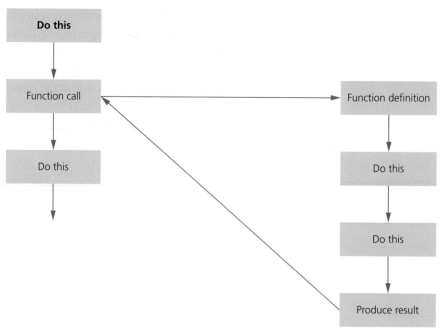

Figure 4.4 Calling a function

When we define a function, we need to provide the following:

- a function name
- any parameters needed by the function; that is, the data that must be fed into the function
- the processing code itself
- the output – usually one output but there can be zero or many outputs.

Here is a simple function written in Python to cube a number. Similar principles, although different syntax, apply to most other languages.

```
#cube a number with a function
'''This function cubes a number'''

def cube(number):
    return number*number*number

print('The cube program')
number=int(input('Input the number to cube '))
print(number,' cubed is ',cube(number))
```

The first two lines are both comments for the benefit of human readers.

The function is then defined with the name 'cube'. Brackets are required after the name to accept any parameters being passed to the function. In this case, there is one parameter defined, called 'number', and it will be the number to be cubed.

The brackets can be left empty if there is no parameter required by the function.

The program actually starts executing with the line `print('The cube program')`.

It asks for a number to be input. The last line then calls the function from an inline position, the function is executed and then the result is printed, all in the same last line.

An important point of interest in this short example is that as well as the function `cube` that we have written, there are in fact three other functions used. These are inbuilt functions `print()`, `int()` and `input()`. Notice that each of these also has brackets after its name where the parameters go. Inbuilt functions and user-defined functions are all called in the same way. As well as programming languages, spreadsheets also provide functions to carry out 'black box' actions.

Note that `int()` returns the integer value of whatever has been input.

Procedures

Procedures are also subprograms that help to support modular programming. The only real difference between a procedure and a function is that a function should return a value. We saw in the cube function example how the function calculated the cube of a number and provided this result as a return value.

Procedures do not have to do this; they are generally a set of commands that act independently of the rest of the program and do not usually return a value to the procedure call. Many languages do not even have procedures as an option and they use the term 'function' even where there is no value to return. In C, everything happens in functions. C functions are defined as a certain type, for example:

```
int add_up (int a, int b)
{
    int result;
    result=a+b;
    return result;
}
```

In this case, the function is set up to return an integer. If there is no return value required; that is, the function is acting as a procedure would in other languages, the return type is declared as void, for example:

```
void birthday_greetings(int age)
{
    printf("Congratulations, you are now\n", age);
    return;
}
```

So, the exact definitions of functions and procedures are a little flexible, depending on which language you are talking about.

Parameter passing

We have seen that functions and procedures can accept values. This makes them flexible so that their internal algorithms are applied to whatever data is being supplied to them. However, it is not quite that simple. There are several different ways in which parameters can be passed to a subprogram. The most commonly known are by reference and by value.

By reference

In some circumstances, the intention of the programmer is to have a function change the value of a variable or more than one variable. An example could be a running total for a bill that has to be updated by various functions and the up-to-date value is always required, no matter which function is accessing it.

One way to do this (apart from the rather dangerous method of using global variables) is to pass the parameters to the function *by reference*. In this case, the function receives a pointer to the actual memory address where the data is stored. This means that the function works directly with the original data and if it changes it, it stays changed.

By value

In other cases, it is not intended for a function to change a variable. An example could be that you have a list or array holding students and their marks in surname order. You might want temporarily to display them in mark order but not disturb the original order. In this case you call the function by value. In this way, a copy of the original data is passed to the function and any changes made are lost as soon as the function is no longer in use.

Here is an example to illustrate this, written in Visual Basic:

```
a=5
b=5

x=doubleByRef(a)
y=doubleByVal(b)
print("a: "+a)
print("b: "+b)
print("x: "+x)
print("y: "+y)

function doubleByRef(num:byRef)
      num=num*2
      return num
endfunction

function doubleByVal(num:byVal)
      num=num*2
      return num
endfunction
```

This will output:

a: 10   **b:** 5   **x:** 10   **y:** 10

Programming languages vary enormously in their provision and syntax for parameter passing.

The IDE

To write program code, all you need is a text editor. To translate it you need an assembler, a compiler or an interpreter (see Chapter 8). To put together compiled code into a complete program you need a linker. It is much easier to do all these things from within a specially designed software package called an IDE (Integrated Development Environment).

For most languages, there are various IDEs available. There are also IDEs that work with a variety of languages. They vary a lot from very basic and simple to large multi-purpose examples that encompass many different aspects of the program development process.

At the very least, an IDE will probably include:

- an editor for writing the **source code**
- facilities for automating the **build**
- a debugger
- features to help with code writing, such as pretty printing and code completion.

Although an ordinary plain text editor is absolutely fine for writing source code, it will not show mistakes and it will require the programmer to use different software to access the translation and completion parts of the work.

Here is the editing window of IDLE – a simple IDE for Python. There is a fragment of program code in it that shows how keywords are automatically separately coloured and indentation has also been automated.

Key terms

Source code This is the code written in a programming language. It can be read and edited by other programmers. This is where the term 'open source' comes from; that is to say, software where the source code is openly available.

Build This term refers to all the actions that a programmer would take to produce a finished working program. It includes writing the source code, compiling it, linking it, testing it, packaging it for the target environment and producing correct and up-to-date documentation.

```
Python 3.4.0: encrypt.py - /home/sean/Desktop/encrypt.py

File  Edit  Format  Run  Options  Windows  Help

msg=input('Enter message ')
key=int(input('Enter key '))
key_bin=(bin(key)[2:])
print(msg)
print(key_bin)
msglength=len(msg)
print(msglength)
key_bin_length=len(key_bin)
print(key_bin_length)

asc_msg=''
repeat_key=''

#generate ascii message
for i in range(0,msglength):
    element=bin(ord(msg[i]))
    asc_msg=asc_msg+(element[2:])
print(asc_msg)
```

Figure 4.6 The editing window of IDLE

IDLE does not have many features but there are other IDEs available, such as ERIC, which incorporate a host of other useful tools for developing a large project. Some can be seen in the screenshot below.

Particularly useful are the debugging tools that allow:

- stepping through a program – you can see what is happening at intermediate points
- inspection of variables – you can check that variables are storing the values that you intend
- setting breakpoints – this stops the program at some set point so that intermediate values of variables can be inspected.

Question

What debugging features are there in your version of Little Man Computer?

Many IDEs have features to allow version control. Some, such as Netbeans® for Java®, show lines of code that have been added, deleted or modified. Such tools make it easier to revert to previous versions if current changes are producing unpromising results. This is particularly useful in large projects where many programmers are working on the same product; see Chapter 6.

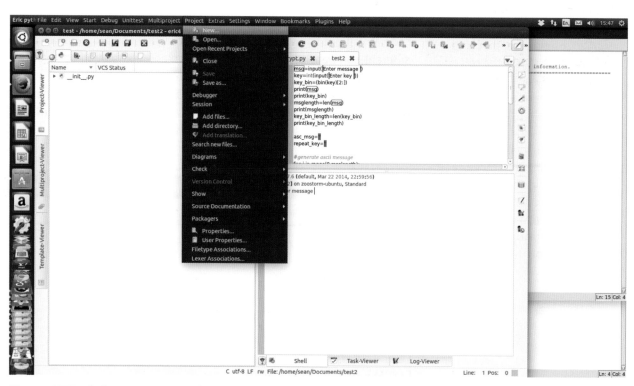

Figure 4.7 Tools for version control

Object-oriented techniques

As you will find out in Chapter 6:

- objects are created from classes
- objects and the classes from which they are derived have attributes, which are their characteristics and methods, which are what they can do
- classes are not objects; they are definitions or blueprints for objects
- instantiation creates a new object – which you can use, based on a class.

Most high-level languages support the creation and use of objects. Many also provide useful pre-made objects.

The Python language provides many objects that can do much of the hard work in your programs. In Python, strings are objects; here are some methods that are supplied with the string object demonstrated in a short piece of code:

```
#string methods
myString=input('Enter your string ')
print('Here is your string:')
print(myString)
print('\nHere is your string in upper case')
print(myString.upper())
print('\nHere is your string in lower case')
print(myString.lower())
print('\nHere is your string in Title case')
print(myString.title())
print('\nHere is your string in with cases swapped')
print(myString.swapcase())
print('\nHere is your string with a change made')
print(myString.replace('o','*'))
print('\nHere is your original string, because we cannot
change strings, only make new ones:')
print(myString)
```

The output from this code is:

```
Enter your string Here is my not very long string
Here is your string:
Here is my not very long string

Here is your string in upper case
HERE IS MY NOT VERY LONG STRING

Here is your string in lower case
here is my not very long string

Here is your string in Title case
Here Is My Not Very Long String

Here is your string in with cases swapped
hERE IS MY NOT VERY LONG STRING

Here is your string with a change made
Here is my n*t very l*ng string

Here is your original string, because we cannot change
strings, only make new ones:
Here is my not very long string
```

Notice (as is usual in most languages) the methods are accessed by dot notation such as `print(myString.upper())`.

Most programmers will want to create their own classes and hence the objects that depend on them. Programming languages have various forms of syntax to do this but it requires the definition of a class first of all, and then the use of a constructor to produce an *instance* of the class; in other words, an object.

In the following Python code, an animal is defined as a class, with an attribute of sound.

Two objects are instanced from this class: dog and cat. In each case they are given a suitable sound attribute.

```python
# accessing class attributes

class Animal(object):
    def __init__(self, sound):
        self.sound=sound

    def __str__(self):
        rep='Animal\n'
        rep+='sound: '+self.sound+'\n'
        return rep

    def talk(self):
        print('self.sound, \n')

#main
dog=Animal('woof')
dog.talk()

cat=Animal('meow')
cat.talk()

print('Dog says:')
print(dog.sound)

print('Cat says:')
print(cat.sound)
```

The output from this program is:

```
Dog says:
woof
Cat says:
meow
```

which is reassuring!

Note the use of the dot notation again to access the object's attributes. (As you will see in Chapter 6, often we will try to avoid this using encapsulation.)

Practice questions

1. What is meant by the instantiation of an object?
2. Describe what happens when a parameter is passed by reference to a function.
3. Here is an algorithm that contains a loop:

```
do while i>10
    print(i)
    i=i-1
endwhile
```

State how many times the algorithm would iterate if the initial value of *i* is
(a) 20
(b) 6
(c) 10
(d) 11.

Chapter 5

Algorithms

Introduction

Algorithms are sets of instructions that can be followed to perform a task. They are at the very heart of what computer science is about. When we want a computer to carry out an algorithm we express its meaning through a program.

There are a number of ways algorithms can be described, including bulleted lists and flowcharts. Computer scientists tend to express algorithms in pseudocode.

This chapter focuses on some of the important algorithms used in computer science. You will be expected to know them for the exam. Trying to commit them to memory by rote probably will not be of much benefit as they are unlikely to stick and you

need to be able to understand and apply them, not just regurgitate them.

The best way to understand these algorithms is to start working through them using pen and paper examples. Each algorithm is accompanied by a worked example to follow. You can then try applying the same algorithm to some of the different data sets provided in the questions. When you have mastered this, the final task is to try implementing them in a program. This will bring challenges of its own, some dependent on your choice of language. Once you have done this, however, you'll be in an excellent position to tackle these questions in the examination.

Search algorithms

Linear search and binary search are used to find items.

Linear search

Linear search involves methodically searching one location after another until the searched-for value is found.

```
pointer=0 WHILE pointer<LengthOfList AND list[pointer]!=searchedFor
   Add one to pointer
ENDWHILE
IF pointer>=LengthOfList THEN
   PRINT("Item is not in the list")
ELSE
   PRINT("Item is at location "+pointer)
ENDIF
```

Worked example

| D | F | C | A | E | B | H | G |

We are looking for A.

| D | F | C | A | E | B | H | G |

And the next …

And the next, where we find A and stop. If we'd got to the end without finding A we would be able to deduce A is not in the list.

Extra info

Short-circuit evaluation

The linear search algorithm shown to the right makes use of short-circuit evaluation. This is when, given a condition made up of multiple parts linked by Boolean operators, the computer only evaluates the second condition if it is necessary, having evaluated the first.

For example:

```
Condition1 OR Condition2
```

If Condition1 is true there is no need to evaluate Condition2 as the statement is true regardless of whether it is true or false.

```
Condition1 AND
Condition2
```

If Condition1 is false there is no need to evaluate Condition2 as the statement is false regardless of whether it is true or false.

Most modern programming languages implement short-circuit evaluation that programmers can use to their advantage. Can you spot the run-time error that might occur if short-circuit evaluation wasn't in use in the line:

```
WHILE
pointer<LengthOfList
AND
list[pointer]!=searched
```

Binary search

Binary search works by dividing the list in two each time until we find the item being searched for. For binary search to work, the list has to be in order.

```
LowerBound=0
UpperBound=LengthOfList-1
Found=False
WHILE Found==False AND LowerBound!=UpperBound
    MidPoint=ROUND((LowerBound+UpperBound)/2)
    IF List[MidPoint]==searchedFor THEN
        Found=True
    ELSEIF List[MidPoint]<searchedFor THEN
        LowerBound=MidPoint+1
    ELSE
        UpperBound=MidPoint-1
    ENDIF
ENDWHILE
IF Found==True THEN
    PRINT("Item found at "+MidPoint)
ELSE
    PRINT("Item not in list")
ENDIF
```

Worked example

This time we will search for E.

We have our list of items in order, with their indexes. We put the lower bound (LB) as the first item, the upper bound (UB) as the index of the last item and work out the midpoint (MP) by adding them together and dividing by 2 to get the midpoint (MP) (0+14)/2=7.

A	B	C	D	E	F	G	H	I	J	K	L	M	N	O
0	1	2	3	4	5	6	7	8	9	10	11	12	13	14

LB   MP   UB

The item at the midpoint location, H, is greater than E so we know E lies between LB and MP. The new upper bound therefore becomes MP−1 (that is, 6). We can then repeat the calculation of getting the midpoint (0+6)/2=3.

A	B	C	D	E	F	G	H	I	J	K	L	M	N	O
0	1	2	3	4	5	6	7	8	9	10	11	12	13	14

LB   MP   UB

The item at 3,D, is smaller than E so we know E lies between MP and UB. The new lower bound therefore becomes MP+1 (that is, 4). The new midpoint is (4+6)/2 =5.

A	B	C	D	E	F	G	H	I	J	K	L	M	N	O
0	1	2	3	4	5	6	7	8	9	10	11	12	13	14

          LB MP UB

F is greater than E so the UB becomes MP−1.

The upper and lower bounds are now in the same position, meaning we have discounted all of the list bar one item. When we check we can see this is the item we are looking for and so E is at position 4. If this had not been the item we were looking for then we could conclude the item was not in the list.

A	B	C	D	E	F	G	H	I	J	K	L	M	N	O
0	1	2	3	4	5	6	7	8	9	10	11	12	13	14

         LB
         UB

Two points should be borne in mind with this example:

1. You may have noticed it took us no fewer steps than linear search would have. Would this still be the case if we'd been searching for M? How about if we'd been searching for the item in a list of 1000 items? The worst case scenario for a binary search on a list of 1000 items would be eight checks; for linear search you would need to check all 1000.

2. Clearly in our example we have nice evenly distributed items going up one letter at a time so we could predict where E would have been. In real life, data is seldom like this. Think about if you were to list all the names in your school or college alphabetically.

Binary search is an example of what we call a 'divide and conquer' algorithm. A divide and conquer algorithm (see Chapter 4) is one that works by repeatedly breaking a problem down into smaller problems and tackling these smaller problems to build an answer to the original problem.

In this section we have looked at binary searches using an iterative approach. As can be seen in Chapter 1 on page 19, it is also possible to implement binary searches recursively.

> **Questions**
>
> 1. This chapter looks at searching, sorting and shortest path algorithms. Find four other types of algorithm.
> 2. Perform a linear search and a binary search to find Peru in the following list:
>
>   Argentina, Bolivia, Brazil, Chile, Colombia, Ecuador, French Guiana, Guyana, Paraguay, Peru, Suriname, Uruguay, Venezuela
> 3. Describe the circumstances in which you might choose to use a linear search over a binary search.

Sorting algorithms

Sorting algorithms are used to put data (usually in an array or list) in order. This data may be numbers, strings, records or objects. The four sorting algorithms you are expected to know are bubble sort, insertion sort, merge sort and quicksort.

Bubble sort

Bubble sort is one of the easiest sorting algorithms to understand and implement; however, as we will see, it is very inefficient compared to its alternatives.

It works as follows:

Create a Boolean variable called swapMade and set it to true.

```
Set swapMade to true
WHILE swapMade is true
        Set swapMade to false.
        Start at position 0.
        FOR position=0 TO listlength-2 i.e. the last but one
                                                      position
                Compare the item at the position you are
                at with the one ahead of it.
                IF they are out of order THEN
                        Swap items and set swapMade to
                        true.
                    END IF
        NEXT position
    END WHILE
```

Worked example

Set swapMade to false.
swapMade=False

B and A are out of order so we swap them and set swapMade to true and move to the second position.

swapMade=True

B and C are in order so no change is made.

swapMade=True

C and F are in order so no change is made.

swapMade=True

F and E are out of order so they are swapped.

swapMade=True

F and D are out of order so they are swapped.

swapMade=True

We are now at the end of the list so check swapMade. It is true so we go back to the start of the list and reset swapMade to false.

swapMade=False

| A | B | C | E | D | F |

Again we move through the list position by position. A and B are in the right order, as are B and C; similarly C and E.

When we get to E, we see E and D are out of order so they are swapped, swapMade becomes True and we move forward to the fifth location.

swapMade=True

swapMade=True

| A | B | C | D | E | F |

E and F are in order.

swapMade=True

Because this example is of a trivially small list, we can see the list is now in order. The algorithm, however, just knows that a swap has been made on this pass and therefore it wasn't in order at the beginning of the pass. swapMade is reset to false and we go back to the first position.

swapMade=False

| A | B | C | D | E | F |

This time we pass through the list without making any changes. The flag remains at False and so the list must be sorted.

Questions

1. Demonstrate how to do a bubble sort on the following lists:
   (a) B, A, E, D, C, F
   (b) F, A, B, C, D, E
   (c) B, C, D, E, F, A
2. (a) Write a program that creates a random array of integers and performs a bubble sort on them.
   (b) Amend the program so it allows you to specify the size of the array and outputs the time taken to perform the sort.
   (c) Compare the time taken to sort lists of 10, 100, 1000 and 10000 integers.
3. Various methods have been used to improve the efficiency of bubble sort. Try to find out some of these and comment on their effectiveness.

Whilst bubble sort is easy to understand it is not terribly efficient.
Consider how bubble sort would tackle this list: I, H, G, F, E, D, C, B, A.

Insertion sort

Insertion sort works by dividing a list into two parts: sorted and unsorted.
Elements are inserted one by one into their correct position in the sorted
section.

```
Make the first item the sorted list, the remaining items
are the unsorted list.
WHILE there are items in the unsorted list
      Take the first item of the unsorted list.
      WHILE there is an item to the left of it which is
      smaller than itself
            Swap with that item.
      END WHILE
      The sorted list is now one item bigger.
END WHILE
```

Worked example

C becomes a member of the 'sorted list'.
A, the first item of the unsorted list is smaller than C so is shuffled to the
left of it.

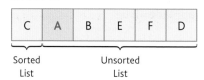

A and C are now both in the sorted list.

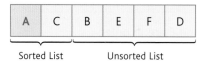

B is now the first item in the unsorted list.

B is less than C so is shuffled to the left of it. B is not less than A
so it does not get shuffled any further. E is now the first item of the
unsorted list.

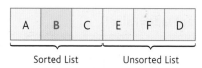

E is not less than C so it does not need shuffling anywhere.

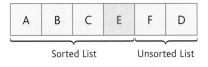

Sorted List   Unsorted List

Similarly F is not less than E so than joins the sorted list without being shuffled.

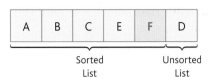

Sorted List   Unsorted List

D is now the only member of the unsorted list. It is less than F so shuffles left.

D is less than E so shuffles left again.

D is not less than C so is now in its correct place.

All items in the list are now members of the sorted list.

Questions

1. Demonstrate an insertion sort on:
   (a) D, G, F, B, A, H, C, E
   (b) A, B, C, D, H, G, F, E
   (c) B, C, D, E, F, G, H, A
2. (a) Write a program that creates a random array of integers and performs an insertion sort on them.
   (b) Amend the program so it allows you to specify the size of the array and outputs the time taken to perform the sort.
   (c) Compare the time taken to sort lists of 10, 100, 1000 and 10 000 integers.

Merge sort

A Level only

To understand merge sort, you first need to understand how we merge lists. If we have two lists in order we can merge them into a single, ordered list, using the following algorithm:

```
WHILE list1 is not empty and list2 is not empty
    If the first item in list1<list2 THEN
        Remove the first item from list1 and add it to
        newlist.
    ELSE
        Remove the first item from list2 and add it to
        newlist.
    ENDIF
ENDWHILE
IF list1 is empty THEN
    Add the remainder of list2 to newlist.
ELSE
    Add the remainder of list1 to newlist.
ENDIF
```

Worked example

List 1   List 2   New List

The first item of List2 (A) is lower than the first item of List1 (B) so we remove it from List2 and add it to the new list.

List 1

| B | C | G | H |

List 2

| D | E | F | | A |

Now the first item in List 1 (B) is the smallest so this is added to the new list.

List 1

| C | G | H |

List 2

| D | E | F |

New List

| A | B |

Again, the first item of List1 (C) is the smallest so this is added to the new list. This process continues until ...

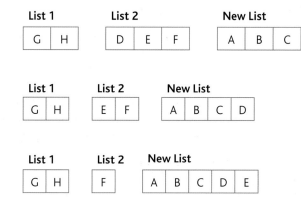

List 1

| G | H |

List 2

| D | E | F |

New List

| A | B | C |

List 1

| G | H |

List 2

| E | F |

New List

| A | B | C | D |

List 1

| G | H |

List 2

| F |

New List

| A | B | C | D | E |

... List 2 is empty. We therefore append the remainder of List 1 onto the new list.

List 1

| G | H |

List 2

New List

| A | B | C | D | E | F |

List 1

List 2

New List

| A | B | C | D | E | F | G | H |

This process of merging lists is used, as the name suggests, in merge sort. The algorithm is:

```
Split a list of n items into n lists of 1 item.
While there is more than 1 list, recursively pair up the
lists and merge each pair into a single list twice the
size.
```

1. Demonstrate a merge sort on:
   (a) D, G, F, B, A, H, C, E
   (b) A, B, C, D, H, G, F, E
   (c) B, C, D, E, F, G, H, A
2. (a) Write a program that creates a random array of integers and performs a merge sort on them.
   (b) Amend the program so it allows you to specify the size of the array and outputs the time taken to perform the sort.
   (c) Compare the time taken to sort lists of 10, 100, 1000 and 10,000 integers.

Computing people

Sir Charles Anthony Richardson Hoare

As well as inventing quicksort, Tony Hoare is famous for proposing Hoare Logic, a system used for formally verifying a program is correct. He is an emeritus professor at Oxford University and a senior researcher at Microsoft. Tony Hoare has received much recognition of his work, including a knighthood and the ACM Turing Award (Computer Science's equivalent of the Nobel Prize).

Figure 5.1 Tony Hoare

Worked example

The list is split into eight single item lists:

Each pair is merged into a list two items big. When merging them we follow the merge algorithm looked at previously in this section.

Again we merge each pair of lists into a single list four items big.

We then merge these into a list eight items big.

We have a single sorted list and so can stop.

Merge sort is also an example of a divide and conquer algorithm. It is common for such algorithms to be tackled recursively.

Quicksort

Quicksort is another divide and conquer sorting algorithm. It was devised by British computer scientist Tony Hoare.

It works as follows:

1. Take the first item in the list, make it a list one item big and call it the pivot.
2. Split the remainder of the list into two sub-lists: those less than or equal to the pivot and those greater than the pivot.
3. Recursively apply step 2 until all sub-lists are pivots.
4. The pivots can now be combined to form a sorted list.

Worked example

| D | F | C | A | E | B | H | G |

Starting with the list above, we take the first element and make it the pivot (technically it doesn't have to be the first element; it can be any). We then create two sub-lists of those items smaller and larger than the pivot. Notice how we make no attempt to sort the sub-lists; items are just added in order.

| C | A | B | D | F | E | H | G |

We now go through exactly the same process for both these sub-lists. C and F become pivots and we generate sub-lists either side of them. In the case of C, as A and B are both less than C an empty list is generated to its right.

Again we repeat for all the sub-lists. A becomes a pivot with the sub-list just containing B to the right of it. E becomes a pivot with no sub-lists and H becomes a pivot with the sub-list G to the left of it.

Now the single item lists G and H become pivots.

| A | | B | | C | | D | | E | | F | | G | | H |

As everything is a pivot we assemble all the pivots to get our sorted list.

| A | B | C | D | E | F | G | H |

Whilst a tremendously powerful method, using recursion on large data sets can be problematic. The computer can run out of memory, causing the dreaded 'stack overflow' error.

To avoid this problem, there is an 'in-place' version of the algorithm that goes through the same process but on a single list without the need for recursive calls. There are a number of variants of the in-place algorithm but all work in a similar way.

```
Place leftPointer at first item in the list and
rightPointer at the last item in the list.
WHILE leftPointer!=rightPointer
  WHILE list[leftPointer] < list[rightPointer]  AND
  leftPointer!=rightPointer
    Add one to leftPointer
  END WHILE
  Swap list[leftPointer] with list[rightPointer]
  WHILE list[leftPointer] < list[rightPointer]  AND
  leftPointer!=rightPointer
    Subtract one from rightPointer
  END WHILE
  Swap list[leftPointer] with list[rightPointer]
END WHILE
```

Worked example

Now the item pointed to by the left and right pointers is in order. We now apply the algorithm to the sub-lists either side of this item and continue this process until the whole list is sorted.

A and D are in order so we move the left pointer across one.

D and F are out of order so we swap them.

| A | D | G | B | E | C | H | F |

→ ←

Now we move the right pointer. D and H are in the right order.

| A | D | G | B | E | C | H | F |

→ ←

D and C are out of order so we swap them.

| A | D | G | B | E | C | H | F |

→ ←

Now it is the turn of the left pointer again.

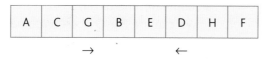

| A | C | G | B | E | D | H | F |

→ ←

G and D are out of order so we swap and go back to moving the right pointer until the items at the pointers are out of order.

| A | C | D | B | E | G | H | F |

→ ←

| A | C | D | B | E | G | H | F |

→ ←

| A | C | D | B | E | G | H | F |

→ ←

We swap C and B and move the left arrow.

| A | C | B | D | E | G | H | F |

→ ←

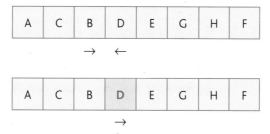

| A | C | B | D | E | G | H | F |

→
←

Now the arrows have met at D, we know D is in the correct place. We apply the algorithm to the sub-lists A,C,B and E,G,H,F. This process is repeated until all items are in the right place.

Questions

1. Demonstrate a recursive or in-place quicksort on:
   (a) D, G, F, B, A, H, C, E
   (b) A, B, C, D, H, G, F, E
   (c) B, C, D, E, F, G, H, A
2. (a) Write a program that creates a random array of integers and performs a quicksort on them.
   (b) Amend the program so it allows you to specify the size of the array and outputs the time taken to perform the sort.
   (c) Compare the time taken to sort lists of 10, 100, 1000 and 10 000 integers.

Complexity

We can evaluate algorithms in terms of how long they take to execute and how much memory they use. Often speed can be increased at the expense of using more memory.

Whilst knowing the time it takes an algorithm to execute can be of use, it should be kept in mind that computers are doubling in power roughly every 18 months. An implementation of an algorithm acting on a given set of data that may have taken five seconds to execute on a top-of-the-range computer 10 years ago might take less than a tenth of second to execute on today's machines.

A more useful way to compare algorithms is their complexity. Complexity doesn't show us how fast an algorithm performs, but rather how well it scales given larger data sets to act upon. An algorithm, like bubble sort, may appear to work well on small sets of data, but as the amount of data it has to sort increases it soon starts to take unacceptable amounts of time to run.

We can use Big-O notation to note an algorithm's complexity. It's called Big-O because it is written $O(x)$ where x is the worst-case complexity of the algorithm. Because we are only interested in how the algorithm scales and not the exact time taken when using Big-O, we simplify the number of steps an algorithm takes.

Let's imagine an algorithm acting on a data set of size n takes $7n^3+n^2+4n+1$ steps to solve a particular problem.

Now look at what happens to the terms as n increases:

n	$7n^3$	n^2	$4n$	1	Total
1	7	1	4	1	13
10	7 000	100	40	1	7 141
100	7 000 000	10 000	400	1	7 010 401
1000	7 000 000 000	1 000 000	4 000	1	7 001 004 001

The larger n gets, the less of an impact n^2+4n+1 has on the total compared to $7n^3$.

As we aren't interested in the exact number of steps needed to solve the problem, but how that number increases with n, we keep only the term that has the most effect (that is, the one with the highest exponent); in this case $7n^3$.

(Note that if we had a term raised to the power of n such as the term 10^n this would be the term we keep as this would have more of an effect on the total than the other terms, as you will see in the next section when we look at *exponential complexity*.)

Similarly, we aren't worried about the actual speed (that will depend on the machine running the algorithm). We can remove any constants that n is multiplied by (if we only have a constant we divide it by itself to get 1). Thus $7n^3$ becomes n^3.

So our algorithm that takes $7n^3+n^2+4n+1$ steps has a time complexity in Big-O notation of $O(n^3)$.

You need to be aware of five different types of complexity: constant, linear, polynomial, exponential and logarithmic.

Key points

- Big-O notation is used to show that the time algorithms take (or space they need) to execute increases as the size of the data set they operate on increases.

- To get the Big-O value:
  - remove all terms except the one with the largest exponent
  - remove any constant factors.

Questions

1. An algorithm takes $2n^4+n-1$ steps to run on a data set n big. Express its time complexity in Big-O notation.

2. An algorithm takes $6n+3$ steps to run on a data set n big. Express its time complexity in Big-O notation.

3. An algorithm takes $2n^2+2n+2$ steps to run on a data set n big. Express its time complexity in Big-O notation.

4. An algorithm takes 10 steps to run on a data set n big. Express its time complexity in Big-O notation.

Figure 5.2 Constant complexity O(1)

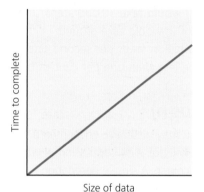

Figure 5.3 Linear complexity O(n)

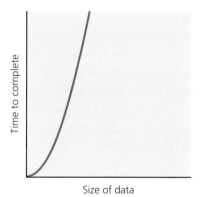

Figure 5.4 Graph showing quadratic complexity; that is, O(n²)

Constant complexity O(1)

Algorithms that show a constant complexity take the same time to run regardless of the size of a data set. An example of this is pushing an item onto, or popping an item off, a stack; no matter how big the stack, the time to push or pop remains constant.

Linear complexity O(n)

Algorithms with linear complexity increase at the same rate as the input size increases. If the input size doubles, the time taken for the algorithm to complete doubles. An example of this is the average time to find an element using linear search.

Polynomial complexity O(n^k) (where k>=0)

Polynomial complexity is that where the time taken as the size increases can be expressed as n^k where *k* is a constant value. As n^0=1 and n^1=n constant and linear complexities are also polynomial complexities. Other polynomial complexities include quadratic O(n²) and cubic O(n³).

Extra info

P vs NP

There is a set of problems in computer science known as NP problems. NP stands for Non-Deterministic Polynomial Time. What this means in simple terms is if you are given a solution to that problem you can check the solution is correct in polynomial time.

Naturally all problems that can be solved in polynomial time (P problems) can have their solutions checked in polynomial time. Therefore all P problems are also NP problems.

Other problems, however, take longer than polynomial time to solve but polynomial time to check. Take the subset sum problem. Given a set of positive and negative integers does there exist a (non-empty) subset that has the total 0?

    {−34, −21, −20, −17, −11, −8, −2, 3, 7, 9, 10, 14, 28}

Finding a solution is difficult, especially as the list grows. An algorithm exists that has a time complexity of O(2$^{n/2}$).

Once given an answer, however, one can quickly verify it is correct. In the example above, given the subset −34, 3, 7, 10, 14 we can get the total as 0 and verify this is a valid solution.

What has been long debated by mathematicians and computer scientists is 'are all NP problems actually also P problems?' Do there exist yet undiscovered algorithms for all NP problems that will solve them in polynomial time? Does P=NP? Most computer scientists believe the answer to this question is 'no' but it is yet to be proved either way. If someone does discover proof there is US$1 000 000 in prize money available.

Exponential complexity O(k^n) (where k>1)

Algorithms with exponential complexity do not scale well at all. Exponential complexity means that as the input *n* gets larger the time taken increases at a rate of k^n where *k* is a constant value.

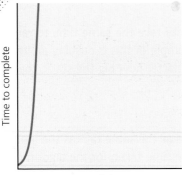

Figure 5.5 Exponential complexity $O(k^n)$

Looking at the graph, exponential growth may seem very similar to polynomial growth. As can be seen from the table below, it grows at a much faster rate:

n	n^2 (polynomial)	2^n (exponential)
1	1	2
10	100	1024
20	400	1048576
30	900	1073741824

To illustrate how a problem can quickly become unsolvable in a practical amount of time (what computer scientists term 'intractable') with exponential growth, consider n=100:

An algorithm with quadratic growth (n^2) would take 10000 steps.

An algorithm with exponential growth of 2^n would take around 1.3×10^{30} steps. A computer performing 10 billion steps per second since the beginning of the universe would still be less than one per cent of the way through solving the problem.

Logarithmic complexity O(log n)

If you are studying A Level mathematics, you may well have encountered logarithms (and if you haven't you certainly will do). A full discussion of what logarithms are is outside the bounds of this course. A simple description is that a logarithm is the inverse of exponentiation (raising to the power of).

If $y=x^z$ then $z=\log_x y$

So 2^3 is 8

$\log_2 8$ is 3 (said as 'log to the base 2 of 8 is 3')

Algorithms with logarithmic complexity scale up extremely well. The rate at which their execution time increases, decreases as the data set increases.

In other words, the difference in execution time between n=100 and n=150 will be less than the difference in execution time between n=50 and n=100.

A good example is binary search. As the size of the data set doubles, the number of items to be checked only increases by one.

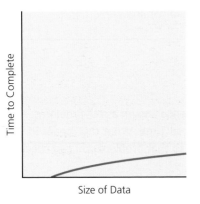

Figure 5.6 Logarithmic complexity

Key points

– Constant complexities take the same number of steps regardless of the size of the data set.

– The steps taken by an algorithm of linear complexity increase at the same rate as the size of data set.

– Polynomial complexities are those that can be written as $O(n^k)$ where k is a positive integer (linear and constant are both polynomial).

– Exponential complexities can be written as $O(k^n)$.

– Logarithmic complexities can be written as $O(\log n)$.

Questions

1. Algorithm A blurs a 1000000 pixel image in 1 second; Algorithm B blurs the same image in 0.7 seconds. One algorithm has a time complexity of $O(n)$ the other $O(n^2)$.
   (a) Is it possible to determine which algorithm has which complexity?
   (b) If the answer to (a) is yes, which algorithm has which complexity? If no, what additional information would you need?
2. Find out the time complexities in Big-O notation to: bubble sort, insertion sort, merge sort and quicksort. For each, decide if they are linear, constant, polynomial, logarithmic or exponential.
3. Find out the time complexities of binary search and linear search. For each, decide if they are linear, constant, polynomial, logarithmic or exponential.

Shortest-path algorithms

Computing people

Edsger Dijkstra

Edsger Dijkstra (1930–2002) was a computer scientist renowned for his work on programming languages and how programs can be proved to work. He invented several algorithms, including the eponymous Dijkstra's algorithm. Dijkstra is well known for his opinions on certain areas of computer science, for example he believed students should not be taught the BASIC programming language, saying 'It is practically impossible to teach good programming to students that have had a prior exposure to BASIC: as potential programmers they are mentally mutilated beyond hope of regeneration.'

He was equally scathing of software engineering as a discipline, saying '[it] should be known as "The Doomed Discipline"'.

In 1972, he received the prestigious ACM Turing Award.

Figure 5.7 Edsger Dijkstra

Often we want to find the shortest path in a graph or tree (you may recall a tree is a graph without cycles). The classic application of this is to find the shortest distance between two places, but as we will see later there are other useful applications. We will look at two shortest-path algorithms: Dijkstra's algorithm and A*-Search. You may wish to skip ahead to Chapter 13 and briefly look at graphs and trees before continuing.

A Level only

Dijkstra's algorithm

Dijkstra's algorithm finds the shortest path between two points and is named after its inventor, Edsger Dijkstra.

The algorithm goes as follows:

```
Mark the start node as a distance of 0 from itself and
all other nodes as an infinite distance from the start
node.
WHILE the destination node is unvisited
    Go to the closest unvisited node to A (initially this
    will be A itself) and call this the current node.
    FOR every unvisited node connected to the current node:
        Calculate the distance to the current plus the
        distance of the edge to unvisited
        If this distance is less than the currently
        recorded shortest distance, make it the new
        shortest distance.
    NEXT connected node
    Mark the current node as visited.
ENDWHILE
```

This, at this stage, probably seems unclear. It is much easier to understand with the aid of an example.

Worked example

Using the graph below, we shall use Dijkstra's algorithm to find the shortest path from A to J.

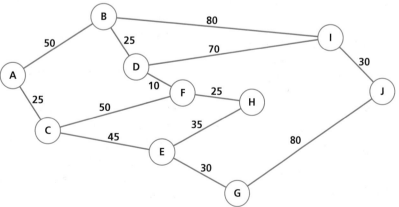

Figure 5.8 Nodes

In this example we want to find the shortest route from node A to node J.

Node	Shortest distance from A	Previous node
A (C)	0	
B	∞	
C	∞	
D	∞	
E	∞	
F	∞	
G	∞	
H	∞	
I	∞	
J	∞	

We begin with the starting node A as the 'current node'.

Next we update the values on the table for all nodes connected to the starting node. So in this case, B becomes 50 and C becomes 25. When we update a value on the table we put the value of the 'current' in the Previous node column.

Node	Shortest distance from A	Previous node
A (C)	0	
B	∞ 50	A
C	∞ 25	A
D	∞	
E	∞	
F	∞	
G	∞	
H	∞	
I	∞	
J	∞	

Now we can mark A as 'visited' and then make the unvisited node with the smallest 'Shortest distance from A' as the new current node – in this case C.

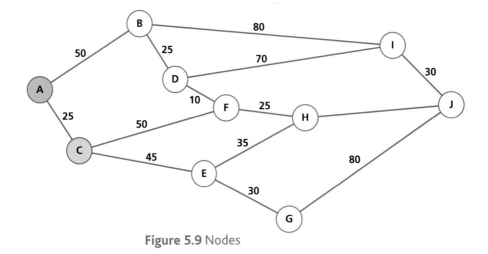

Figure 5.9 Nodes

We now need to update all the unvisited nodes connected to the current node, C. To do this, we add the distance of the current node C from A (in this case 25) to the distance from the current node C to the connecting nodes. In our example the distance to F is 75 (that is, 25+50) and the distance to E is 70 (that is, 25+45).

We only update the values in the table if the values we have calculated are less than the values already in the table.

In this case, the values in the table for E and F are infinity so we update them both and put the current node in the Previous node column. (The route for the current shortest distance from A to F involves the edge C–F and the route for the shortest distance from A to E involves the edge C–E.)

Node	Shortest distance from A	Previous node
A (V)	0	
B	∞ 50	A
C (C)	∞ 25	A
D	∞	
E	∞ 70	C
F	∞ 75	C
G	∞	
H	∞	
I	∞	
J	∞	

We can now mark C as visited and repeat the process. B is now the closest unvisited node to A so this becomes the current node.

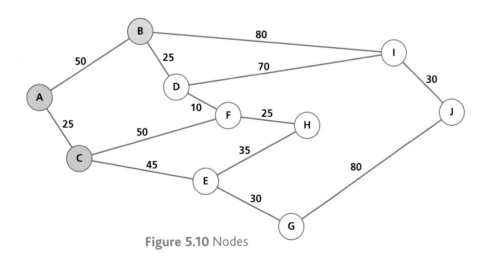

Figure 5.10 Nodes

Next update the connecting nodes D (50+25=75) and I (50+80=130) and put B as their previous node.

Node	Shortest distance from A	Previous node
A (V)	0	
B (C)	∞ 50	A
C (V)	∞ 25	A
D	∞ 75	B
E	∞ 70	C
F	∞ 75	C
G	∞	
H	∞	
I	∞ 130	B
J	∞	

E now becomes the current node and we update G and H.

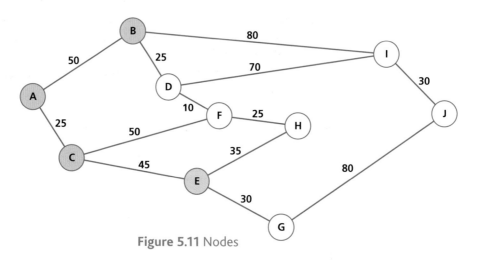

Figure 5.11 Nodes

Node	Shortest distance from A	Previous node
A (V)	0	
B (V)	∞ 50	A
C (V)	∞ 25	A
D	∞ 75	B
E (C)	∞ 70	C
F	∞ 75	C
G	∞ 100	E
H	∞ 105	E
I	∞ 130	B
J	∞	

We now have two nodes, D and F, which are the shortest distance from A (that is, 75). We can pick either of these arbitrarily to be the new current node. We shall pick D.

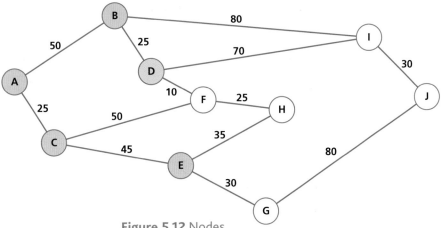

Figure 5.12 Nodes

We calculate the distance from A, via D, for the connecting nodes and get I to be 145 (that is, 75+70) and F to be 85 (that is, 75+10). The value of 145 is higher than the existing value for I on the table 130. **We therefore do not update the table.**

Likewise 85 is greater than F's existing value of 75, so again the table is not updated.

Node	Shortest distance from A	Previous node
A (V)	0	
B (V)	∞ 50	A
C (V)	∞ 25	A
D (C)	∞ 75	B
E (V)	∞ 70	C
F	∞ 75	C
G	∞ 100	E
H	∞ 105	E
I	∞ 130	B
J	∞	

F now becomes the current node. The calculated distance for H is less than the existing value of 105 so we update the table and the new previous node for H is F.

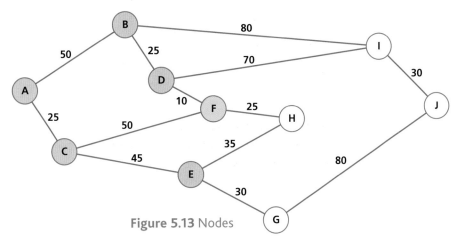

Figure 5.13 Nodes

Node	Shortest distance from A	Previous node
A (V)	0	
B (V)	~~∞~~ 50	A
C (V)	~~∞~~ 25	A
D (V)	~~∞~~ 75	B
E (V)	~~∞~~ 70	C
F (C)	~~∞~~ 75	C
G	~~∞~~ 100	E
H	~~∞~~ ~~105~~ 100	~~E~~ F
I	~~∞~~ 130	B
J	∞	

The next node 'current node' could be G or H. We will arbitrarily pick G and update accordingly.

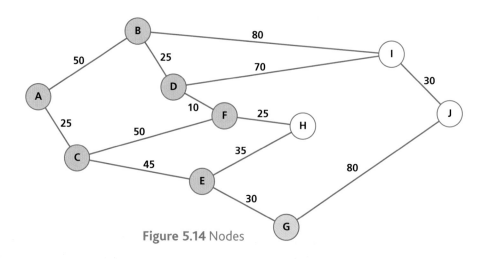

Figure 5.14 Nodes

Node	Shortest distance from A	Previous node
A (V)	0	
B (V)	~~∞~~ 50	A
C (V)	~~∞~~ 25	A
D (V)	~~∞~~ 75	B
E (V)	~~∞~~ 70	C
F (V)	~~∞~~ 75	C
G (C)	~~∞~~ 100	E
H	~~∞~~ ~~105~~ 100	~~E~~ F
I	~~∞~~ 130	B
J	~~∞~~ 180	G

We now have a value for J but must not stop yet. **We continue until J has been visited.** Next we make H current. As all nodes connected to H have been visited we don't need to update the table.

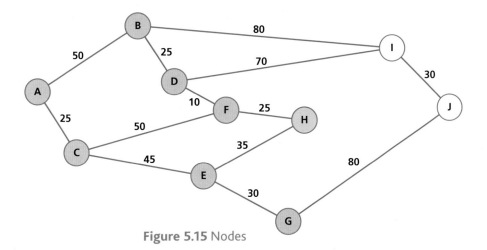

Figure 5.15 Nodes

Node	Shortest distance from A	Previous node
A (V)	0	
B (V)	∞ 50	A
C (V)	∞ 25	A
D (V)	∞ 75	B
E (V)	∞ 70	C
F (V)	∞ 75	C
G (V)	∞ 100	E
H (C)	∞ ~~105~~ 100	~~E~~ F
I	∞ 130	B
J	∞ 180	G

We mark H as visited and I as current. The distance to J via I is 160 (that is, 130+30). As 160 is smaller than the existing value in the table, 180, we update the table accordingly.

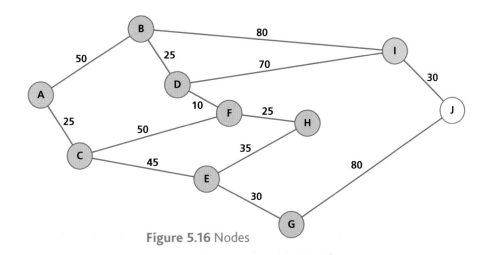

Figure 5.16 Nodes

Node	Shortest distance from A	Previous node
A (V)	0	
B (V)	~~∞~~ 50	A
C (V)	~~∞~~ 25	A
D (V)	~~∞~~ 75	B
E (V)	~~∞~~ 70	C
F (V)	~~∞~~ 75	C
G (V)	~~∞~~ 100	E
H (V)	~~∞~~ ~~105~~ 100	~~E~~ F
I (C)	~~∞~~ 130	B
J	~~∞~~ ~~180~~ 160	~~G~~ I

Now J becomes the current node. As the current node, we know it is the shortest unvisited node from A. The value in the table for J represents the shortest possible distance to it.

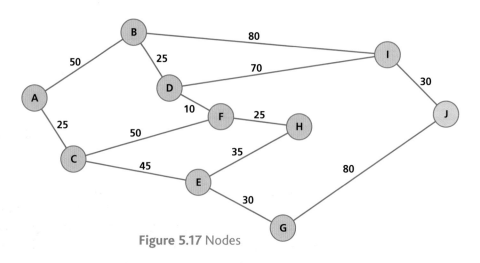

Figure 5.17 Nodes

Node	Shortest distance from A	Previous node
A (V)	0	
B (V)	~~∞~~ 50	A
C (V)	~~∞~~ 25	A
D (V)	~~∞~~ 75	B
E (V)	~~∞~~ 70	C
F (V)	~~∞~~ 75	C
G (V)	~~∞~~ 100	E
H (V)	~~∞~~ ~~105~~ 100	~~E~~ F
I (V)	~~∞~~ 130	B
J (C)	~~∞~~ ~~180~~ 160	~~G~~ I

We know the shortest distance from A to J is 160. All that remains is to establish the route. We have the information we need to do this in the Previous node column and just need to work backwards from J to A. The node previous to J is I, previous to I is B and previous to B is A.

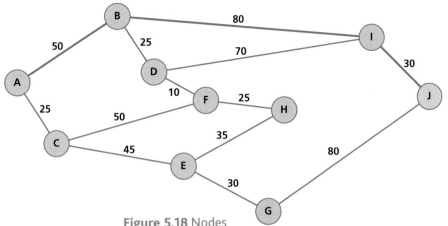

Figure 5.18 Nodes

Node	Shortest distance from A	Previous node
A (V)	0	
B (V)	∞ 50	A
C (V)	∞ 25	A
D (V)	∞ 75	B
E (V)	∞ 70	C
F (V)	∞ 75	C
G (V)	∞ 100	E
H (V)	∞ ~~105~~ 100	~~E~~ F
I (V)	∞ 130	B
J (C)	∞ ~~180~~ 160	~~G~~ I

Question

Use Dijkstra's Algorithm to find the shortest path from A to J on this graph:

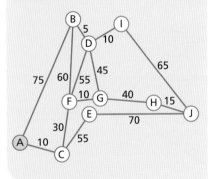

Question

Apply Dijkstra's algorithm to find the shortest path from A to J on the graph to the right.

In the previous example we looked at, we visited every other node before visiting our destination node. This will not always be the case. Dijkstra's algorithm always finds the shortest route but doesn't go about this in a particularly efficient way. Look at the following graph. It is clear looking at it that the shortest route is edge A–G–J.

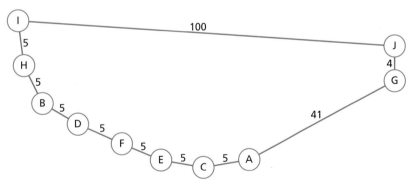

Figure 5.19 Nodes

A* search

A* search (pronounced 'A star') is an alternative algorithm that can be used for finding the shortest path. It performs better than Dijkstra's algorithm because of its use of **heuristics**. You will recall from Chapter 3 that a heuristic is when existing experience is used to form a judgement; a 'rule of thumb', as it were. In A* search, the heuristic must be *admissible*; that is to say, it must never make an overestimate.

The A* search algorithm works as follows:

```
Begin at the start node and make this the current node.
WHILE the destination node is unvisited
FOR each open node directly connected to the current node
        Add to the list of open nodes.
        Add the distance from the start (g) to the
        heuristic estimate of distance left (h).
        Assign this value (f) to the node.
NEXT connected node
Make the unvisited node with the lowest value the
current node.
ENDWHILE
```

Worked example

We will now work through the same example as we did with Dijkstra's algorithm.

The heuristic we will use is the straight line distance between a node and the end node. This is admissible as a straight line is always the shortest distance between two points. (Note that the graph is an *abstraction* of a set of roads. Unlike the edges in a graph, real roads are often not straight. Therefore in the graph you will find edges like G–J that have a weight with a higher distance than the straight line distance.)

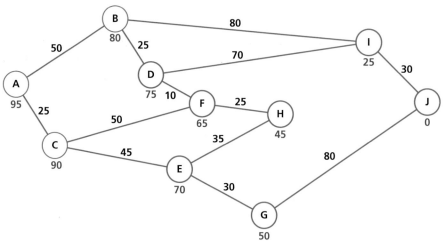

Figure 5.20 Nodes

Starting with A, as the current node we can 'open' and calculate the values for the connecting nodes B and C. The value for B becomes the path value of 50 plus its heuristic value of 80, making 130. Similarly, C becomes the path value of 25 plus its heuristic value of 90, making 115. We note we have reached B and C from their 'previous node' A.

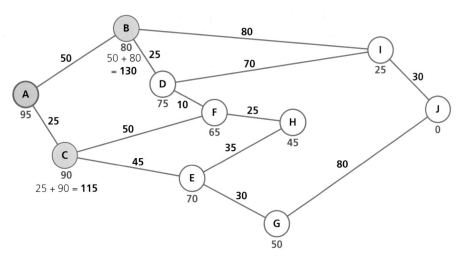

Figure 5.21 Nodes

Node	Path distance (g)	Heuristic distance (h)	f=g+h	Previous node
A	0	95	95	
B	50	80	130	A
C	25	90	115	A
D		75		
E		70		
F		65		
G		50		
H		45		
I		25		
J		0		

We close A and the smallest open node is now C so this becomes the current node, meaning we open and calculate F and E, noting we have arrived at them from the Previous node C.

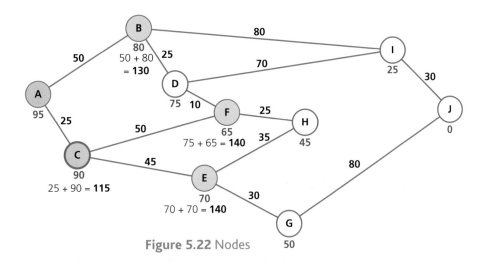

Figure 5.22 Nodes

Node	Path distance (g)	Heuristic distance (h)	f=g+h	Previous node
A	0	95	95	
B	50	80	130	A
C	25	90	115	A
D		75		
E	70	70	140	C
F	75	65	140	C
G		50		
H		45		
I		25		
J		0		

B is now the open node with the lowest value. We mark C as closed, make B current and open and calculate D and I and record that we arrived at them from the Previous node B.

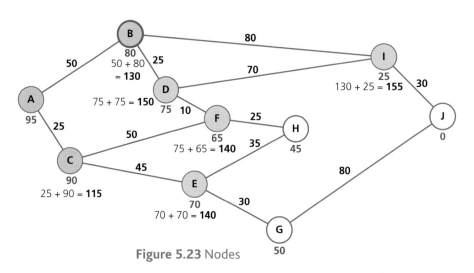

Figure 5.23 Nodes

Node	Path distance (g)	Heuristic distance (h)	f=g+h	Previous node
A	0	95	95	
B	50	80	130	A
C	25	90	115	A
D	75	75	150	B
E	70	70	140	C
F	75	65	140	C
G		50		
H		45		
I	130	25	155	B
J		0		

Next we can make F or E current. We can pick either so shall pick F. We open and calculate for H (noting we got there from F). As an updated value for D (85+75=160) would be worse than its existing value we leave it alone.

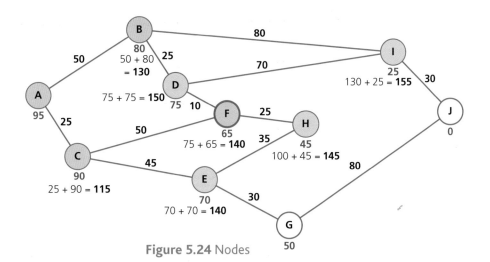

Figure 5.24 Nodes

Node	Path distance (g)	Heuristic distance (h)	f=g+h	Previous node
A	0	95	95	
B	50	80	130	A
C	25	90	115	A
D	75	75	150	B
E	70	70	140	C
F	75	65	140	C
G		50		
H	100	45	145	F
I	130	25	155	B
J		0		

Next step, close F and make E current. We can't improve on H as (105+45)>145 so we just open and calculate G.

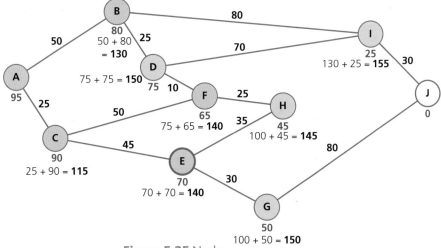

Figure 5.25 Nodes

Node	Path distance (g)	Heuristic distance (h)	f=g+h	Previous node
A	0	95	95	
B	50	80	130	A
C	25	90	115	A
D	75	75	150	B
E	70	70	140	C
F	75	65	140	C
G	100	50	150	E
H	100	45	145	F
I	130	25	155	B
J		0		

Moving forward a few steps:

- H becomes current node. It cannot improve on F so just gets closed.
- We can now open D or G; we shall arbitrarily pick D.
- Going to I via D gives a calculated value of 170, which is worse than 155.
- We therefore close D without updating it, make G current and open and calculate J.

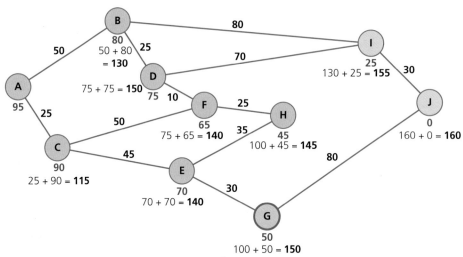

Figure 5.26 Nodes

Node	Path distance (g)	Heuristic distance (h)	f=g+h	Previous node
A	0	95	95	
B	50	80	130	A
C	25	90	115	A
D	75	75	150	B
E	70	70	140	C
F	75	65	140	C
G	100	50	150	E
H	100	45	145	F
I	130	25	155	B
J	180	0	180	G

We have a value for J but don't yet know this is the shortest path. To be sure, we have to wait until J is current. Next we close G and I becomes current. The calculated value for J via I is 160, which is smaller than the existing so we update J accordingly, making sure we record we get the new value via the 'previous node' I.

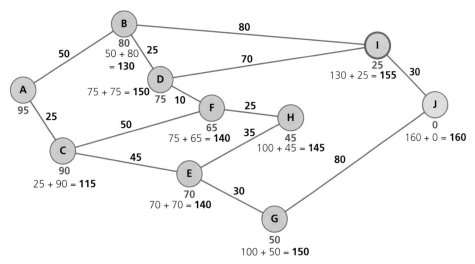

Figure 5.27 Nodes

Node	Path distance (g)	Heuristic distance (h)	f=g+h	Previous node
A	0	95	95	
B	50	80	130	A
C	25	90	115	A
D	75	75	150	B
E	70	70	140	C
F	75	65	140	C
G	100	50	150	E
H	100	45	145	F
I	130	25	155	B
J	180	0	~~180~~ 160	~~G~~ I

Finally I is closed, J becomes current and we stop.

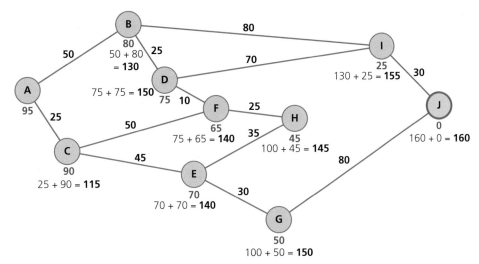

Figure 5.28 Nodes

Question

Use A* search to find the shortest path from A to J on this graph:

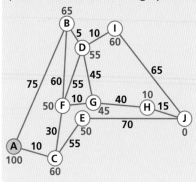

Node	Path distance (g)	Heuristic distance (h)	f=g+h	Previous node
A	0	95	95	
B	50	80	130	A
C	25	90	115	A
D	75	75	150	B
E	70	70	140	C
F	75	65	140	C
G	100	50	150	E
H	100	45	145	F
I	130	25	155	B
J	180	0	180 160	G I

We can now work backward through the 'previous node' column to determine the shortest path, just as we did with Dijkstra's algorithm.

You may at this stage be wondering why one would choose to use A* search over Dijkstra's algorithm. In this example we have had to visit every node in the graph (just like Dijkstra's) to get to the same answer.

Now think back to the other example:

Question

Perform an A* search to find the shortest path from A to J.

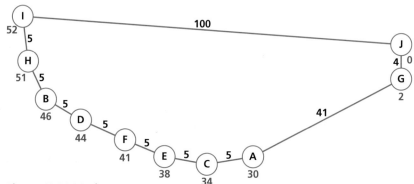

Figure 5.29 Nodes

A* search (using an admissible heuristic) and Dijkstra's algorithm will both always find the best solution, but A* can find it quicker. How much quicker depends on the effectiveness of the heuristic.

After tackling the questions above, you may have realised Dijkstra's algorithm is a particular case of an A* search where the heuristic estimate for the distance to the end node is always 0.

While we commonly tend to think of shortest-path problems in terms of distance, we can apply this thinking to a much wider range of problems. It might be the shortest path of moves needed to win a game or to solve a puzzle. We will now look at such an example.

Questions

1. What would happen if A* used a heuristic that wasn't admissible (that is, overestimated the distance to the end node)?
2. As a heuristic underestimates the distance more and more, how does this affect A*'s effectiveness.

Applying algorithms to a problem – the 'fifteen puzzle'

You may be familiar with slide puzzles where you have a grid of tiles with one space blank. By sliding tiles into the space, the challenge is to rearrange the tiles to form a picture, or, in our case, to order the numbers 1 to 15.

1	2	3	4
5	6	7	8
9	10	11	12
13	14	15	

There are 16! (over 2×10^{13}) different arrangements of the 15 tiles and space. Many of these are not possible to get to from an initial starting layout of the tiles in order and so are outside our search space.

Let's begin with a starting arrangement that is possible to solve:

5	1	7	6
10	9	2	4
13	3	8	
15	11	14	12

We need to decide on a data structure to represent the problem. We could use a graph but as we never want to return to a previously visited state a tree would be better.

The starting arrangement will be the root of the tree and its children the three possible moves that can be made from this state.

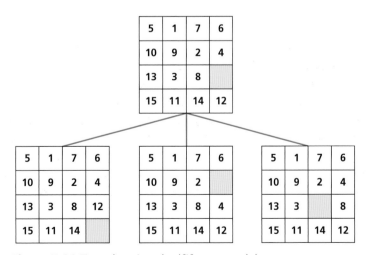

Figure 5.30 Tree showing the 'fifteen puzzle'

Question

For the given starting order show the first ten nodes to be generated by:
(a) a depth-first search
(b) a breadth-first search.

If we continue generating all the possible moves for the leaf nodes we will eventually come across a state with the tiles in order. By doing this in a depth-first manner, we may never get to the correct state; breadth first will eventually get there but will take a long time. (See Chapter 13 for depth- and breadth-first searches.)

While sometimes referred to as the 'A* algorithm', its full name is the 'A* Search Algorithm'. A* is a search algorithm in the same way that breadth-first and depth-first are searches; it is used to search for a given state space and in doing so finds the shortest path to it.

Let's look at how A* search can be applied to this problem. We add the start node and to the list of visited nodes and expand it. We apply A* Search in the following way:

```
Create two lists Open States and Closed States.

Calculate the heuristic value of the root node and put it
in the Open States list.

WHILE the destination state is not the current node.

    Remove the lowest scoring node from the Open States
    and make it the current node.

    Expand the current node, ignoring any child nodes
    that are already in the Open States or Closed States.

    FOR each child node from the expansion

            give it a score of its depth + heuristic value
            and add it to the Open States

    NEXT child node

    Put the current node in the Closed States list.

ENDWHILE
```

It may not seem it at first glance, but the above code is performing the same process as we performed using A* on the graph in the last section. This should become clear as we apply it to our fifteen puzzle.

Each of the children is added to the list of open nodes. Next we need a heuristic to estimate the number of moves left.

There are several different heuristics that can be used. In this example we shall use of one of the simplest, which is to count the number of tiles out of order.

heuristic estimate = 14   heuristic estimate = 15   heuristic estimate = 15

Question

Research and describe an alternative heuristic that could be used: The sum of the Manhattan distances. Is this better or worse than the one suggested to the right?

5	1	7	6
10	9	2	4
13	3	8	12
15	11	14	

5	1	7	6
10	9	2	
13	3	8	4
15	11	14	12

5	1	7	6
10	9	2	4
13	3		8
15	11	14	12

Figure 5.31 Fifteen puzzle

It is clear at the moment there is a long way to go to the correct solution. Each node is given the value of the number of moves needed to get to that node (in this instance 1) plus the heuristic estimate.

Node value = Moves so far + Heuristic

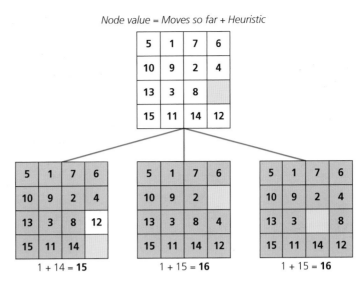

Figure 5.32 Fifteen puzzle

The next step is to move the most promising node (in this case the left-most) from the 'open list' to the 'visited list' and expand it. When expanding the node, we check the visited list to check we haven't already encountered that state. One possible child by moving the 12 down is:

5	1	7	6
10	9	2	4
13	3	8	
15	11	14	12

This of course is the starting configuration and on our visited list and so we do not generate this node. This leaves only one possible child we can generate.

Node value = Moves so far + Heuristic of how far

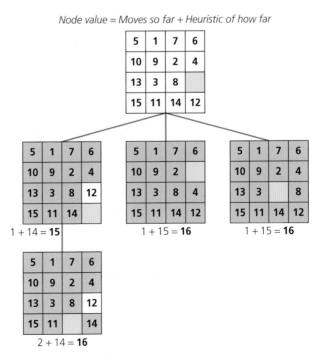

Figure 5.33 Fifteen puzzle

We now have three possible nodes to expand, all of equal values. We can pick any and shall simply go with the left-most.

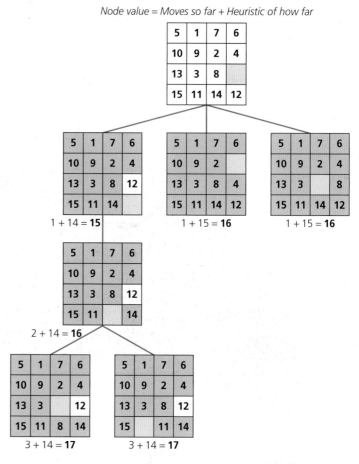

Node value = Moves so far + Heuristic of how far

Figure 5.34 Fifteen puzzle

The lowest valued nodes are now 16 so we would expand one of these. The algorithm continues until the Closed States list contains a square with the numbers 1 to 15 in order.

Practice questions

1. Write a program that generates an 'eight puzzle' (that is, the numbers 0–8 on a 3×3 grid). It should randomly shuffle the puzzle then allow the user to solve it. (It is important it shuffles the puzzle rather than just generating a random order, as it may otherwise not be solvable.)
2. Extend your program so it has a 'solve' option that will solve it using A* search.

Topic 3 Computer systems

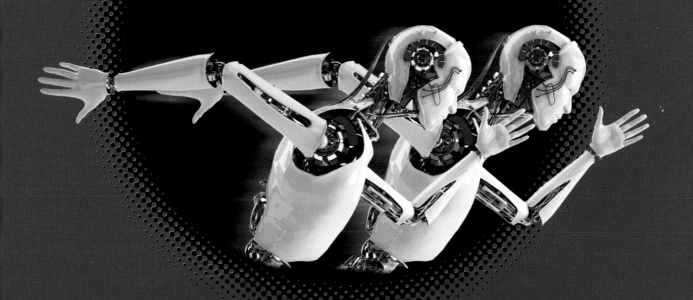

Chapter 6

Types of programming language

Introduction

There are many different types of programming language. In this chapter we will look at some of those types, their features and why they might be used.

The need for different paradigms

Key terms

Procedural programming A program where instructions are given in sequence; selection is used to decide what a program does and iteration dictates how many times it does it. In procedural programming, programs are broken down into key blocks called procedures and functions. Examples of procedural languages include BASIC, C and Pascal.

Logic programming Rather than stating what the program should do, in logic programming a problem is expressed as a set of facts (things that are always true) and rules (things that are true if particular facts are true). These facts and rules are then used to find a given goal. The most commonly used logic language is Prolog.

Functional programming A function, in mathematics, takes in a value or values and returns a value, for example:

double(4) would return 8
highestCommonFactor(36,24) would return 12

In functional programming, a description of the solution to a problem is built up through a collection of functions. Examples include Haskell and ML.

A *paradigm* is a way of thinking. We can apply different paradigms to how we program.

A common paradigm in programming is *imperative programming*. In linguistics, the imperative mood means the language we use to give orders, for example: Sit down. Eat up. Open the box. These sentences are all imperative – they're giving orders. Imperative programming languages are those in which we tell the computer what to do; we tell it how to solve a problem. **Procedural** and **object-oriented programming** are imperative paradigms.

In procedural programming, we use the program to tell the computer the steps we want the computer to go through to solve a problem. An alternative approach is *declarative programming*.

With declarative programming, we tell the computer the qualities the solution should have. A common example of declarative programming is SQL (Structured Query Language), as discussed in Chapter 15, where we describe what results we want from a database query but don't need to explain how we to get them. There are a number of subtypes of declarative language, including **logic** and **functional programming**.

Some languages allow programming in multiple paradigms. Python, for example, can be used procedurally but also supports object-oriented programming and some functional programming.

You will need to know about object-oriented programming for this course and so we will examine it in more detail later in this chapter.

A programming language is referred to as 'Turing Complete' if it can solve all the problems it has been proved computers can solve. Most programming languages across different paradigms are Turing Complete. We don't therefore have different programming paradigms because some problems can only be solved in a particular type, but rather because some problems are better suited to being solved in a particular paradigm. A lot of work has been done, for example, using logic programming for natural language processing. By defining a language by facts and rules, it is possible to get a computer to infer some meaning from the sentences we use.

> **Key points**
>
> - There are many different programming paradigms, each with many different languages.
> - Procedural programming uses sequence, selection and iteration to build procedures and subroutines.
> - Other paradigms include object oriented, functional and logical.
> - Each paradigm is best suited to a particular type of problem.

Assembly language (Little Man Computer)

Low-level languages

All computer programs are executed as machine code in the CPU. Each line of machine code consists of an instruction (opcode) that may be followed by an item of data (operand). This is then executed during a cycle of the fetch–decode–execute cycle.

Most programs are written in high-level languages such as C#, BASIC, Java and Python. A single line of code may represent multiple machine code instructions and are converted to this form using a compiler or an interpreter (as described in Chapter 8).

Assembly code is what is known as a low-level language. Each assembly code instruction represents a machine code instruction. This means that assembly code programs can often be much longer than their high-level equivalents. Rather than having to remember which binary sequence represents which instruction, assembly code allows us to use mnemonics to represent these sequences.

Each family of processors has its own **instruction sets** available. This means a program written in the assembly language for one instruction set will not work with another; for example an assembly language program written for a Raspberry Pi that uses an ARM processor will not work on a PC that uses an x86 processor.

Little Man Computer

For the examination, you will be expected to be able to program using the instruction set for the conceptual 'Little Man Computer'. This set of 11 instructions is much smaller than that of a real processor (which may contain hundreds) but the underlying concepts are the same.

Mnemonic	Instruction
ADD	Add
SUB	Subtract
STA	Store
LDA	Load
BRA	Branch always
BRZ	Branch if zero
BRP	Branch if positive
INP	Input
OUT	Output
HLT	End program
DAT	Data location

Question

Download a Little Man Computer implementation so you can work through the examples in this chapter.

You can find a list of LMC implementations at www.hodderplus.co.uk.

A simple Little Man Computer program

As with any programming, the only way to truly get to grips with assembly code is through lots of practice. There are several implementations of LMC online, and while they may have slightly different mnemonics for their instructions they all work in pretty much the same way.

Each line of LMC code can have up to three parts: a label, a mnemonic and some data (there may be an additional comment after these but this has no bearing on the program's execution).

The label is used as an identifier to give a name to that line of code. They are also used with the DAT mnemonic to give a label to refer to a memory location. This is effectively a variable.

Let's start with an example of adding two numbers together.

```
        INP
        STA     Num1
        INP
        ADD     Num1
        OUT
Num1    DAT
```

The first part of the program to take note of is actually the final line. Num1 DAT tells the assembler you want to have a data location, which you will refer to in the program as Num1.

- The first line (INP) means the user must input a number, which is then stored in the accumulator (sometimes referred to in LMC as the calculator).
- The next tells it to store the contents of the accumulator in the data location Num1.
- The third line means another number is input and stored in the accumulator.
- The line ADD Num1 tells the computer to add whatever is stored at location Num1 (that is, the first number we entered) to whatever is stored in the accumulator (that is, the second number we entered). The result of this calculation is stored back in the accumulator.
- Finally, OUT outputs the contents of the accumulator (that is, the numbers we added together).

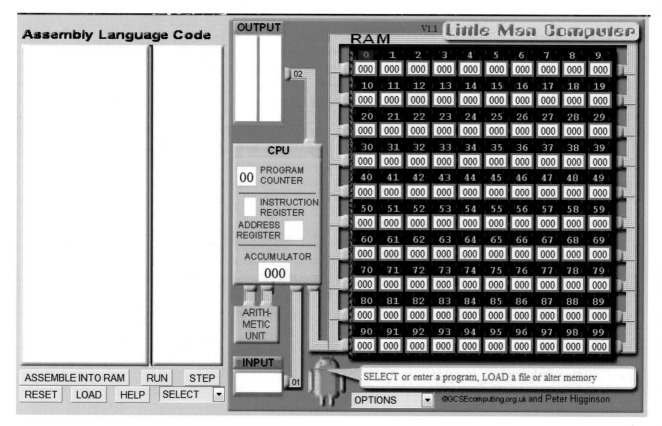

Figure 6.1 Program to add two numbers having been run on an online LMC simulator (http://peterhigginson.co.uk/LMC/)

Selection in Little Man Computer

You will recall that in high-level languages selection takes place with the use of `if..else` and sometimes `switch..case` or equivalent. In LMC we use the *branch* instructions BRP (branch if positive) and BRZ (branch if zero) Let's look at them being used in a program. The following program asks for a number, which it will output. The maximum number we want entered is 100 so any number higher than that will get output as 100.

In a high-level language we might write something along the lines of:

```
if num1>100 then
        print 100
else
        print num1
endif
```

In LMC we don't have access to operators such as > or <. We do, however, know that if `num1` is greater than 100 then 100 minus `num1` will be negative. We can use this to create a selection instruction. Let's start with a program that takes in a number and subtracts it from 100. Note the use of # for comments.

```
          INP                    #Ask for a number
          STA    Num1            #Store the number
          LDA    Hundred         #Load the contents of Hundred in
                                 the accumulator
          SUB    Num1            #Subtract Num1 from the
                                 accumulator
          OUT                    #Output accumulator to screen
Hundred   DAT    100             #Create location 'Hundred' and
                                 store 100 in it.
Num1      DAT                    #Create location called 'Num1'
```

You may find, depending on the implementations of the LMC you are using, if you type in a number greater than 100 you won't actually get a negative number but (what appears to be) a larger positive number instead. The reason for this is that some versions only store positive numbers in the accumulator (using 500–999 to represent negative numbers using 10's complement). You don't need to worry about this – a flag is set when a negative number is in the accumulator and it is this the BRP causes to be checked.

Now we can take our program a step further. Instead of outputting the result we will use the BRP mnemonic. This tells the program to jump to a given label if the value in the accumulator is positive; otherwise it just moves to the next line.

```
          INP                    Ask for a number
          STA    Num1            Store the number
          LDA    Hundred         Load the contents of Hundred in the accumulator
          SUB    Num1            Subtract Num1 from the cont
          BRP    numIsOK         Jumps to label numIsOK if accumulator is positive
          LDA    Hundred         Loads the contents of 'Hundred' into the
                                 accumulator
          OUT                    Outputs the contents of the accumulator
          HLT                    Stops program
numIsOK   LDA    Num1            Loads the contents of 'Hundred' into the
                                 accumulator
          OUT                    Outputs the contents of the accumulator
          HLT                    Stops program
Hundred   DAT    100             Create location 'Hundred' and store 100 in it.
Num1      DAT                    Create location called 'Num1'
```

Let's look at the two routes of flow for the program. First a number greater than 100:

INP		*User enters 150*
STA	Num1	*150 is stored in Num1*
LDA	Hundred	*100 is loaded into the accumulator*
SUB	Num1	*150 is subtracted from 100, putting –50 in the accumulator*
BRP	numIsOK	*–50 is not positive so the program does not jump*
LDA	Hundred	*100 is loaded into the accumulator*
OUT		*100 is output*
HLT		*Program stops*
numIsOK LDA	Num1	
OUT		
HLT		
Hundred DAT	100	
Num1 DAT		

Now let's look at where the number is less than 100:

INP		*User enters 60*
STA	Num1	*60 is stored in Num1*
LDA	Hundred	*100 is loaded into the accumulator*
SUB	Num1	*60 is subtracted from 100, putting 40 in the accumulator*
BRP	numIsOK	*40 is positive so the program jumps to numIsOK*
LDA	Hundred	
OUT		
HLT		
numIsOK LDA	Num1	*Program jumps here and loads 60 to accumulator*
OUT		*60 is output*
HLT		*program stops*
Hundred DAT	100	
Num1 DAT		

<aside>
Questions

1. Write an LMC program that outputs the larger of two numbers.
2. BRZ branches when 0 is stored in the accumulator. Write an LMC program that takes in two numbers and outputs 1 if they are the same and 0 if they are different.
</aside>

Iteration in Little Man Computer

When we want to perform iteration (or looping) in a high-level language we usually have access to constructs such as `for` and `while`. If we want a program that keeps asking the user for a number until they enter one under 100, in a high-level language it may look something like this:

```
num1=input("Enter a number less than 100")
while num1>100
    num1=input("Enter a number less than 100")
endwhile
```

As with selection, to perform iteration in LMC we use branches and labels. On this occasion we want to loop back to the top if the number entered is greater than 100. To do this, we subtract 101 from the number entered. If the result is positive the number must be greater than 100. Little Man Computer treats zero as a positive number.

(Note that we have called the label 'loop' for clarity – but the label doesn't have to be called this. Indeed, a real assembly program is likely to have multiple loops and it would be important for the labels each to be assigned meaningful names.)

```
loop         INP                    Ask for a number
             STA    Num1            Store the number
             SUB    HundAndOne      Subtract One hundred and one from
                                    the accumulator
             BRP    loop            If the result is positive go to the label
                                    loop
             LDA    Num1            Otherwise load Num1 to the
                                    accumulator
             OUT                    Output the accumulator
             HLT                    Stop program
HundAndOne   DAT    101             Create location 'HundAndOne' and
                                    store 101 in it
Num1         DAT                    Create location called 'Num1'
```

The above is the equivalent to a condition-controlled loop (such as `while`). We can get something more akin to a count-controlled loop (such as `for`) using the following approach:

```
             INP
             STA    times
loop         LDA    times
             SUB    count
             BRZ    end            jump to end if accumulator is zero
             LDA    count
             ADD    one
             STA    count
             OUT    times
             BRA    loop           always jumps to loop
end          HLT
count        DAT    0
times        DAT
one          DAT    1
```

Questions

1. Describe what the code to the right does. (If you are unsure, try running it.)
2. Rewrite the code so the program does exactly the same but this time only using BRP and not BRZ or BRA.

Location	Contents
0	
1	
2	
3	
4	
5	
6	85
7	
8	
9	

Memory addressing

A Level only

When we want to access memory locations in assembly code there are different methods of doing so.

Direct addressing

In the previous LMC examples, we have used direct addressing. This means the operand represents the memory location of the data we want.

Using direct addressing, the line STA 6 in this case means store the contents of location 6 in the accumulator. So 85 gets stored in the accumulator.

Immediate addressing

With immediate addressing, the operand is the actual value we want.

Using immediate addressing, STA 6 means store 6 in the accumulator.

Location	Contents
0	
1	
2	
3	
4	
5	
6	85
7	
...	
83	
84	
85	21
86	
87	

Indirect addressing

Indirect addressing is where the operand is the address of the data we want. This can be useful as we have a limited number of bits we can use for the operand (some of which are taken up by the opcode from the mnemonic). By being able to use all the bits in the memory location for an address, we access a much wider range of memory locations.

In this case, using indirect addressing, STA 6 means store the contents of the location addressed at location 6 in the accumulator; in other words, put 21 in the accumulator.

Indexed addressing

One of the registers in the CPU is the index register. This is used for index addressing. In index addressing, the address given is the base address. This is then added to the value in the index register. By incrementing the index register, it is possible to iterate efficiently through an array.

Object-oriented programming

In object-oriented programming, we represent the solution to a problem through objects.

Each object has attributes (sometimes referred to as properties) that are variables that store information about that object. It also has methods. Methods are actions an object can carry out. These are the equivalent to subroutines.

Example

In the exam pseudocode, you will see methods represented with the terms 'procedure' and 'function' to denote whether or not they return a value, but really they should be referred to as methods. Real languages have different approaches. Java, for example, uses the keyword 'void' if it doesn't return a value or the data type/object type returned if it does.

Java method that doesn't return a value:

```
public void changeVolume(int newVol)
{
    volume=newVol;
}
```

Exam pseudocode for method that doesn't return a value:

```
public procedure changeVolume(newVol)
    volume=newVol
endprocedure
```

Java method that returns a value:

```
public int getVolume()
{
    return volume;
}
```

Exam pseudocode for method that returns a value:

```
public function getVolume()
    return volume
endfunction
```

Classes and objects

We can think of a class as a template. It defines what attributes and methods an object should have. It is the equivalent to a biscuit cutter, with our objects being the biscuits themselves. One of the benefits of object-oriented programming is that once a class has been written it can be reused in other programs.

```
class Monster
    private poisonous
    private strength
    private name
    public procedure new(givenPoisonous, givenStrength,
    givenName)
        poisonous=givenPoisonous
        strength=givenStrength
        name=givenName
    endprocedure
    public procedure eat()
        print(name+" eats a hero. Mmmmmm Delicious!");
    endprocedure
    public procedure sleep()
        print("Snore, Snore, Snore")
    endprocedure
endclass
```

This class tells us that all objects of type *Monster* have the attributes poisonous, strength and name and the methods eat and sleep.

The section starting `public procedure new(...` is what is called a constructor. It describes what happens when an object of this type is created. In this case, it uses the values of the parameters passed to it to set the monster's attributes.

In the main program we can have the lines:

```
monsterOne = new Monster(true, 5, "Alvin")
monsterTwo = new Monster(false, 7, "Wilfred")
```

The objects `monsterOne` and `monsterTwo` are created. Monster one is poisonous, has a strength of 5 and the name Alvin. Monster two is not poisonous, has a strength of 7 and the name Wilfred.

We can then use the method eat():

```
monsterOne.eat()
```

This would cause the following to be displayed:

```
Alvin eats a hero. Mmmmmm Delicious!
```

Inheritance

Often we will need classes that have similarities to another class but also their own distinct differences, for example in a company, all employees might have a salary, date of joining and email address. Different categories of employee might have additional attributes. A manager might have the additional attribute *department*. An engineer might have the additional method *repair*.

Questions

1. In an object-oriented language of your choice, find out how to write a class, recreate the monster class here and create the objects `monsterOne` and `monsterTwo`.
2. Add the method greet to the monster class, which should make the monster introduce themselves. Test this method works.

Inheritance allows us to create a class that has all the methods and attributes of another class as well as attributes and methods of its own.

Going back to our example of Monster, let's create a new class *Vampire*.

```
class Vampire inherits Monster

endclass
```

Notice how the class line uses 'inherits'. This keyword tells us that Vampire has all the methods and attributes of Monster. (The pseudocode you will see in the exam will use the keyword `inherits`; real languages have different alternatives. Java uses `extends`, C# and C++ use a colon `:`. They all function in the same way.) We refer to Monster as the super (or parent) class and Vampire as the sub (or child) class.

At this stage, we could create objects of type Vampire but they would be exactly the same as objects of type Monster. We want Vampire to have the attribute `hasCastle` (as to whether or not they own a castle) and the additional method `drinkBlood`.

```
class Vampire inherits Monster

    hasCastle=true

    public procedure drinkBlood()

        print(name+", the vampire, drinks the hero's
        blood")

    endprocedure

endclass
```

If we write the code in the main part of the program:

```
vampireOne=new Vampire(false, 10,"Dracula")
```

A new Vampire is created, using the constructor from Monster. We can now use the method `drinkBlood`:

```
vampireOne.drinkBlood()
```

Likewise, we can still do:

```
vampireOne.sleep()
```

Vampires don't tend to snore when they sleep (because they don't breathe). We therefore want the sleep method for a Vampire to be different. We can do this by *overriding* the Monster's sleep method. Overriding is when a method in a subclass is used to replace a method inherited from the super class.

```
class Vampire inherits Monster

    hasCastle=true

    public procedure drinkBlood()

        print(name+", the vampire, drinks the hero's blood")

    endprocedure

    public procedure sleep()

        print("The vampire sleeps silently")

    endprocedure

endclass
```

Now:

```
vampireOne.sleep()
```

will display

```
The vampire sleeps silently
```

Key points

– Inheritance allows a class to have all the methods and attributes of another class.
– The subclass can also have its own methods and attributes.
– The subclass can override methods of the superclass.

Questions

1. In an object-oriented language of your choice, find out how to use inheritance and create a Vampire class.
2. Create a Goblin class. Goblins like to collect gold so ensure they have a `goldCoins` attribute, storing how many they have, and a method for them to tell the program how many they have.
3. Goblins are noisy eaters – override the eat method to reflect this.

It would be better in this case if Vampire had its own constructor. This would allow us to set a starting value for `hasCastle`. Also, as no vampires are poisonous we don't need to take in a value for poisonous when creating a new vampire. To do this, we override the superclass's (Monster) constructor. In overriding it we still, in this case, want to use the superclass constructor. We can do this with the keyword `super`. (Note this keyword can be used to call any other methods from the superclass too.)

```
class Vampire inherits Monster
    hasCastle=true
    public new(givenHasCastle, givenStrength, givenName)
        hasCastle=givenHasCastle
        super.new(false, givenStrength, givenName)
    endprocedure
    …
    …
endclass
```

We can now give Dracula a castle, creating him in the following way:

```
vampireOne=new Vampire(true, 10, "Dracula")
```

Polymorphism

The word 'polymorphism' comes from the Greek meaning 'many forms'. You may well have come across polymorphism, depending on the programming language you have used, without realising it.

Consider the following code:

```
a="Hel"
b="lo"
c=a+b
print(c)
```

Now compare it with:

```
a=1
b=2
c=a+b
print(c)
```

In both cases we use the + symbol, but in each case it has different meanings. In the first example, + means concatenate as it is being used with two strings. In the second it means add these two numbers together, as it is being used with two integers. In other words, + has different forms according to its context.

Let's assume I want a monster zoo, which I am going to store in an array. There are going to be all sorts of monsters in this array but if my array is of type Monster, I can store all subclasses of Monster (Vampire, Goblin, and so on) in there. The technical term for this is a 'polymorphic array'.

Now I have this array I may wish to iterate through it and send all my monsters to sleep. Some monsters will have different sleep methods (for example we overrode the Vampire sleep method in the last section). This is no problem as polymorphism means (just as with the + in our example earlier) the correct sleep method will be called depending on the object type.

```
monsterA=new Goblin(23, false, 7, "Frank")
zoo[0]=monsterA
monsterB=new Monster(true,8, "Medusa")
zoo[1]=monsterB
monsterC=new Vampire(true, 10, "Dracula")
zoo[2]=monsterC
for i=0 to 2
    zoo[i].sleep()
next i
```

Encapsulation

Imagine you have written a class called Airplane that is used as part of a program to calculate the fuel necessary for a flight and that this class has the attributes `passengers`, `cargoWeight` and `fuel`. What could go wrong if other classes had direct access to these attributes and could change them freely?

One possibility is that a weight is assigned that is too heavy for the plane to carry.

```
plane=new Airplane()
plane.weight=99999
```

It might be that the weight is updated but no code is run to update the fuel to take into account the new weight. More passengers could be added, which would add to the weight and fuel needed but these too might not be updated.

This is the sort of situation we wish to avoid. To do this we use *encapsulation*.

Encapsulation is the pattern of making attributes in a class private but allowing them to be changed and accessed through public methods.

The keyword `private` means that the method or attribute following it is only accessible from within that class. If the Airplane class had the weight as `private` then any attempt to change it outside the class would result in an error.

Airplane class:

```
class Airplane
    private weight
    private fuel
    private passengers
    ...
```

Main program:

```
plane=new Airplane()
plane.weight=99999       ← this line would cause an error
```

We then provide a method to change the attribute and make this public. As the method is in the same class as the attribute, it is able to change it. By only allowing access via this method, the attribute can only be changed in the way we specify, for example:

Airplane class:

```
class Airplane
    private weight
    private fuel
    private passengers
    ...
    public procedure setWeight(enteredWeight)
            if enteredWeight>maxWeight then
                print("Too heavy")
            else
                weight=enteredWeight
                updateFuel()
            endif
    endprocedure
    public function getWeight()
            return weight
    endfunction
endclass
```

Main program:

```
plane=new Airplane()
plane.setWeight(500)
```

Typically when using encapsulation, each attribute will have a 'get' method (for example getWeight), sometimes called the accessor, which allows other classes to see the value of an attribute and a set method (for example setWeight), sometimes called the mutator, which allows the attribute value to be changed.

It should be remembered that encapsulation isn't there to stop malicious attempts to change attributes. It is there to reduce the chance of mistakes occurring through attributes being altered in an unforeseen way by other objects (which may well have been coded by the same person who coded the encapsulated class).

Practice question

Using the Monster class you made earlier, use encapsulation to ensure the strength can only be set to a value between one and twenty.

Chapter 7

Software

Introduction

Software is the programs that run on a computer system. We categorise software according to its function. Types of software include applications, utilities and systems software.

Applications

Applications software is that which allows a user to perform a task or produce something. People tend to think of applications in terms of the software they use on a daily basis, such as:

- **word processors:** Used for writing letters, reports and other documents
- **spreadsheet packages:** These allow a user to model complex situations, and are often used for financial calculations
- **presentation software:** Used to make on-screen slide shows to accompany presentations
- **desktop publishing software:** Used for documents where layout is important, such as newsletters
- **image editors:** Used to alter and amend images such as photographs
- **web browsers:** Allow a user to browse the world wide web.

It should be remembered that there are many other types of applications available. Computer-aided design packages allow engineers to build accurate designs; management information systems allow data to be stored and processed; and video games provide a common form of entertainment. All these are examples of applications.

As the speed of internet access increases and processing power becomes cheaper, it is becoming increasingly common for applications to become 'cloud based'. By accessing applications over the internet, users don't have to worry about installing or updating software and can have access to it regardless of what computer they are using and where they are in the world.

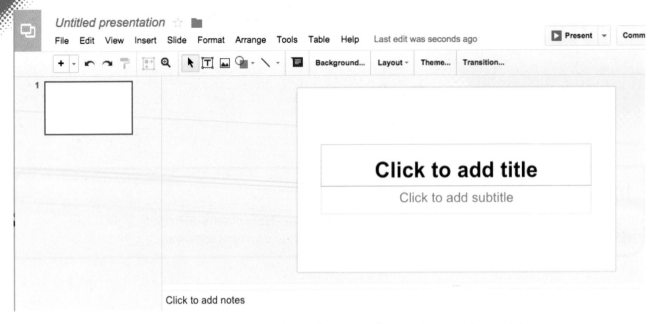

Figure 7.1 Google Docs™ allows presentations to be made using software that runs in a web browser

Utilities

A utility is a relatively small program that has one purpose, usually concerned with the maintenance of the system.

Examples of utilities are:

Anti-virus programs: Viruses are malicious programs, often designed to harm a computer system in some way and spread to others. Anti-virus software detects and removes viruses.

Disk defragmentation:

Figure 7.2 Programs and data are stored on the hard disk

Figure 7.3 When files get deleted they create 'free space' on the hard drive

When new files are added they may not fit entirely into this free space. On these occasions, they are split across different areas of free space.

Figure 7.4 When new files are added, they are sometimes split across different areas of free space

Over time, lots of files can be split up into multiple sections and spread out over a hard disk. This means a computer has to find and read each part when loading them. This takes time and slows down the operation of the computer. A disk-defragmentation program groups all the parts of each file together so they can be read in one go.

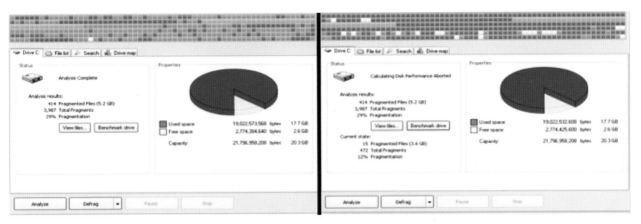

Figure 7.5 Defraggler® is an example of a defragmentation utility; this image shows it before and after running on a hard disk: red blocks indicate fragmented files

Compression: Compression programs reduce the amount of space data takes up in storage. Often these **algorithms** make use of the fact that patterns of data are regularly repeated. You can find out more about some of the algorithms used by compression programs in Chapter 17.

File managers: These allow files and directories to be moved, copied, deleted and renamed.

Backup utilities: These allow backups to be automatically made of specified data.

Questions

1. Discuss what applications might be used by a hotel.
2. Explain the difference between an application and a utility.
3. Research and describe an example of utility you might use to free up space on your hard disk.
4. Find out why you should not use defragmentation utilities on a solid state drive.

What is an operating system?

The first computers programmed through wires and switches and would continue running that program until it was set up differently. As computers developed, they were expected to run a number of programs (sometimes at the same time), cater for different users (again sometimes at the same time) and interact with increasing amounts of hardware. To do all this, computers need an operating system.

An operating system is the software that manages the computer. Modern operating systems have several purposes:

- to manage the hardware of the system
- to manage programs installed and being run
- to manage the security of the system
- to provide an interface between the user and the computer.

You may be familiar with the following operating systems:

Operating System	Description
Android®	Android is developed by Google™ to run on mobile devices. It is based on Linux®.
iOS®	iOS is Apple's mobile operating system used on iPhones®, iPads® and Apple TV®.
GNU Linux®	Linux, based on Unix, is open source. There are many variants of Linux currently available.
Unix®	Unix has been around since the 1970s and has achieved widespread use. It is the basis of Apple's OS X® operating system and the operating system on which Linux is based.
Windows®	Probably one of the best-known operating systems, written by Microsoft®, Windows is commonplace on most desktop and laptop PCs. More recent versions of Windows are designed to run on PCs and mobile devices.

Most operating systems will come with utilities that can help with their maintenance.

Different types of operating system

There are a number of types of operating system.

Multi-tasking

When you use a computer, you will often be running several programs at once, for example while typing a report on a word processor you might have music playing, a web bowser with a social network open and at the same time your virus checker may be performing a scan. This is organised by a multi-tasking operating system.

While modern processors may have multiple cores, they may have to deal with more processes than they have cores. Multi-tasking allows for this and has been around since single-core processors were commonplace.

The reason multi-tasking is possible is the speed processors work at. As you will see in Chapter 10, processors carry out billions of instructions per second. This speed is significantly faster than that at which any of the other components work. This means that the CPU can carry out processing for one program and then switch its attention to another while the peripherals are dealing with the output of that processing. By rapidly switching between programs in this manner, a processor gives the illusion of running multiple programs at once.

Multi-user

Your computer at home may allow different login accounts for different people. This does not necessarily mean it is running a multi-user operating system. A true multi-user operating system must allow more than one person to share a computer's resources at the same time. Multi-user operating systems are common on mainframe computers where there may be many users accessing them simultaneously.

Distributed operating system

Sometimes we want to combine the power of a group of computers to work together on a single task. We can do this with a distributed operating system. A distributed operating system can control and co-ordinate many computers, presenting them to the end user as though they were a single system.

Embedded operating system

When we talk about computers, we don't just mean desktops and laptops but also embedded computers; that is to say, computers built into devices such as television set-top boxes, high-end printers, cars, ATMs and washing machines. An embedded system will likely only have one job and is not likely to have a need for multi-tasking.

Some (but not all) embedded devices run on an embedded operating system. Embedded operating systems are often specifically designed for the device on which they run and with efficiency in mind to operate on low-powered CPUs with little RAM.

Real-time operating system

Real-time operating systems are those that are designed to carry out actions within a *guaranteed* amount of time even when left running for long periods. Usually the expected response time is within a small fraction of a second. Safety critical systems will often run on real-time operating systems. Consider the consequences of a plane's autopilot system having unexpected delays (even by a second or two) in adjusting the plane's flight path.

Most operating systems will have more than one of these properties, for example many real-time operating systems are also embedded.

> ### Key points
>
> – Operating systems are an important piece of systems software.
> – They help control the hardware, allow other software to be installed, provide a user interface and help control system security.
> – There are many operating systems in use. The most common include Windows®, OS X®, GNU Linux® and Android®.
> – Operating systems can be categorised in different ways, including: single or multi-user, multi-tasking, embedded, real-time, distributed.

> ### Questions
>
> 1. Explain why it would be important for the safety system of a nuclear power plant to run on a real-time operating system.
> 2. Describe what is meant by a multi-tasking operating system.
> 3. Find out what type of operating system Windows 10 is.

How operating systems work

Kernel

The kernel is the very core of the operating system. It helps manage the system resources, including memory management and scheduling. Any applications running use the kernel to send and receive data to and from devices. The kernel lies below the user interface. When a system uses Linux, the 'Linux part' is technically only the kernel; a separate user interface runs over the top of it. This means Linux users can change their user interface without affecting the rest of their setup.

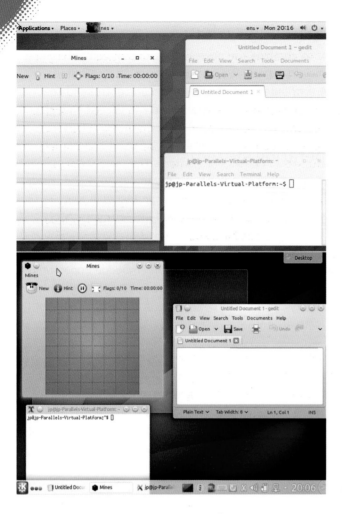

Memory management

One of the key jobs of an operating system is the management of memory. Memory stores the programs and data in use by the system. Memory management allows programs to be stored in memory safely and efficiently.

First let's look at the safety aspect.

Each different program will be using its own data. Without memory management, one program could change the data of another. It would also be possible for a maliciously coded program to access or amend the data of another program. The memory management aspect of operating systems restricts each program to accessing and amending its own area of data.

Sometimes two programs may have a valid need to share data; again, it is the operating system's memory management that allows this.

The next consideration is efficiency. Let's assume we store all programs continuously, one after another, as they are loaded into memory.

Figure 7.6 Screenshot of Ubuntu Linux® running the GNOME (top) and KDE (bottom) environments

---

Example

Consider the following situation.

Figure 7.7 Programs A, B and C are stored in memory

Figure 7.8 Program B is no longer needed and closed

Figure 7.9 Now program D is needed: there is no continuous block of free space it will fit into, but there is enough free space across the whole of memory

We could 'shuffle' C along so it starts immediately after A, leaving all the free space together. While this is possible, it is inefficient, and having to constantly rearrange programs in memory in this way would have a negative effect on system performance.

An alternative solution is to split programs up. In the example above, we could have part of D in the first section of free memory and the remainder in the second section.

The next decision is *how* we split these programs up. One option is to do it logically, splitting it into blocks containing modules or routines; we call this *segmentation*.

The alternative is to split programs up into blocks of the same physical size; we call this *paging*. Each physical unit (typically several kilobytes) is a page. The operating system uses a page table to keep track of where the pages are stored. This means all the pages of a process don't have to be stored contiguously.

Most modern operating systems use a combination of paging and segmentation in their memory management.

Virtual memory

RAM is significantly more expensive that secondary storage. A computer system will often have hundreds of times more secondary storage than RAM.

When a system is running low on physical memory (that is, RAM) it is able to use an area of the hard disk as **virtual memory**. When the operating system believes a page is not likely to be needed in the near future, it is moved from RAM to virtual memory. Then when the page is needed at a later point it is moved back into physical memory.

This process is slower than keeping everything in physical memory so we don't want to use it too often. If the RAM is full, the operating system can end up moving pages back and forth between physical and virtual memory often. This will significantly slow the system down and is referred to as *disk thrashing*.

Questions

1. Page sizes are traditionally 4 Kb, but modern systems offer the option of significantly larger page sizes. Discuss what the advantages and disadvantages might be of larger sized pages.
2. Describe what is meant by *disk thrashing*.
3. Explain why adding RAM to a computer system can improve its performance.

Scheduling

Multi-tasking operating systems need to make sure that multiple processes can run alongside each other, apparently simultaneously. Multi-user operating systems may have a number of users sharing a system without any apparent delay. For this to be possible, operating systems need to carry out scheduling and this is the job of a *scheduler*.

A scheduler is a program that manages the amount of time different processes have in the CPU. There are a number of different algorithms a scheduler can use, including: round robin, first come first served, shortest job first, shortest remaining time and multi-level feedback queues.

- **Round robin:** In round robin scheduling, each process is given a fixed amount of time. If it hasn't finished by the end of that time period, it goes to the back of the queue so the next process in line can have its turn.
- **First come first served:** With first come first served, is just like queuing in a shop. The first process to arrive is dealt with by the CPU until it is finished; meanwhile, any other processes that come along are queued up for their turn. Just like in a shop when the person in front has a particularly full shopping trolley, if a process being run takes a lot time the other processes have to wait.
- **Shortest job first:** Shortest job first picks the job that will take the shortest time and run it until it finishes. Naturally this algorithm needs to know the time each job will take in advance.

- **Shortest remaining time:** In this algorithm, the scheduler estimates how long each process will take. It then picks the one that will take the least amount of time and runs that. If a job is added with a shorter remaining time the scheduler is switched to that one.
- **Multi-level feedback queues:** As the name suggests, a multi-level feedback queue uses a number of queues. Each of these queues has a different priority. The algorithm can move jobs between these queues depending on the jobs' behaviour.

When choosing a scheduling algorithm, there are certain aspects to be considered. With some algorithms it is possible that a job never gets processed, for example imagine the scenario where a scheduler is running a shortest-job-first algorithm. What happens if there is a fairly long job waiting to be serviced and shorter jobs regularly being added? The alternative problem can be the time spent waiting for a job. All jobs ultimately get processed but some may take an unacceptably long time.

Interrupts

The CPU needs to know when a device needs its attention. There are two ways of doing this: *interrupts* and *polling*. Polling is when the CPU keeps checking each peripheral to see if it needs attention. This is a waste of the CPU's time; imagine if a teacher were to ask every single student in the class if they had any questions continuously throughout a lesson. The alternative is interrupts. This is when a device sends a signal to the processor, to get attention. This is similar to what happens in most classrooms where a student will put their hand up if they have a question. An interrupt will have a priority indicating how urgently it requires attention. When an interrupt is raised, the operating system runs the relevant interrupt service routine.

Interrupt service routines (ISR)

When a peripheral or software routine requires attention, an interrupt is raised to tell the CPU. Each interrupt has a priority level. If its priority is higher than the process currently being executed it needs to be serviced first. The operating system has interrupt service routines that determine what happens when a particular interrupt is carried out.

At the end of each iteration of the fetch–decode–execute cycle, the processor checks to see if there are any interrupts. If there are and they are of a higher priority than the current task the following steps are carried out:

- The contents of the program counter and the other registers are copied to an area of memory called a stack.
- The relevant interrupt service routine can then be loaded by changing the program counter to the value of where the ISR starts in memory.
- When the interrupt service routine is complete, the previous values of the programs counter and other registers can be restored from memory to the CPU.

It is of course possible that while one interrupt is being serviced another, higher priority, interrupt will be raised. In this case, the interrupt currently being serviced is added to the stack in memory and the new interrupt is serviced. Once this new interrupt is finished (assuming it too isn't interrupted and added to the stack) the previous interrupt is taken off the stack and continued. You can find out more about stacks in Chapter 13.

Device drivers

Operating systems are expected to communicate with a wide variety of devices, each with different models and manufacturers. It would be impossible for the makers of operating systems to program them to handle all existing and future devices. This is why we need device drivers.

A device driver is a piece of software, usually supplied with a device, that tells the operating system how it can communicate with the device.

Questions

1. Describe what is meant by the round robin scheduling algorithm.
2. Describe what happens in the processor when an interrupt is generated.
3. Explain why it is often necessary to install a device driver when installing a new printer.

Virtual machines

It is possible to write a program that has the same functionality as a physical computer. We call such programs 'virtual machines'.

A common use of virtual machines is to run operating systems within another operating system. This might be because a program is needed that will not run on the host operating system or it might be because it offers a convenient way to test a program being developed on multiple platforms.

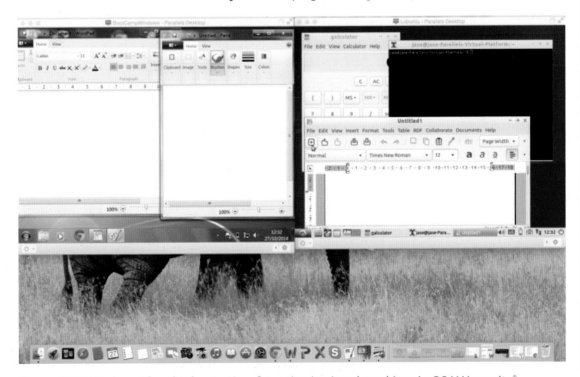

Figure 7.10 Windows 7® and Lubuntu Linux® running in virtual machines in OS X Yosemite®

Because virtual machines are just a programs and data, they have advantages over physical machines. They can be backed up and duplicated and more than one can be run at one time on a physical machine. It is for these reasons that many organisations are virtualising their network infrastructure, making their servers a group of virtual machines running from a cluster of physical machines.

Another common use of virtual machine is for interpreting intermediate code. As you will discover in Chapter 8, when programs are compiled to machine code, that code will only run on processors with the same **instruction set**. An alternative is to use an interpreter but this is slow and means the **source code** is freely available.

Intermediate code offers a compromise between these two approaches. A compiler converts the source code into something called byte code. This isn't machine code but is a much more efficient representation than the original source code. Because it isn't machine code it can't be run directly on a processor. Instead, a virtual machine is used to read the code. Any device with this virtual machine can read this intermediate code. This means code can be highly portable. As hardware becomes cheaper and more powerful, virtual machines are likely to become more commonplace.

Example

Java®

Java® is one of the best-known examples of a language that uses intermediate code, hence its slogan 'Write once, run anywhere'. Devices with the Java Virtual Machine are able to run Java intermediate code, be they computers with different types of processor, smartphones, tablets or even TV set-top boxes.

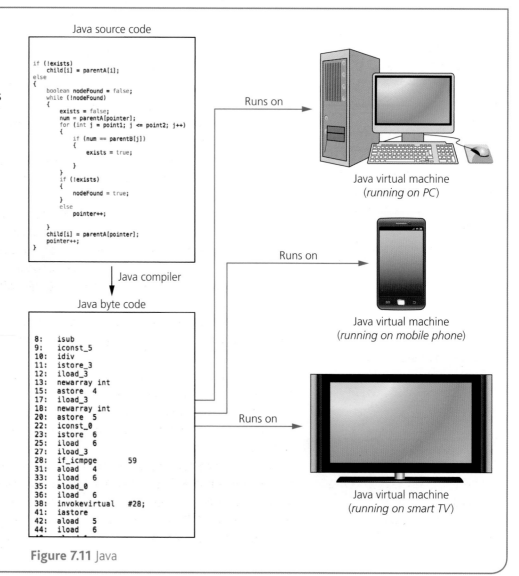

Figure 7.11 Java

BIOS

BIOS stands for *basic input/output system*. When a computer is first switched on it looks to the BIOS to get it up and running, and so the processor's program counter points to the BIOS's memory.

The BIOS will usually first check that the computer is functional, memory is installed and accessible and the processor is working. This is called the *power-on self-test* (POST). Once it has done this, it can use a boot loader program to load the operating system's kernel into memory.

The BIOS is usually stored on flash memory so that it can be updated. This also allows settings such as boot order of disks to be changed and saved by the user.

Open and closed source software

When software is sold commercially it is compiled to machine code. This means users can run it without having to translate it. Most users would have no need for the program's source code. It would not be wise for the company making the software to supply it as it would mean users could amend their software and steal their work.

There is a type of software called *open source software* (OSS) where source code is made publicly available. This means that users can modify software to suit their needs. It also means that anyone can have a part in the development of software.

One of the best-known pieces of open source software is the operating system Linux. There are now many variants of Linux and it was used as the basis for the Android™ operating system.

There are many advantages and disadvantages to OSS. One of the biggest advantages is price. As the source code is freely available, there would be little point in charging for it, therefore most OSS is free. Some companies make money by offering the software for free then offering paid support contracts to businesses that want it.

Open source projects tend to be supported by armies of volunteer coders and testers. While they are often very competent, they may not have the resources and organisation available to a software house's paid programming team. For this reason, open source projects can lack the polish of their commercial, closed source counterparts. On the other hand, large open-source projects may have many programmers and testers working on them, which means software can be quickly and regularly updated.

Whether open source systems are more or less secure is subject to debate. Some argue that as source code is freely available anyone can find security holes in the code. Proponents of open source would counter that this is what makes it so secure; there are many people checking the code to identify such problems.

Key points

- A virtual machine is a piece of software that replicates the functionality of a physical machine.
- The BIOS is what allows the computer to start up.
- Open source software is that which has its source code freely available.

1. Describe the purpose of a BIOS.
2. Explain how a software developer may make use of a virtual machine.
3. Discuss whether schools should move to using open source software where they can.

Chapter 8

Applications generation

Introduction

Chapter 7 looked at different types of software, but how is software made? Programming languages are used to write programs, but how does the code written by the programmer become a program that can be executed by the computer's CPU? The answer is using a translator.

A translator is a program that converts **source code** (the code written in a programming language) into the machine code (the ones and zeros executed by the processor). This chapter examines the different types of translators and how they work.

Machine code

Processors only understand machine code; that is to say, binary sequences representing instructions and data. The sequences representing instructions we call *opcodes*. For the very first computers there was no choice but to write programs in machine code.

This laborious task would be error prone. What's more, different processors had different **instruction sets**; the binary sequence to add two numbers for one processor could be different from that of another. One could even have instructions in one processor that were not available in another.

This meant that a program would need rewriting for different computers.

Question

Find out about Windows RT®. Why did Microsoft® release this particular version of Windows 8®?

Assembler

A mnemonic is a memory device; something that makes difficult things easier to remember. One of the most commonly used mnemonics is 'Richard Of York Gave Battle In Vain' to remember the colours of the rainbow (red, orange, yellow, green, blue, indigo, violet).

x86 assembly code

```
section .data
msg     db      'Hello, World!', 0AH
len     equ     $-msg
section .text
global  _start
_start: mov     edx,    len
        mov     ecx,    msg
        mov     ebx,    1
        mov     eax,    4
        int     80h
        mov     ebx,    0
        mov     eax,    1
        int     80h
```

By using mnemonics to represent the opcodes, code became somewhat easier to read and write. We call this assembly code. You found out about assembly code in Chapter 6.

The assembly code to the left displays 'Hello, World' on a machine with an x86 processor. Compare this to the code used to produce the same in a high-level language below.

An assembler is a program that converts assembly language into object code. There is usually a one-to-one relationship between assembly and object code; that is to say, each mnemonic and operand in assembly code will translate into an opcode and operand in machine code. This means that on the simplest level an assembler just needs to translate each line of code into its binary equivalent.

As with machine code, assembly code isn't very portable. Assembly code for one processor is unlikely to work on another.

Compilers and interpreters

In the late 1950s, the limitations of writing assembly code were becoming clear. Even with the significantly higher relative cost of hardware back then compared to now, companies were still finding they were spending much more on the development of software than purchasing hardware.

The solution to this was the first high-level language, called Fortran. A high-level language is one that consists of more easily human-readable statements. People quickly saw the benefits of coding in high-level languages and started writing programs in this way. Over time, many high-level languages have been created. Examples include BASIC, C, C++, JavaScript and Python. You found out about high-level languages in Chapter 6.

The code to the left is Fortran code to display 'Hello, World'. Compare this in length with the assembly code version above. Both code extracts are from the site RosettaCode.org, which shows examples of code for different tasks in many different languages. Have a look at some examples on there and see if you can spot the similarities and differences between different languages.

While high-level languages are easier for humans to understand, we need a way of converting them into a form a CPU can use. There are two types of translator program used to do this: *interpreters* and *compilers*.

An interpreter takes each line of a high-level language program, converts it to machine code and runs it.

This is useful when debugging a program as the program can start running straight away and will stop at a line if it finds an error. The downside of this is that an interpreted program runs slowly. Every time the program is run, the user has to wait for the translation of each line as well as the execution. When iterating through a loop, the interpreter may have to translate the same line many times. To run the code, the user needs access to an interpreter (which itself will take up some of the system's resources).

Fortran code

```
print *,"Hello, World!"
```

Questions

1. Why is JavaScript usually provided as high-level code that is then interpreted?
2. Why is most commercial software provided as compiled code?

A compiler is a program that takes a program written in a high-level language and converts it to object code. This object code can then be distributed to anyone with a compatible system without the need for any additional programs. Once the code is compiled, it can be run as often as needed and at a much faster speed than an interpreted program. Also, if the source code were distributed commercially, people could amend this, removing anti-piracy measures, rebrand the product and sell it on or copy any innovative ideas into their own product, thus stealing a company's hard work. As machine code is not human-readable, doing any of these things is much harder.

Small programs such as the ones you might write on an A Level course will compile in a matter of seconds. Compilation for more complex programs, however, may take minutes or even hours.

Object code

You will often see the term 'object code' being used apparently interchangeably with 'machine code'. Object code is an intermediary step sometimes taken before pure machine code is produced. The object code contains placeholders where library code needs to go. Once a linker has been used machine code that can be run directly on the processor is produced.

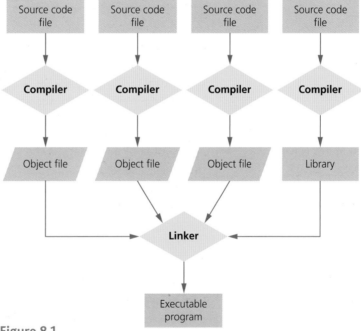

Figure 8.1

How a compiler works

A compiler works by going through a sequence of stages, each moving closer to the machine code. While the exact process varies between compilers, most will include the following steps: lexical analysis, syntax analysis, code generation and optimisation.

Lexical analysis

All comments and whitespace are removed from the program. (Remember comments are there for the benefit of the programmers but are of no use to the computer.)

This stage sees the high-level code turned into a series of *tokens*. Just as while you are reading this your brain is recognising the individual words and punctuation symbols, the compiler tries to pick out **reserved words**, operators, variables and constants. Tokens are specific strings of characters.

The code below to the left may be converted into the tokens shown in the table.

```
IF pincode==1234 THEN

     PRINT("Access Granted")

ELSE

     PRINT("Access Refused")

ENDIF
```

IF	pincode	==	1234	THEN	
PRINT	(	"	Access Granted	"	)
ELSE					
PRINT	(	"	Access Refused	"	)
ENDIF					

During compilation, the compiler needs to keep track of the variables and subroutines within the program. To do this it uses a symbol table. During the lexical analysis the names are added to the table. Later on other information will be added such as the data types and scope.

Syntax analysis

The syntax of a language is the set of rules that govern its structure. Take the English sentence:

The horse jumped over the wooden fence.
The order of the words is important.
If I change it to:
The wooden horse jumped over the fence.

the meaning has changed somewhat and the sentence becomes somewhat less believable. This is because in English we usually put an adjective in front of the noun it describes.

If we look at this code:

```
a=1
b=2
a=b+1
```

we can see how in many programming languages order also matters. If the order of the last line is changed to:

```
b=a+1
```

the line of code has new meaning.

If the syntax of a language is broken it can stop having meaning altogether:
Wooden jumped the over horse fence.

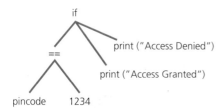

Figure 8.2 An abstract syntax tree (AST)

Similarly the code:

```
=ab1+
```

would be nonsense.

Syntax analysis is when the compiler checks that the code that has been written uses a valid syntax. Where code does not follow the rules of a language the compiler will generate a list of syntax errors to alert the programmer as to why it cannot be compiled.

Syntax analysis will produce an abstract syntax tree (AST) that will represent the program. You can find out more about trees in Chapter 13. If the tokens will not fit into an abstract syntax tree then this would mean there is a syntax error; in other words, someone has written something against the rules of the language.

Code generation

By this stage, the program is represented as an abstract syntax tree. Code generation is when the compiler converts this into object code.

Optimisation

Usually we want the code to run as quickly as possible (or sometimes using as little memory as possible); this is the role of optimisation. There are a number of tricks the optimiser can use. If it finds lines of code that have no effect on what the program does it will remove these. It will also look at instructions, or groups of instructions, to see if they can be replaced by any more efficient alternatives. Optimisation will usually take place during and after code generation.

Computing people

Frances Allen

In 2006, 40 years after it was first awarded, Frances Allen became the first woman to win the ACM Turing award. She spent her career working for IBM and also helped the NSA to build a code-breaking language. Her work at IBM focused on compilers, specifically optimization, and it is her work in this area for which she is best known. Frances laid the groundwork for optimisation that has been built upon ever since.

Libraries

You have probably heard the expression 'There's no point reinventing the wheel', meaning that it is pointless spending time making something that has already been made perfectly well. This adage is very apt when it comes to software development. Often code to perform complex tasks has already been written. This code can be reused by other programmers.

It is usually best to use a library where possible. Often libraries are designed to tackle complex tasks such as graphics or cryptography. These require a certain amount of expertise and may be time consuming to program from the beginning.

Here are two examples of libraries being imported into a Python program. 'PyGame' is a freely available library designed for game making; 'time' is a library that comes with Python and is designed for time-based calculations and functions. By including these lines at the top of a Python file, the programmer can then make calls to these libraries within the file.

For example, here a programmer has called the 'sleep' function from the time library, which pauses the program for a given number of seconds.

```
import pygame
import time


time.sleep(5)
```

Programmers use the library through an API (Application Programming Interface). A library may be written in one language and then have APIs designed to work with other languages.

Figure 8.3 Minecraft was written in Java but uses OpenGL for its graphics

Linkers and loaders

A Level only

Once code has been generated and optimised, it is still not quite ready to be run. There is a good chance it will rely on code from libraries. The job of a linker is to include this library code and all the compiled files into the final single executable program. Linkers can either be static linkers or dynamic linkers (which are really loaders).

When using static linking, all the library code needed is put directly into the program when it is compiled. This means that the final program can be large in size and a computer could have a number of different programs, each with their own separate copy of library routines embedded within them. Dynamic linking tries to circumvent this problem. Compiled versions of the library are stored and the operating system links a program to them when it is run. A loader is part of the operating system and is responsible for loading a program into memory.

Key points

- The stages of compilation are: lexical analysis, syntax analysis, code generation and optimisation.
- Lexical analysis is when code is split into tokens.
- During syntax analysis, the tokens are used to build an abstract syntax tree.
- The code generation phase is when the abstract syntax tree is converted to machine code.
- The code is made more efficient (either to run quicker or in less space) during the optimisation stage.
- Libraries contain existing code that developers may wish to reuse.
- Linkers are used to incorporate library code into the final program.

Practice questions

1. Describe what is meant by the term 'assembler'.
2. Explain what happens during the lexical analysis stage of compilation.
3. Explain why the length of variable names and amount of comments in a program's source make no difference to the size of a compiled program.
4. Explain why, while developing a program, a programmer might prefer to use an interpreter over a compiler.
5. Describe, using an example, why the compiler might generate an error during syntax analysis.
6. Describe the purpose of a linker.

Chapter 9

Software development

Introduction

Building large pieces of software can be an expensive business. Complex programs require large teams of highly paid analysts, programmers and testers working for months, even years. In this chapter we look at the different approaches to working on large software projects.

Question

Find three examples of failed IT projects. Briefly describe:
(a) what they were meant to do
(b) what went wrong
(c) what lessons you think could be learned.

Example

NHS IT Project

In 2002 the UK Government commissioned an ambitious IT project for the NHS (National Health Service). It had multiple aims, including making all patients' records easily accessible across the health service. It was planned to cost just over £2 billion and take about three years to develop. Ten years later the project was still nowhere near completion at a cost of over £12 billion. (To put this in context, £12 billion is the cost of running the entire UK's police forces for a year.) As a result, the project was largely abandoned (with some parts of it being passed on to smaller teams).

Such a project is an example of how things can go wrong. As time and costs spent on a project spiral, it becomes harder to call things to a halt. You might assume it would make sense to add more programmers to a project to speed things up. This can often make things worse. As well as increasing costs, adding programmers to a software project that is already running late makes it later. This is referred to as Brook's law, named after software engineer Fred Brooks who wrote about the phenomenon in his book about his experiences with an overly delayed project at IBM – *The Mythical Man Month*.

Figure 9.1 Computers in the NHS

Elements of software development

Feasibility study

As we have established, software development is costly. If we can tell that a project is likely to fail in advance then it is better off not being started. This is the purpose of a feasibility study – to determine if a project is likely to be successful. There are a number of reasons a project might fail, including:

- the budget may not be big enough or the cost of the project too high compared to the benefits; in other words, the project may not be economically feasible
- it might be that the project would break laws about data protection and privacy – it might not be legally feasible
- the project could be overly ambitious and go beyond what current hardware or **algorithms** can achieve – it might not be technically feasible.

Because of all these reasons, the first step of any project should be a feasibility study. That way, any issues that make a project unviable can be addressed and, if necessary, the project can be set aside until such a time when it becomes possible.

Requirements specification

At the heart of any project is what the end user needs the final system to be able to do. These are the 'requirements'. They should be easily understandable and measurable. The process of determining these requirements is called 'requirements elicitation'.

This can be a challenge in itself. The user may have a clear idea of what they want from a system but the analyst needs to make sure they accurately extract this information from them. Sometimes the customer might not fully appreciate what they need from the system.

How the customer explained it

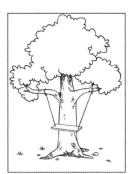
How the project leader understood it

How the engineer designed it

How the programmer wrote it

How the sales executive described it

How the project was documented

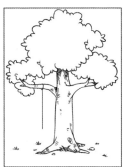
What operations installed

How the customer was billed

How the helpdesk supported it

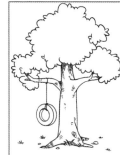
What the customer really needed

Figure 9.2 Software has to be tested to ensure it can handle users making mistakes

The determining of requirements is traditionally done in the requirements elicitation phase, which usually culminates in a document called the 'requirements specification'. This document lists every requirement of the final system and can become the focal point for the remaining stages of the project.

When the project is signed off, it will be the requirements specification that the system is tested against in what is known as 'acceptance testing'. This gives the end user the assurance that the project will meet their needs and the developer the confidence that they are producing what the user wants and that the user isn't going to come up with any unexpected demands.

Testing

Testing should take place continually during the coding process. Every time a module of code is written, it should be tested to be certain it works. In theory, if you know all the modules work on their own all you then need to test is how they work together.

Testing should include 'destructive testing' where testers try to cause a program to crash or behave unexpectedly. This might be, for example, by entering a different value in a text box from what it is supposed to accept or trying to open a corrupt data file. As Edsger Dijkstra (see Chapter 5) put it: 'Testing can be used very effectively to show the presence of bugs but never to show their absence'.

Once the code is complete and free of obvious bugs, the company can undertake *alpha testing*. This is where the product is used within the company by people who haven't worked on the project.

The problem is real users don't always use software in the same way that coders envisage. This is where *beta testing* can be of use. In beta testing, a small group of users from outside the software company use the software to see if they encounter any bugs or usability problems not picked up during the previous testing.

The final stage of testing is *acceptance testing*. This is when the user tests the program against every requirement in the requirements specification. Once this testing is successful the project can be signed off.

Documentation

Written documents are produced during the software engineering process. One such document is the requirements specification, which details exactly what the system should be able to do. The system's design may be documented to allow the programmers to understand what it is that they are making. This might include algorithms, screen layout designs and descriptions of how data will be stored, for example entity-relationship diagrams (see Chapter 15).

As the system is built, it may be documented to allow software engineers to be able to understand and maintain it in the future. This is referred to as the *technical documentation*. The technical documentation will often include descriptions of the code, its modules and their functionality. A lot of tools exist that allow this documentation to be automatically generated from special comments put in the code.

Another important type of documentation is *user documentation*. This is effectively the manual that tells the user how to operate the designed system. This may include tutorials on how to use the system, descriptions of error messages and a troubleshooting guide on how to overcome common problems.

Methodologies

To ensure software projects are delivered on time and on budget, different methodologies have been developed. These methodologies will all have the above elements but take different approaches as to when they are used and to what extent.

The waterfall lifecycle will typically involve large amounts of documentation, whereas extreme programming aims to minimise documentation produced, relying instead on verbal communication and clear code.

The waterfall lifecycle

The waterfall life cycle is a well-known (and often criticised) development model.

It consists of a sequence of stages. In its most basic form, each stage is started only after the previous is complete. This of course is only going to work if each stage is completed perfectly the first time. Even the person credited with first describing this process, William Royce, didn't feel this was a realistic way to approach a project, stating that this model 'is risky and invites failure' (Winston W. Royce [1970]: 'Managing the Development of Large Software Systems' in: *Technical Papers of Western Electronic Show and Convention* [WesCon], August 25–28, 1970, Los Angeles, USA, page 329 [www.cs.umd.edu/class/spring2003/cmsc838p/Process/waterfall.pdf]).

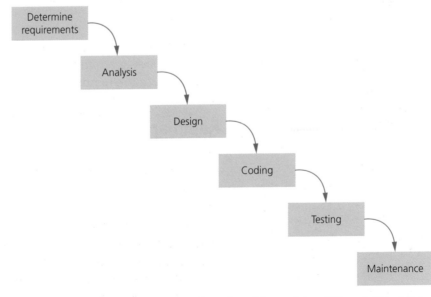

Figure 9.3 Royce never actually referred to this model as 'Waterfall' but it is clear how it soon got its name; the one-way flow down through the stages is similar to the flow of water in a waterfall

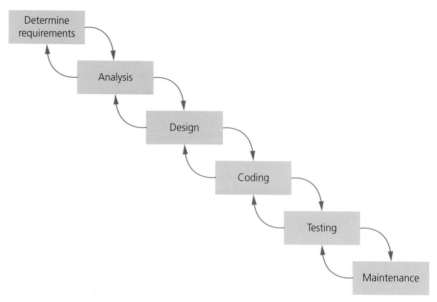

Figure 9.4 Royce proposed that it could be improved by allowing iteration between adjacent stages

Now if the coders find that part of the design is causing issues they can send it back to the design team. Likewise if the designers find there is an issue as a result of them not knowing exactly what the user wants they can go back to the analysts.

Advantages and disadvantages of the waterfall model

An advantage of the waterfall lifecycle is its simplicity. This makes it easy to manage.

Everyone on the project can be clear on their responsibilities at each stage and, as there is an expected output at the end of each stage, it is clear to see whether or not a project is running to schedule. Its ease of management and measuring if it is running to time make it suitable for large-scale projects.

The biggest issue with the model is the risk it carries. It really isn't until the project reaches the testing stage that the end user gets to see something tangible. If their requirements have been misunderstood it may be very difficult, given the time and money already expended, to rectify any issues. For this reason, the waterfall approach is best suited to less complex projects in which the requirements are very clearly understood.

Rapid application development

Rapid application development (RAD) involves the use of prototypes. A prototype is a version of system that lacks full functionality. This could be anything from some screen mock-ups to a partially working version of the final program. This means there is something to show the user early on. If there is an aspect the user doesn't like, this can be amended before effort is expended into adding the functionality behind it. The end user evaluates the prototype and, based on their feedback, it is improved further, ready to be evaluated again.

This cycle of prototyping and evaluation continues until the program has all the functionality the user wants and they approve it. At this stage it becomes the final product.

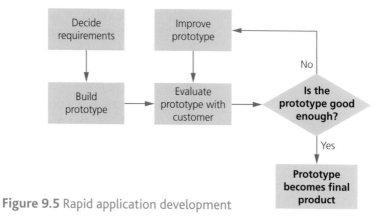

Figure 9.5 Rapid application development

Advantages and disadvantages of rapid application development

Rapid application development is well suited to projects where the requirements aren't entirely clear from the outset. With the continuous feedback from the client, the end product is likely to have excellent usability. As the focus is on the usability of the final product rather than *how* it works, RAD is not suited to projects where efficiency of code is important.

It is important to have continual contact with the client throughout the process to get regular feedback from them – RAD is unsuitable where the client is unable to make this commitment or such a commitment is impractical. RAD doesn't scale well and so is less suited to large projects with big teams.

Spiral model

Software development can involve high amounts of risk. Projects can run out of time, requirements can change and competitors can come out with better alternatives. The spiral model is designed to take into account risks within the project. By focusing on managing risks, these can be dealt with before they become issues.

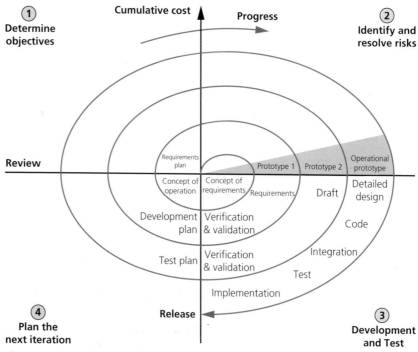

Figure 9.6 Spiral model

The model consists of four stages, each forming a quadrant of the spiral. The first stage is to determine the objectives of that rotation of the spiral. In the first instance, this may be determining the main requirements of the project. These should be chosen according to the biggest potential risks.

In the next stage, the possible risks are identified and alternative options considered. This may involve building a prototype of the system. If risks are considered too high at this stage, the project may be stopped.

The third stage allows the part of the project being worked on to be made and tested. After this, there is a stage to determine what will happen in the next iteration of the spiral. There will be a 'product' at the end of each cycle of the spiral, but this isn't necessarily a version of the program. The earlier cycles are likely to produce increasingly detailed requirements.

Advantages and disadvantages of the spiral model

The fact that risk is at the heart of the spiral model is its biggest advantage and would make it the ideal choice for projects with the potential to be high risk. Large projects in particular tend to involve large amounts of risk and as such are suitable for this model.

Risk analysis is in itself a very specialised skill – the model is only as good as the risk analysts working on it. Good risk analysts are expensive, adding to the cost of the project.

Agile programming

In the early 2000s, the concept of agile programming emerged. Agile programming isn't a single methodology but a group of methods. These methods are designed to cope with changing requirements through producing the software in an iterative manner; that is to say, it is produced in versions, each building on the previous and each increasing the requirements it meets. This means that if on seeing a version the user realises they haven't fully considered a requirement, they can have it added in a future iteration.

Compare this to the waterfall model where the user may not realise the deficiency in the system until it has been entirely coded.

Extreme programming

An example of an agile programming methodology is extreme programming, often abbreviated to XP. Extreme programming doesn't, as its name might suggest, involve snowboards or parachutes, but is a model that puts the emphasis on the coding itself.

A representative of the customer becomes part of the team. They help decide the 'user stories' (XP's equivalent of requirements), decide what tests will be used to ensure they been correctly implemented and answer any questions about any problem areas the programmers might have.

Like rapid application development, XP is iterative in nature (the program is coded, tested and improved repeatedly), but unlike RAD the iterations in XP are much shorter – typically a week long.

Also, while RAD uses prototyping, each iteration in XP produces a version of the system (albeit lacking some of the requirements) with code of a good enough quality to be used in the final product. At the start of each iteration, the team goes through 'the planning game'. This involves deciding what the next set of user stories will be and how the team will divide the work.

One of the key features of XP is *pair programming*. In pair programming, code is written with two programmers sitting next to each other. Typically one programmer ('the driver') will use the keyboard to write the code while the other ('the navigator') analyses what is being written.

The two programmers will switch roles regularly, collaborating to ensure the code works. Advocates of paired programming suggest it can result in as much code being produced as would be from two individual programmers but of a higher quality as mistakes and problems are more easily spotted. Programmers are encouraged to regularly 'refactor' code; that is, make it more efficient without changing what it does.

The programmers all have to code to a clear set of standards as every programmer is responsible for the entire program. Tired programmers make mistakes, so to ensure code stays of a high quality, one of the principles of XP is that programmers should work no more than a 40-hour week. In other methodologies it would be common for programmers to be virtually living at their computers as project deadlines draw near.

Rather than being a separate phase, in XP, testing is carried out continuously. Every module of code is tested as soon as it is programmed in what is called 'unit testing'. Once a module is known to work, it is immediately integrated into the main code version so everyone has access to it.

Advantages and disadvantages of extreme programming

With such an emphasis on programming, the quality of the final code is likely to be very high.

A project carried out using extreme programming requires a team of programmers who are able to collaborate well together and work in the same building (it is not likely to work well if they are distributed across the globe).

The client needs to be able to commit to having a representative working with the team.

Key points

- There are many different software development methodologies.
- The waterfall model divides the process into sequential stages.
- Rapid application development involves building a prototype. This is evaluated and refined over multiple iterations until it becomes the final product.
- The spiral model is designed to manage risk and requires risks to be identified and evaluated at each stage.
- Agile methods are designed to deal with projects where there may be changing requirements.
- Extreme programming is an agile method where the focus is on producing high-quality code.

Practice questions

1. Explain which methodology you would recommend and why for the following scenarios:
   (a) building a website for a shop
   (b) building an operating system
   (c) building a video game.
2. Find out about and describe an agile method other than extreme programming.
3. 'Waterfall is dead, long live agile.'
   Discuss to what extent you agree with this statement.
4. Explain why an agile approach is suitable for the A-Level project.

Chapter 10

Computer systems

Introduction

Computer systems are made of hardware and software. You can find out more about software in Chapter 7. Hardware is the description given to the physical components of a computer system.

A computer system has a central processing unit and memory. There is usually some form of storage and devices to input data into and output information from the computer. A *peripheral* is the term given to devices external to the processor. Peripherals are either input, output or storage devices.

The central processing unit (CPU)

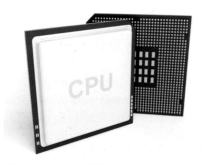

Figure 10.1 A CPU

The CPU is often described as the 'brain' of the computer. This is slightly misleading as it doesn't actually *think*, but it does carry out instructions given to it. Inside a processor there are billions of transistors (effectively electronic switches). Transistors can be combined to build the logic gates seen in Chapter 14, which in turn can be used to build the circuitry inside a processor.

Gordon Moore, founder of Intel®, one the world's best-known processor companies, predicted in 1965 that the number of transistors on a processor would double approximately every two years. This has held true since then, though we are starting to reach the physical limits of how long this can feasibly continue. Doubling the number of transistors (into the same space) increases the speed of the processor. Processor speed has continued to increase exponentially. There are smartphones today with faster processors than desktop computers of ten years ago.

Example

Raspberry Pi ®

There is a flip side to Moore's law, which is that a processor that may have been top of the range 15 years ago can be produced at little cost today. This is the thinking behind the Raspberry Pi computer. Its processor is the equivalent of what may have been found in a desktop PC in the late 1990s. Today it can be produced at such a price that the whole computer can be sold for around £20.

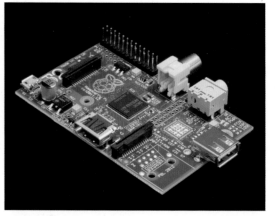

Figure 10.2 Raspberry Pi

Processors work at incredible speeds, which are so far removed from our day-to-day experiences that they are hard to conceptualise. Just like an army marches to the beat of a drum, the processor runs to the timings of a clock signal. The speed of this signal or clock speed is measured in hertz.

Unit	Pulses per second
1 Hertz	1
1 Kilohertz	1000
1 Megahertz	1000000
1 Gigahertz	1000000000

Modern desktop processors tend run in the order of Gigahertz. A 4 Ghz processor is capable of up to 4000000000 instructions per second (that's literally over a billion calculations in the blink of an eye). Clock speed is one way to compare processors but it is possible for a processor with a lower clock speed to outperform one with a higher clock speed. This is because, as we will see later in this chapter, there are other factors that influence a processor's performance, notably cache size, pipelining and number of cores.

Processors work by continually fetching instructions from memory, decoding them and executing them. This is known as the fetch–decode–execute cycle.

Inside the processor

You should note that the model of the processor we are looking at is an *abstraction*; a simplified version to make it easier to understand. Modern processors are extremely complex.

Registers

Registers are memory locations within the processor itself. They work at extremely fast speeds so can be used by the processor without causing a bottleneck. (A bottleneck is the slowest part of a system that limits the speed of the system as a whole.)

Program counter (PC): The program counter keeps track of the memory location of the line of machine code being executed. It gets incremented to point to the next instruction, with each cycle of the fetch–decode–execute cycle allowing the program to be executed in sequence one by one. (In the case of the Little Man Computer, the program counter is always incremented by one during the fetch phase of the fetch–decode–execute cycle.) The program counter is also changed by instructions that alter the flow of control; in the case of the Little Man Computer: Branch if zero (BRZ), Branch always (**BRA**) and Branch if positive (**BRP**).

Memory data register (MDR): The memory data register stores the data that has been fetched from or stored in memory.

Memory address register (MAR): The memory address register stores the address of the data or instructions that are to be fetched from or sent to.

Current instruction register (CIR): The current instruction register stores the most recently fetched instruction, waiting to be decoded and executed.

Key points

– The CPU carries out all the instructions in a computer.

– It is made up of billions of transistors.

– The clock speed is the speed at which it works and is measured in Gigahertz.

– It works by fetching, decoding and executing instructions.

Accumulator (ACC): The accumulator stores the results of calculations made by the ALU. In the Little Man Computer, the instruction LDA loads the contents of a given memory location into the accumulator and STA stores the contents of the accumulator in a given memory location.

General purpose registers: Processors may also have general purpose registers. These can be used temporarily to store data being used rather than sending data to and from the comparatively much slower memory.

Buses: Buses are the communications channels through which data can be sent around the computer. You will probably be familiar with the USB (universal serial bus), which is used to transfer data between the computer and external devices.

When looking at the fetch–decode–execute cycle, there are three buses inside the computer we need to consider: the data bus, control bus and address bus. The data bus carries data between the processor and memory, the address bus carries the address of the memory location being read from or written to and the control bus sends control signals from the control unit.

Arithmetic logic unit (ALU): The arithmetic logic unit, or ALU, carries out the calculations and logical decisions. The results of its calculations are stored in the accumulator.

Control unit (CU): The control unit sends out signals to co-ordinate how the processor works. It controls the how data moves around parts of the CPU and how it moves between the CPU and memory. Instructions are decoded in the control unit.

Example

How the processor executes Little Man Computer code

Let's see how all this works on some Little Man Computer code. You may wish to refresh your memory with how LMC works by referring to Chapter 6.

This code will load two numbers from memory, add them and store the result in memory.

```
        LDA     Num1

        ADD     Num2

        STA     Total

        HLT

Num1    DAT     5

Num2    DAT     10

Total   DAT
```

In practice, memory will contain binary representations of the instructions and data but we shall show them as LMC assembly code so we can follow what is going on.

When the program is put into memory, the instructions are loaded in, followed by the data for Num1, Num2 and Total. Wherever the program has

referred to these three locations, the names can be substituted by these memory locations. Using names in assembly code to represent memory locations is called *symbolic addressing*.

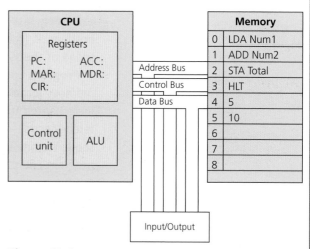

Figure 10.3

We start with the **fetch** step. The PC starts at 0. This value, 0, is loaded into the MAR. The control unit then orchestrates the step. A fetch signal is sent down the control bus and the value 0 down the address bus, denoting fetch the contents of memory location 0.

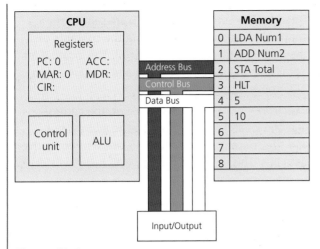

Figure 10.4

The contents of location 0 (that is, LDA Num1) are sent down the data bus. The contents are stored in the CIR.

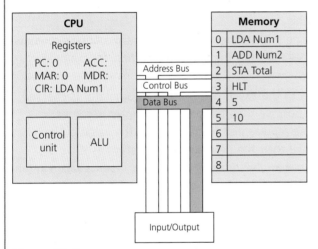

Figure 10.5

We then increment the PC by one.

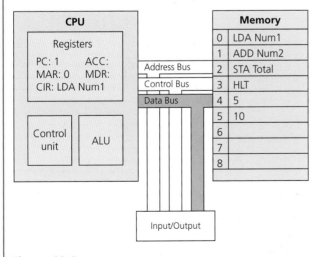

Figure 10.6

With the instruction fetched we now move to the **decode** step.

The contents of the CIR are sent to the control unit. It decodes the instruction as 'Load the contents of Num1 into the Accumulator'. As we will be executing the instruction on Num1, this location is loaded into the MAR.

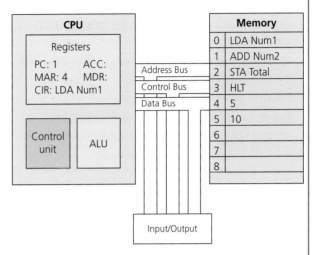

Figure 10.7

Finally the **execute** step. The control unit sends a fetch instruction down the control bus and the value in the MAR (that is, Num1) down the address bus. The contents of memory address 4 are sent to the processor down the data bus and loaded into MDR and then sent to the accumulator.

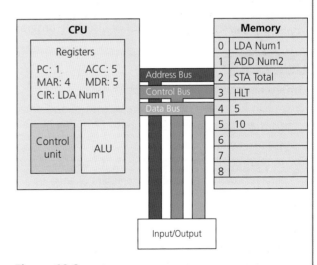

Figure 10.8

This concludes the first run of the fetch–decode–execute cycle. We now repeat the process for the next line of code.

Fetch: The PC is copied into the MAR and the contents of location 1 are fetched and loaded into the CIR. The PC is incremented.

Decode: The contents of the CIR are sent to the control unit and decoded as: Add the contents of Num2 (that is, location 5) to the contents of the accumulator.

Execute: The contents of memory location 5 are fetched from memory and loaded into the MDR and then from here to the ALU. The ALU performs an addition, adding the 10 to the 5 in the ACC. The result, 15, is stored in the ACC.

Now we are ready for another cycle.

Fetch: The PC is copied into the MAR and the contents of location 2 are fetched and loaded into the CIR. The PC is incremented to 3.

Decode: The contents of the CIR are sent to the control unit and decoded as Store the contents of the ACC in Total (that is, location 6). The location for 'total', 6, is loaded into the MAR and contents of the ACC copied to the MDR.

Execute: A write signal is sent down the control bus, the location 6 is sent down the address bus and the contents of the MDR, 15, are sent down the data bus. This results in the value 15 being written to memory location 6.

Fetch: The PC is copied into the MAR and the contents of location 3 are fetched and loaded into the CIR. The PC is incremented to 4.

Decode: The contents of the CIR are sent to the control unit and decoded as 'Halt'.

Execute: The program terminates.

All programs work in this manner. If a program has a branch instruction that is carried out then during the execute phase the program counter's contents become the location pointed to by the branch instruction, for example:

```
BRP   numIsOK
```

When this line comes to the execute stage, the accumulator is checked. If the accumulator is positive then the program counter becomes the location of the line represented by numIsOk. If the value in the accumulator is negative then the program counter stays as it is.

Where a program has an INP or OUT instruction, input is taken in (and stored in the MDR) or output displayed during the execute phase.

Many LMC implementations allow you to watch how memory changes as the program runs. It is highly recommended you try this with some sample programs.

Questions

1. Describe the purpose of the ALU.
2. Explain how each of the address, control and data buses are used in the fetch phase of the fetch–decode–execute cycle.
3. You may recall the code to the right from Chapter 6. Explain how the processor's registers change as this code is run.

```
          INP
          STA     Num1
          LDA     Hundred
          SUB     Num1
          BRP     numIsOK
          LDA     Hundred
          OUT
          HLT
numIsOK   LDA     Num1
          OUT
          HLT
Hundred   DAT     100
Num1      DAT
```

Improving CPU performance

Clock speed is one aspect of a CPU that affects its performance. Most modern CPUs use cache memory, multiple cores, pipelining and integrated GPUs to improve performance.

Cache memory

RAM, while fast compared to storage devices, is still slower than the processor. This makes RAM a bottleneck in the speed at which a processor can operate. To get round this, processors have a small amount of fast memory called cache. Cache memory is built into the processor itself, reducing the distance data has to travel to it. By anticipating the data and instructions that are likely to be regularly accessed and keeping these in cache memory, the overall speed at which the processor operates can be increased.

There is a catch with the way cache is built. As well as being expensive, the larger cache becomes the slower it operates. Therefore modern processors have multiple (often three) levels of cache. When data is required, the smallest (and therefore fastest) cache is checked first, followed by the next largest, and so on, until the RAM is checked.

Multiple cores

You have no doubt come across the terms 'dual core' and 'quad core' processors. Each core is a distinct processing unit on the CPU. As well as having its own cache, the cores will also share a higher-level cache. When multitasking, different cores can run different applications. It is also possible for multiple cores to work on the same problem. As we will see later in this chapter, when looking at *parallel processing*, having four cores does not mean a processor will work at four times the speed.

Figure 10.9 Cache memory

Random access memory → L3 cache → L2 cache → L1 cache → CPU core

Extra info

Four for the price of two

A major portion of the cost of a processor is down to the research and development rather than the silicon itself. Processor manufacturers often want to sell quad core processors to users in need of larger amounts of processing power and then dual cores as a cheaper alternative.

When manufacturers have already designed the circuitry for a quad core processor and set up the manufacturing process, it is cheaper to disable two of the cores on a quad core processor than completely redesign a dual core processor. This is exactly what they do. In the past, some users have been able to re-activate the extra two cores, allowing them to effectively get a four core for the price of two.

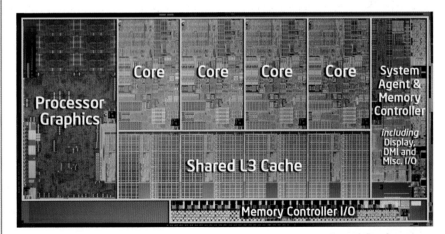

Figure 10.10 Cores in a CPU

Pipelining

A Level only

Imagine you and three friends are tasked with making 1000 jam sandwiches. You only have one block of butter, one pot of jam and one sharp knife to cut the sandwiches. The less sensible option would be one of you could butter all the bread then when finished the next person could put the jam on all of them then when they have finished the final person can cut them all.

What would be eminently more sensible would for person one to spread the butter on the first sandwich. They can then pass it to person two who will spread the jam on, meanwhile person one can be spreading the butter for the next sandwich. When they have both finished, person two passes the sandwich to person three to cut, they receive the second sandwich from person one so they can spread the jam on that and person one can spread butter on the third sandwich.

	Person one Spreads butter	Person two Spreads jam	Person three Cuts sandwich
Step one	Sandwich one		
Step two	Sandwich two	Sandwich one	
Step three	Sandwich three	Sandwich two	Sandwich one
Step four	Sandwich four	Sandwich three	Sandwich two

This process is known as 'pipelining'. Being able to apply pipelining to a problem is an example of **computational thinking**.

Pipelining is used in modern processors. While one instruction is being executed, the next instruction is being decoded and the one after that fetched.

	Fetch	Decode	Execute
Step one	Instruction one		
Step two	Instruction two	Instruction one	
Step three	Instruction three	Instruction two	Instruction one
Step four	Instruction four	Instruction three	Instruction two

Pipelining does have its limitations. It is not always possible accurately to predict what instruction needs to be fetched and decoded next. Imagine in the example above that Instruction two, when executed, branches to Instruction nine as the result of a condition (perhaps the equivalent to a BRP has been used). In this case we have to 'flush the pipes' of the existing instructions.

	Fetch	Decode	Execute
Step one	Instruction one		
Step two	Instruction two	Instruction one	
Step three	Instruction three	Instruction two	Instruction one
Step four	Instruction four	Instruction three	Instruction two
Step five	Instruction nine		

The more often we have to flush the pipeline, the less of a benefit pipelining gives us.

Graphics processing unit (GPU)

A graphics processing unit is specifically designed to perform the calculations associated with graphics. Modern 3D graphics require significant computation and, as is the case with games and simulations,

Extra info

Bitcoin mining

Bitcoin is a 'virtual currency'. Unlike real world currencies that have their value linked to physical wealth such as gold, BitCoin is linked to the 'mining' of solutions to hashes. As described in

Chapters 13 and 15, a hash is a one-way function. A BitCoin is mined by finding the value that gives the hash as a result. Bitcoins are set up such that as more coins are mined, more coins become increasingly harder to find.

Initially people mined, for Bitcoins using CPUs. They soon realised however that GPUs could check many hashes in one go and so GPUs were commonly used instead. As Bitcoins became harder and harder to find, the use of GPUs has now been replaced by specially designed circuitry known as application-specific integrated circuits (ASIC).

need to be rendered in real time. GPUs have **instruction sets** specifically designed for the sorts of calculations required in graphics processing.

Often when rendering graphics, the same calculation needs to be applied to multiple points on the screen. To speed this up, graphics processors have the ability to process these pieces of data in parallel; what is referred to as *single instruction multiple data* (SIMD).

People who run applications that require detailed graphics to be produced in real time (for example games enthusiasts and 3D animators) are likely to use a graphics card. This card will contain a fast GPU with its own memory. For most other users a GPU embedded onto the main processor, sharing the system's memory, will be sufficient.

Uses of GPUs

GPUs are clearly used for graphics for gamers, designers and 3D animators. Over recent years they have started to be applied to different situations. The ability of GPUs to process the same instruction across multiple pieces of data at one time has made GPUs attractive to scientists and engineers. Uses of GPUs include:

- modelling physical systems
- audio processing
- breaking passwords
- machine learning.

Questions

1. Look at the following specification for a CPU. Describe what each of the characteristics means:

   Lightning processor
   Quad core
   3.2 GHz
   6 MB L3 Cache

2. Explain why a statistician might use a GPU.

3. Explain how a carwash could be made more efficient by applying the principle of pipelining.

Key points

- Cache memory is a special type of fast memory used for instructions and data likely to be needed by the processor.
- Cores are separate processing units. Modern processors contain multiple cores.
- Pipelining is the practice of fetching one instruction while decoding another and executing one further.
- Graphics processing units are other processors specifically designed to deal with the mathematics involved with producing graphics on screen. Many modern CPUs have an integrated GPU.

Input, output, storage and memory

Input and output devices

Input devices allow data to be entered into a computer. Examples include keyboards, mice, microphones, scanners and joysticks.

Output devices allow information to be retrieved from a computer. Examples include printers, speakers, monitors and actuators (devices that cause movement).

You are not expected to know the detailed workings of any of these devices for the examination, but you are expected to be able to choose suitable input and output devices for a given scenario.

Storage devices

Storage devices fall into three categories: magnetic, flash and optical. When looking at storage there are three considerations:

- cost (how much it costs to purchase per MB)
- speed (how quickly it can be read from and written to)
- capacity (how much data it can store).

Magnetic storage uses a magnetisable material. Patterns of magnetisation are then used to represent binary sequences. Examples include hard disk drives and magnetic tape (often used to back up servers). Magnetic storage tends to have a high capacity at a low cost.

Optical storage such as CDs, DVDs and Blu-ray discs™ work by using a laser and by looking at its reflection, determining where there are pits on a surface representing 1s and 0s. Optical media tend to be cheap to distribute and fairly resilient. You can drop a DVD, submerge it in water, even eat your dinner off it and put it in the dishwasher and it is still likely to work.

Flash media work by using a special type of ROM that can be overwritten. Flash memory is used in USB memory sticks and camera memory cards. It has a good number of advantages. It can be read from and written to at high speeds.

Some hard disks now use flash memory. Solid state drives (SSDs) are an alternative to a hard drive, but with no moving parts. While technically SSDs can use technologies other than flash, in practice nowadays the overwhelming majority use flash. Magnetic hard drives can get damaged if the device they are in is dropped or moved sharply while they are writing data.

As flash memory has no moving parts, it doesn't have this issue. Its lack of moving parts also means it consumes less power than other types of media. These advantages make flash media well suited to portable devices. There is a trade-off however. Flash media are significantly more expensive than magnetic or optical media. Each storage location in a flash medium has a limited number of times it can be written to (usually up to 100 000 times, but it depends on the quality of the flash memory).

To get round this, most flash devices have a controller on board that moves frequently written-to files to different locations in the device. In the case of good quality SSDs, there is usually enough reserved extra space that can be used, such that the SSD will have a life expectancy to match a traditional magnetic hard drive. Cheap USB memory sticks and SD cards, however, may well develop faults over time.

Because of the way data is stored on an SSD there is little benefit to be gained from defragmenting it. In fact, because of the amount of rewriting of files involved, regular defragmenting of an SSD can decrease its life expectancy.

Memory

RAM

Random-access memory (RAM) is where the programs and data being run by a computer are temporarily stored. The random aspect of it is that the processor can access its locations equally as quickly as any other location. Access to RAM is much quicker than to a storage device. When power to the computer is lost, RAM loses its contents; it is what we call **volatile**.

Extra info

Hybrid drives

Hybrid hard drives are becoming increasingly common. These aim to combine the capacity available on magnetic drives with the speed of solid state drives. Hybrid drives have a magnetic component where the majority of data is stored. There is also a smaller solid state component. This usually contains commonly accessed files (for example parts of the operating system) so they can be loaded quickly.

With high bandwidth internet connections becoming common, people are increasingly using virtual storage. This involves storing data in the 'cloud' rather than locally on their computer. This has the advantage that they have large amounts of storage available, automatically backed up. While we refer to this storage as 'virtual', it is of course physically stored, just in a data centre somewhere rather than locally on the user's computer.

Key points

- Input devices put data into a computer.
- Output devices give the user information from a computer.
- Storage devices permanently store data.
- Storage can be magnetic, optical or flash.
- RAM and ROM are different types of memory.
- RAM temporarily stores programs and data being used by the computer.
- ROM cannot be written to and is often used to store the boot program for the computer.

ROM

Read-only memory is memory that, as its name suggests, can be read from but not written to. A common use for it is storing the program to boot up a computer. As ROM retains its contents when the computer's power is lost, it is referred to as being **non-volatile**.

Questions

1. Describe the input and output devices that might be used in a doctor's surgery.
2. Find some examples of magnetic hard drives, recordable Blu-ray discs and solid state drives for sale online. Work out the average price per Gb for each of these media.
3. Explain why it is often advised that you disable virtual memory on an SSD. You should refer to disk thrashing in your answer. (See Chapter 7.)
4. Explain why software is often distributed on DVD.
5. Find out one other way RAM can be measured other than by its storage capacity.

Computer architectures

The Von Neumann architecture

The model of the processor we have looked at is known as the Von Neumann architecture after its creator John von Neumann. The Von Neumann architecture describes a computer with a single control unit that sequentially works through instructions. One of its most distinctive characteristics is that instructions and data are stored in memory together. You will recall that in the LMC, the instructions were stored in memory locations 0 to 3 and the data in locations 4 to 5 all in the same memory unit. As you will recall from the example above, the instructions and data are both sent along the data bus. This means that instructions can't be fetched at the same time data is being sent along the bus, causing what is refered to as the 'Von Neumann Bottleneck'.

Computing people

John von Neumann

Born in 1903 in Hungary, John von Neumann was a gifted mathematician and physicist. In his late 20s, he moved to America where, after a few years, he became an American citizen. Because of his expertise in how explosions can be mathematically modelled, he was recruited to work on the Manhattan Project (the project to design the first atomic bomb) during the Second World War.

John von Neumann made significant contributions to computer science. He invented the merge sort **algorithm** (see Chapter 5) and did much work looking at how (sufficiently) random numbers can be generated by computers. He was a consultant on the building of the EDVAC computer, which was used for performing ballistics calculations.

As a result of a report he wrote on this project, the EDVAC's architecture became known as the Von Neumann architecture – much to the displeasure of the other scientists who worked on the project.

Figure 10.11 John von Neumann

The Harvard Architecture

In the Harvard Architecture, data and instructions are store in separate memory units with separate buses. This means that while data is being written to or read from the data memory, the next instruction can be read from the instruction memory. The Harvard Architecture tends to be used by RISC processors.

Parallel processing

Parallel processing is when a computer carries out multiple computations simultaneously to solve a given problem. There are different approaches to this. One, as we have seen with GPUs, is *single instruction multiple data* (SIMD), where the same operation is carried out on multiple pieces of data, at one time. The other approach is *multiple instructions multiple data* (MIMD); here, different instructions are carried out concurrently on different pieces of data. This can be carried out using multiple cores on a CPU. MIMD takes place on a much larger scale on supercomputers. Supercomputers are massive parallel machines. The top super computers in the world contain tens of thousands of multicore processors (often accompanied by thousands of GPUs). Such computers cost phenomenal amounts of money to buy and run (due to their massive power consumption). Over recent years, an alternative approach to parallel computing has become viable, thanks in part to the internet: distributed computing. In distributed computing, each computer across a network takes on part of a problem.

It's worth bearing in mind that adding 100 more processors to a problem doesn't necessarily make solving it 100 times quicker. Some problems naturally lend themselves to parallelisation. Take the example of adding a billion numbers. With 100 processors, the first processor could add the 10 million numbers, the next could simultaneously add the next 10 million, and so on. Then the totals could be added together. This would take nearly one-hundredth of the time it would take a single processor to do this.

Other problems are not parallelisable at all, for example the Fibonacci sequence. Each Fibonacci term is generated by adding the previous two terms together: 1 1 2 3 5 8 13 21 34 …

As each term depends on the previous, having more processors available will not speed things up.

In practice, most problems are partially parallelisable. If a problem is only 50 per cent parallelisable then no matter how many processors you use on it you will only ever be able to get close to running it in half the time of one processor, and no faster.

RISC vs CISC

As processors became more sophisticated, they have acquired a wider range of instructions in their instruction set. Some instructions are designed to match the functionality available in high-level code. A big advantage of this is that programs require less memory as they can be implemented in fewer complex instructions. Often these instructions will require data being read from memory and can take several clock cycles to complete.

Extra info

SETI@Home

SETI@Home is a volunteer-distributed computing project. SETI stands for *search for extra terrestrial intelligence*. Users can download the SETI@Home client. This client can either use spare processor time when the user is working or run when the computer is idle.

Each client is tasked with analysing radio waves detected by telescopes for signs of them being the result of transmissions by intelligent beings. Using this distributed method, SETI has the equivalent computing power of approximately half a million computers.

Key points

- In the Von Neumann architecture, instructions and data are stored together in memory; instructions are executed one at a time in sequence.
- In the Harvard architecture, separate memory and buses are used for data and instructions.
- Parallel processing is when multiple processors work together to solve a problem.
- RISC is an alternative to CISC in which less complex instructions are easy to pipeline.

An alternative approach taken to this is RISC: reduced instruction set computing. In a RISC system the number of instructions is streamlined, for example only the load and store instructions access memory; all other instructions operate on the registers. This is one of the reasons RISC systems tend to have fewer addressing modes (see Chapter 6) and more general purpose registers than non-RISC processors. All instructions in a RISC system should execute in roughly the same, small, number of clock cycles (ideally one). This allows RISC systems to use pipelining.

The term CISC (complex instruction set computing) is used to describe non-RISC processors.

As RISC processors tend to involve fewer transistors, they have the added bonus that they tend to produce less heat, consume less power and cost less to produce than their CISC counterparts. On the other hand, a compiler for a RISC system has a harder job as it must determine how the functionality specified in the high-level code can be built from the more limited set of available instructions.

The boundaries between RISC and CISC are becoming increasingly blurred as RISC manufacturers try to incorporate elements of CISC into their processors and vice versa.

Practice questions

1. To find out if a number is 'happy', take its digits, square each one and add them together. Repeat the process on the answer, and continue until you reach the number 1, in which case it is happy, or you cycle through a sequence forever.

   23 is happy: $2^2+3^2=13$ $1^2+3^2=10$ $1^2+0^2=1$

   24 is not happy: $2^2+4^2=20$ $2^2+0^2=4$ $4^2=16$ $1^2+6^2=37$ $3^2+7^2=58$, and so on until it cycles back to 4.

   Explain to what extent can determining if a number is happy or not be sped up by using more processors.

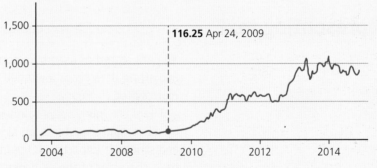

Figure 10.12

2. Why might the following organisations use supercomputers?
   (a) The Meteorological Office
   (b) GCHQ (the UK government's code-breaking organisation)
   (c) A Formula 1 Racing Team
3. ARM is a big producer of RISC processors. The graph below shows ARM's share price over the last decade. Why do you think ARM's share price started rising in 2009 and has continued to rise since?

Chapter 11

Data types

Why we need data types

When we look at data, we instinctively recognise the type of data from our experience. When we see the list: 6, hat, 12.95, we recognise 6 as an integer, hat as text and 12.95 as decimal. Different data types are stored and processed in different ways and, since computers do not have the instinctive ability to recognise data types, we have to tell the computer what type data is so that appropriate facilities for processing and storing it can be made available.

Data types

The main data types we use are:

Type	Description	Example
Character	Single letter, digit, symbol or control code	S, g, 7, &
String	A string of alphanumeric characters	hat, Fg7tY6, %7&*j
Boolean	One of two values	True or False
Integer	Whole number values with no decimal part	6, −12, 9, 143
Real	Numbers with decimal or fractional parts	12.3, −18.63, 3.14

Whatever the data type, the computer stores the value in binary.

Representing text

All data stored or used by a computer is in binary and the character and string data types identified at the start of this chapter are also represented in binary.

There are many ways to represent data but for data to be readable by all computer systems, an agreed method of representing characters and strings is important. One important approach to this is ASCII, where each character of the alphabet and some special symbols and control codes are represented by agreed binary patterns. The ASCII character set was originally based on an 8-bit binary pattern using seven bits plus a single parity bit and was able to represent 128 separate characters. The extended ASCII set uses eight bits and can represent 256 separate characters.

ASCII TABLE

Decimal	Hexadecimal	Binary	Octal	Char	Decimal	Hexadecimal	Binary	Octal	Char	Decimal	Hexadecimal	Binary	Octal	Char
0	0	0	0	[NULL]	48	30	110000	60	0	96	60	1100000	140	`
1	1	1	1	[START OF HEADING]	49	31	110001	61	1	97	61	1100001	141	a
2	2	10	2	[START OF TEXT]	50	32	110010	62	2	98	62	1100010	142	b
3	3	11	3	[END OF TEXT]	51	33	110011	63	3	99	63	1100011	143	c
4	4	100	4	[END OF TRANSMISSION]	52	34	110100	64	4	100	64	1100100	144	d
5	5	101	5	[ENQUIRY]	53	35	110101	65	5	101	65	1100101	145	e
6	6	110	6	[ACKNOWLEDGE]	54	36	110110	66	6	102	66	1100110	146	f
7	7	111	7	[BELL]	55	37	110111	67	7	103	67	1100111	147	g
8	8	1000	10	[BACKSPACE]	56	38	111000	70	8	104	68	1101000	150	h
9	9	1001	11	[HORIZONTAL TAB]	57	39	111001	71	9	105	69	1101001	151	i
10	A	1010	12	[LINE FEED]	58	3A	111010	72	:	106	6A	1101010	152	j
11	B	1011	13	[VERTICAL TAB]	59	3B	111011	73	;	107	6B	1101011	153	k
12	C	1100	14	[FORM FEED]	60	3C	111100	74	<	108	6C	1101100	154	l
13	D	1101	15	[CARRIAGE RETURN]	61	3D	111101	75	=	109	6D	1101101	155	m
14	E	1110	16	[SHIFT OUT]	62	3E	111110	76	>	110	6E	1101110	156	n
15	F	1111	17	[SHIFT IN]	63	3F	111111	77	?	111	6F	1101111	157	o
16	10	10000	20	[DATA LINK ESCAPE]	64	40	1000000	100	@	112	70	1110000	160	p
17	11	10001	21	[DEVICE CONTROL 1]	65	41	1000001	101	A	113	71	1110001	161	q
18	12	10010	22	[DEVICE CONTROL 2]	66	42	1000010	102	B	114	72	1110010	162	r
19	13	10011	23	[DEVICE CONTROL 3]	67	43	1000011	103	C	115	73	1110011	163	s
20	14	10100	24	[DEVICE CONTROL 4]	68	44	1000100	104	D	116	74	1110100	164	t
21	15	10101	25	[NEGATIVE ACKNOWLEDGE]	69	45	1000101	105	E	117	75	1110101	165	u
22	16	10110	26	[SYNCHRONOUS IDLE]	70	46	1000110	106	F	118	76	1110110	166	v
23	17	10111	27	[ENG OF TRANS. BLOCK]	71	47	1000111	107	G	119	77	1110111	167	w
24	18	11000	30	[CANCEL]	72	48	1001000	110	H	120	78	1111000	170	x
25	19	11001	31	[END OF MEDIUM]	73	49	1001001	111	I	121	79	1111001	171	y
26	1A	11010	32	[SUBSTITUTE]	74	4A	1001010	112	J	122	7A	1111010	172	z
27	1B	11011	33	[ESCAPE]	75	4B	1001011	113	K	123	7B	1111011	173	{
28	1C	11100	34	[FILE SEPARATOR]	76	4C	1001100	114	L	124	7C	1111100	174	|
29	1D	11101	35	[GROUP SEPARATOR]	77	4D	1001101	115	M	125	7D	1111101	175	}
30	1E	11110	36	[RECORD SEPARATOR]	78	4E	1001110	116	N	126	7E	1111110	176	~
31	1F	11111	37	[UNIT SEPARATOR]	79	4F	1001111	117	O	127	7F	1111111	177	[DEL]
32	20	100000	40	[SPACE]	80	50	1010000	120	P					
33	21	100001	41	!	81	51	1010001	121	Q					
34	22	100010	42	"	82	52	1010010	122	R					
35	23	100011	43	#	83	53	1010011	123	S					
36	24	100100	44	$	84	54	1010100	124	T					
37	25	100101	45	%	85	55	1010101	125	U					
38	26	100110	46	&	86	56	1010110	126	V					
39	27	100111	47	'	87	57	1010111	127	W					
40	28	101000	50	(	88	58	1011000	130	X					
41	29	101001	51	)	89	59	1011001	131	Y					
42	2A	101010	52	*	90	5A	1011010	132	Z					
43	2B	101011	53	+	91	5B	1011011	133	[					
44	2C	101100	54	,	92	5C	1011100	134	\					
45	2D	101101	55	-	93	5D	1011101	135	]					
46	2E	101110	56	.	94	5E	1011110	136	^					
47	2F	101111	57	/	95	5F	1011111	137	_					

Figure 11.1 ASCII table

With just eight bits available, the number of characters in the character set is limited to 256, making it impossible to display the wide range of characters for other alphabets or symbols sets. Unicode was originally a 16-bit code allowing for more than 65,000 characters to be represented, but this was quickly updated to remove the 16-bit restriction by using a series of code pages with each page representing the chosen language symbols. The original ASCII representations have been included as part of the Unicode character set with the same numeric values.

A string is simply a collection of characters and uses as many bytes as required, so if using the ASCII 8-bit character set, the string 'HODDER' would require one byte per character, or six bytes, to store the string.

Boolean data

Boolean is a data type that can only take one of two values: TRUE or FALSE, using 1 to represent TRUE and 0 to represent FALSE. It is clear that Boolean data only requires one bit to store a value, but the values are often stored in one byte for convenience. Boolean data types are often used to flag if an event has occurred.

Key points

— There are basically five data types: character, string, Boolean, integer and real. Other data types are represented using these formats, for example date and time is represented as an integer.

— All data types are represented in the computer in binary: 0s and 1s.

Representing positive integers in binary

Questions

1. Convert the following binary numbers into denary:
   (a) 10111001
   (b) 00010001
   (c) 11111111
   (d) 00000000
2. What is the largest denary value that can be stored in an 8-bit binary integer?

Key points

— Binary is a number system based on 2; the column values are the powers of 2 starting at 2^0 (1).

— Denary is the number system we commonly use based on 10; the column values are the powers of 10 starting at 10^0 (1).

— Integers are represented in binary using powers of 2. We add up the column value where there is a 1 in the binary number to get the denary equivalent.

— To convert from denary to binary, we simply divide by 2 repeatedly and write down the remainder at each stage.

Questions

Convert the following integers to binary:
1. 49
2. 131
3. 127
4. 255
5. 203

When we write a number in base 10 (denary), we simply combine a quantity of 1s, 10s, 100s, and so on to represent the value, for example: 397 is three 100s plus nine 10s plus seven 1s. We often show these as column headings:

Column value	$1000 = 10^3$	$100 = 10^2$	$10 = 10^1$	$1 = 10^0$
Denary number	2	4	3	6
Is:	2*1000+	4*100+	3*10+	6*1

Base 2, binary, uses a similar approach, but the column headings are based on 2 rather than 10.

Example

Column value	$128 = 2^7$	$64 = 2^6$	$32 = 2^5$	$16 = 2^4$	$8 = 2^3$	$4 = 2^2$	$2 = 2^1$	$1 = 2^0$
Binary number	1	0	0	1	1	0	1	1
Is	128+	0+	0+	16+	8+	0	2+	1

which is 128+16+8+2+1=155 in denary.

The conversion from binary to denary is really very straightforward: add the column values together for every column containing a 1 in the binary number.

Converting denary numbers to binary can be done by dividing repeatedly by 2 and recording the remainder until we reach 0.

Example

163 in denary into binary is:

163 ÷ 2 = 81 remainder 1 (*This is the number of 1s*)

81 ÷ 2 = 40 remainder 1 (*This is the number of 2s*)

40 ÷ 2 = 20 remainder 0 ...

20 ÷ 2 = 10 remainder 0 ...

10 ÷ 2 = 5 remainder 0 ...

5 ÷ 2 = 2 remainder 1 ...

2 ÷ 2 = 1 remainder 0 ...

1 ÷ 2 = 0 remainder 1 (*This is the number of 128s*)

So 163 in binary is 10100011

Check: 128+32+2+1 = 163 ✓

Representing negative integers in binary

There are two ways to represent negative integers in binary.

Sign and magnitude

We can follow the convention used in denary and store a sign bit, a + or −, as part of the number. Simply use the left-hand bit, the one with the largest value, often called the **most significant bit (MSB)** to store these as a binary value; 0 for + and 1 for −.

This approach to storing integers is known as sign and magnitude. This modifies the column headings to:

Column value	Sign bit	64	32	16	8	4	2	1

Questions

1. Convert the following denary numbers to binary sign and magnitude using eight bits:
   (a) −81
   (b) 52
   (c) −127
   (d) 127
2. What are the largest and smallest values that can be stored in eight bits using sign and magnitude?

Example

So to store −103 we will need to set the sign bit to 1 and set the remaining columns to store the magnitude, 103.

Column value	Sign bit	64	32	16	8	4	2	1
Binary number	1	1	1	0	0	1	1	1

To store +27 in sign and magnitude representation, we set the sign bit to 0 and the remaining seven bits for the magnitude to:

Column value	Sign bit	64	32	16	8	4	2	1
Binary number	0	0	0	1	1	0	1	1

Two's complement

While we are quite happy to deal with a sign and a magnitude, the processing required to handle this is quite complicated and a more effective approach is to make the most significant bit (MSB) a negative value. This changes the column headings for 8-bit numbers to:

Column value	−128	64	32	16	8	4	2	1

Example

To store −103 we record −128 + 25 or:

Column value	−128	64	32	16	8	4	2	1
Binary number	1	0	0	1	1	0	0	1

Check −128 + 16 + 8 + 1 = −103 ✓

so +27 is:

Column value	−128	64	32	16	8	4	2	1
Binary number	0	0	0	1	1	0	1	1

1. Convert the following denary numbers to two's complement binary using eight bits:
   (a) −81
   (b) 52
   (c) −128
   (d) 127
2. What are the largest and smallest values that can be stored in eight bits using two's complement?

Representing numbers in hexadecimal

Computers do not work in **hexadecimal** – base 16 – but it is often used to represent numbers stored in a computer because it is simpler for humans to read and remember, for example FDA5 is much easier to recognise and remember than its binary equivalent 1111110110100101. It also gives us a direct representation of the binary since the base value 16 is 2^4 or four bits.

In hexadecimal, the column headings are:

Column value	$4096 = 16^3$	$256 = 16^2$	$16 = 16^1$	$1 = 16^0$

The main problem is that we have digits to represent the values 0 to 9 but as we reuse these to form numbers 10 or larger, we need extra digits to represent the values 10 to 15 in hexadecimal. We use A to F for this purpose.

Denary	Hexadecimal		Denary	Hexadecimal
0	0		8	8
1	1		9	9
2	2		10	A
3	3		11	B
4	4		12	C
5	5		13	D
6	6		14	E
7	7		15	F

To convert a hexadecimal number into denary, we use the column values as we did for binary.

Questions

Convert the following hexadecimal numbers to denary:
1. 12
2. FF
3. 3D
4. 2BE
5. AB5

Example

A2C as a denary number is:

Column value	$4096=16^3$	$256=16^2$	$16=16^1$	$1=16^0$
Hexadecimal number		A	2	C
Denary value		10*256	2*16	12

A2C is 2560+32+12 = 2604 in denary.

To represent a denary number in hexadecimal, we repeatedly divide by 16, recording the remainders, as we did for binary.

Example

163 denary in hexadecimal:

163 ÷ 16 = 10 remainder 3 *(This is the number of 1s)*

10 ÷ 16 = 0 remainder 10 *(This is the number of 16s)*

Using our table of symbols above, 163 denary is A3 in hexadecimal.

One important feature of hexadecimal numbers is their link to binary. The base value is 16, which is 2^4, meaning each digit can be represented using four binary digits (often called a nibble or nybble).

Binary	Hexadecimal		Binary	Hexadecimal
0000	0		1000	8
0001	1		1001	9
0010	2		1010	A
0011	3		1011	B
0100	4		1100	C
0101	5		1101	D
0110	6		1110	E
0111	7		1111	F

This makes converting between binary and hexadecimal straightforward. Simply convert each hexadecimal digit to its equivalent binary nibble:

Example

A3FD as a binary value is:

1010 0011 1111 1101

To convert a binary value to its hexadecimal equivalent, divide it into a set of nibbles and convert to the hexadecimal equivalent.

Example

1011 0101 1100 0111

  B   5   C   7

Images, sound and instructions

All data stored and used by the computer is represented in binary. And all images, sound and instructions are represented by binary patterns.

Images

A simple black and white graphic, such as those in the early space invader video games, is made up of black and white dots. The character can be represented in binary by simply choosing 1 for black and 0 for white. Each row is one byte and the whole character is described by eight bytes:

Figure 11.2 A simple black and white graphic represented in binary

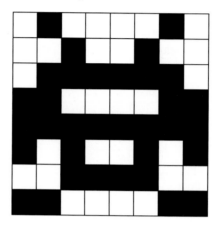

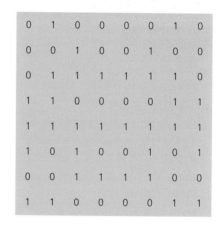

In reality, images are far more complex than this, with several colours to be represented. In a single bit we can only represent two colours; for more colours we need to use more bits.

- Using two bits can represent 2^2 or four colours.
- Using three bits can represent 2^3 or eight colours.
- Using eight bits we can represent 2^8 or 256 and with 16 bits 2^{16} or 65,536 colours.

This is part of the binary used to store an image of some flowers:

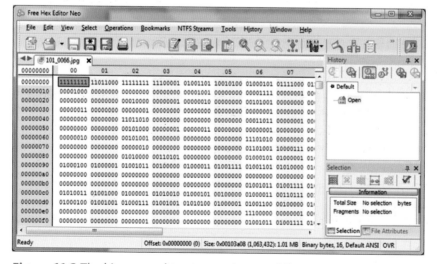

Figure 11.3 The binary used to store an image of flowers

The image of the flowers uses 24 bits per pixel compared to the one bit per pixel for the space invader graphic, and the computer needs to have information about the data to reproduce the images accurately.

This data about the data is called **metadata**. This is the metadata for the image of the flowers:

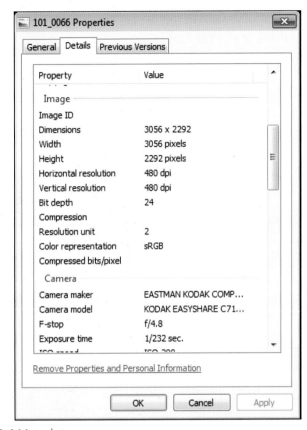

Figure 11.4 Metadata

This metadata includes information about the number of bits per pixel, or **colour depth**, the **resolution** of the image in dots per inch and the width and height in pixels.

Image files are stored in a variety of formats, but basically either as a set of pixels in bitmap form or as a vector form. In vector graphics, formats images are made up of primitive shapes such as lines, arcs and ellipses together with other information about the shape, including a set of control points the shape must pass through.

When an enlarged bitmap image becomes *pixelated*, the pixels become larger and more visible and we can see the blocks that make up the image. With vector graphics, that does not happen because the information about the shapes that makes up the image is simply recalculated and the primitive shapes redrawn.

To store large or high resolution images, a bitmap needs to store more information and the size of the file increases with size and resolution. Since the definitions for the primitive shapes and control points remain unchanged, the file size for vector graphics files is not affected by the size of the image.

Sound

Sound is continuously varying (analogue) data, but if the computer is to represent or store sound files they must be converted to binary (digital) data. The analogue sound data is sampled at set intervals and the values that are sampled are used to represent the sound in digital format.

The **sample rate** determines the quality of the sound recorded. If we sample at a low rate then we use few samples and there is a poor match between the original and the sampled sounds.

If we sample at a high rate then we use a large number of samples, improving the match between the original and sampled sounds.

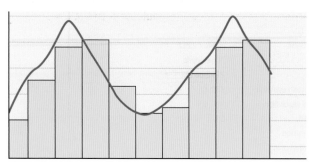

Figure 11.5 Sampling at a low rate

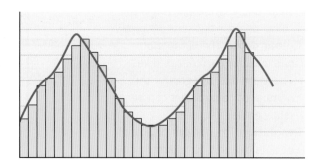

Figure 11.6 Sampling at a high rate

Another factor that affects the quality of the sound recorded is the *accuracy* of the values sampled. To record an accurate value requires more bits to store each individual sampled value.

The **bit rate** is the space available for each sample and is measured in kilobits per second (Kbits/s). A typical bit rate for an MP3 track is 128 Kbits/s, whereas an audio CD uses 1411.2 Kbits/s.

There is a trade-off to be made when recording sound digitally. The higher the sample rate and bit rate, the better the quality, but higher sample rates and bit rates require more storage space and increase the file size.

Instructions

Program instructions and data are both stored by the computer in binary. When a program is run, the CPU is directed to the start address for the first instruction. The binary number stored at that address is fetched and decoded into two parts: the operator and the operand.

The operator is a binary pattern that represents a machine-level instruction, for example an instruction to add a value to the accumulator.

The operand is the data part and contains either a value to be dealt with or the information needed to locate the data to be dealt with, for example it might be the binary value for a location containing the data to be used.

Example

In a simple 8-bit instruction, 1001 represents the instruction to add the value found in a memory location to the accumulator. If the following instruction is fetched:

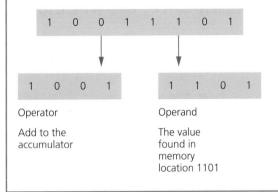

| 1 | 0 | 0 | 1 | 1 | 1 | 0 | 1 |

| 1 | 0 | 0 | 1 | | 1 | 1 | 0 | 1 |

Operator

Add to the
accumulator

Operand

The value
found in
memory
location 1101

The computer has no way of differentiating between data and instructions and interprets what it finds based on what it expects to find. If it is told to run a program from a certain start location, it will interpret data it finds at that location as an instruction. If there are errors in the program, it might fetch what is meant to be data but interpret it as an instruction.

Practice questions

1. Convert the denary number 273 into:
   (a) a 16-bit binary number
   (b) a hexadecimal.
2. Convert −89 into binary using:
   (a) 8-bit sign and magnitude representation
   (b) 8-bit two's complement representation.
3. Explain how the image size and colour depth affect the size of an image file.
4. What metadata is stored with an image file?
5. Explain how bit rate and sample rate affect the size of a sound file.
6. Explain how instructions are coded in binary in a computer and how the computer is able to distinguish between instructions and data.

Chapter 12

Computer arithmetic

Adding and subtracting integers in binary

The process for adding together two numbers in binary is very similar to that which we use for denary, for example if we add 85 and 67 the steps are:

- Add 5 and 7, this is 12, so we write down 2 and carry the 1 to the next column
- Add 8, 6 and the carried 1 to get 15, we write down the 5 and carry the 1:

$$
\begin{array}{r}
85 \\
67 \\
\hline
152 \\
\scriptstyle 1\ 1
\end{array}
$$

The carried values

Example

For example adding 1011 and 10011011:

$$
\begin{array}{r}
0\,0\,0\,0\,1\,0\,1\,1 \\
1\,0\,0\,1\,1\,0\,1\,1 \\
\hline
1\,0\,1\,0\,0\,1\,1\,0 \\
\scriptstyle 1\ 1\quad\ 1\ 1
\end{array}
$$

The carried values

	Carry	Sum
0 + 0	0	0
0 + 1	0	1
1 + 0	0	1
1 + 1	1	0
1 + 1 + 1	1	1

In binary when we add 0s and 1s we have the following possible outcomes:

When subtracting in denary, if the one we are subtracting is larger than the one we are subtracting it from, we borrow a 'ten' from the next column, for example 85–67.

We cannot subtract 7 from 5 so we borrow a ten from the 8, leaving 7, and we subtract 7 from 15:

Borrowing 1 from the 8 adds 10 to the next column

$$
\begin{array}{r}
\scriptstyle 7\ 15 \\
8\,5 \\
6\,7 \\
\hline
1\,8
\end{array}
$$

The process is the same in binary, except when we borrow from the next column, we borrow a 2, for example:

```
  0 2
1 1 1̶ 0
0 1 0 1
1 0 0 1
```

> Borrowing 1 from the second column adds 2 to the next column

We often have to borrow from columns much further away in binary, but the process follows the same pattern.

Example

```
      1 2
    0̶ 2̶
1 0 1 1 0 0 1
0 0 1 0 1 1 1
1 0 0 0 0 0 0
```

> Borrowing 1 from the fourth column adds 2 to the third column; we then borrow one of these to make a 2 in the second column

Questions

Complete the following binary additions and subtractions:

1. 10100110 + 110011
2. 1111 + 1001
3. 10010 − 1011
4. 10000 − 1111
5. 10101010 − 10111

Adding using two's complement numbers

Adding two's complement values is the same process as adding standard binary integers, but adding two large numbers together does illustrate an interesting phenomenon.

The two large numbers when added together are too large to store in the 8-bit two's complement integer and the value overflows the available bits, creating a negative number.

If the calculation were to result in a number that was too small to represent, then this would be called underflow.

Subtracting using two's complement numbers

Subtracting two's complement numbers is a relatively straightforward process. We convert the number to be subtracted into a negative two's complement number and add.

Example

Adding together the two two's complement integers 01101111 and 01110011:

01100111	in denary $\quad$ 64 + 32 + 4 + 2 + 1 = 103
+ 01110011	in denary $\quad$ 64 + 32 + 16 + 2 + 1 = 115
= 11011010	in denary $\quad$ −128 + 64 + 16 + 8 + 2 = −38

Key term

One's complement Changing 0s to 1s and 1s to 0s in a binary number.

> The 1 overflows the space and is lost, leaving the correct positive two's complement value in the 8-bits

Example

To complete the subtraction 73 − 58 in two's complement, we can follow a simple process using the **one's complement** (change 1s to 0s and 0s to 1s).

58 in binary	**00111010**
one's complement	**11000101**
Add 1	**11000110** (This is −58 in two's complement form)
73 in binary	**01001001**
Add $\quad$ (1)	**00001111** (Check this is 15 in denary ✔)

Questions

In the following questions, use two's complement binary in eight bits and check your answers in denary.

1. 10011001 + 00111100
2. 11100011 + 01110010
3. Show the addition in two's complement form of 58 + 73.
4. Show the subtraction in two's complement form of 68 − 17.
5. Show the subtraction in two's complement form of 55 − 63.

Representing real numbers in binary

To represent denary fractions (decimals), it is customary to use a standard form so 123.456 is written as 1.23456×10^2 and 0.00167 as 1.67×10^{-3}.

The power of 10 shows how many places the decimal point has 'floated' left or right in the number to make the standard form.

The first part of these representations is called the **mantissa** and the power to which the 10 is raised, the **exponent**.

In binary, we use a similar standard form called floating point, for example a 16-bit floating point number may be made up of a 10-bit mantissa and a 6-bit exponent, as follows:

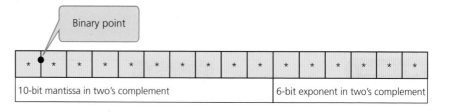

Binary point

| 10-bit mantissa in two's complement | 6-bit exponent in two's complement |

Real numbers have fractional parts to them; in binary these fractional parts are $\frac{1}{2}, \frac{1}{4}, \frac{1}{8}$, and so on.

So the column values associated with the mantissa are:

| Column value | −1 | $\frac{1}{2}$ | $\frac{1}{4}$ | $\frac{1}{8}$ | $\frac{1}{16}$ | $\frac{1}{32}$ | $\frac{1}{64}$ | $\frac{1}{128}$ | $\frac{1}{256}$ | $\frac{1}{512}$ |

The column values for the exponent are:

Column value	−32	16	8	4	2	1

Example

The floating point number 0100101000 000100 has:

mantissa 0.100101000 and exponent 000100

The exponent is 4 in denary, which means the binary point has 'floated' four places to the left.

If we undo this, we get a mantissa part 1001.01000:

1001 is 9 in denary

.01000 is $\frac{1}{4}$ (or 0.25) in denary.

Our binary floating point number 0100101000 000100 is 9.25 in denary.

In this case, both the mantissa and exponent were positive. If the two's complement values start with a 1 then they are negative values and converting these into their sign and magnitude form is a convenient way of completing the calculation.

Example

The 8-bit two's complement integer 11011101 can be converted from two's complement to sign and magnitude by:

	11011101
1. Convert all 1s to 0s and 0s to 1s	00100010
2. Add 1	00100011

11011101 is −00100011

Check

11011101 = −128 + 64 + 16 + 8 + 4 + 1 = −35

−00100011 = −(32 + 2 + 1) = −35 ✔

The exponent in this example was positive. In the binary floating point number 0101000000 111100 (using the same format of 10-bit two's complement mantissa and 6-bit two's complement exponent), the exponent is 111100, which is negative.

Example

The floating point number 0101000000 111100 has mantissa 0.101000000 and exponent 1111110.

Taking the two's complement of the exponent, the exponent becomes −000010 or −2.

If we undo this the mantissa becomes 0.00101 or $\frac{1}{8} + \frac{1}{32}$ (or 0.125 + 0.03125) in denary.

The floating point binary number 0101000000 111100 is 0.15625 in denary.

Example

If the mantissa starts with a 1 then the value will be negative and the binary number 110011000 000110 (using a 10-bit two's complement mantissa and 6-bit two's complement exponent) can be split into:

The floating point number 110011000 000110 has:

mantissa 1.10011000 and exponent 000011

The exponent is 2 + 1 = 3, which means the binary point has been floated three places to the left.

Taking the two's complement of the mantissa:

original number 110011000

one's complement   001100111

add 1   001101000

110011000 in two's complement is −001101000.

If the binary point is moved three places to the right, to undo the exponent the mantissa becomes −0011.01000 or −(2 + 1 + 0.25) = −3.25.

The floating point binary number 110011000 000110 is −3.25 in denary.

One other possibility is when the mantissa and exponent are both negative, for example 101100000 111110.

Example

The floating point number 101100000 111110 has:

mantissa 1.01100000 and exponent 111110
The two's complement of the exponent is −000010
The two's complement of the mantissa is:
original number   101100000
one's complement   010011111
add 1   010100000
101100000 in twos complement is −010100000.

The exponent is −2 in denary so the binary point needs to be floated two places to the left, making the mantissa −0.0010100000 or −(0.125 + 0.03125) = −0.15625.

The floating point number 101100000 111110 is −0.15625 in denary.

Key points

- A floating point number is a binary representation for real numbers using a mantissa (the digits in the number) and an exponent (the number of places the binary point has been moved from its original position).

- The mantissa and exponent are two's complement binary numbers.

- To normalise a floating point number, we 'float' the binary point to be in front of the first significant digit and adjust the exponent accordingly.

- We normalise numbers in this way to maximise the accuracy of the value stored and to avoid multiple representations of the same number.

Questions

In all of these questions, the floating point numbers use a 10-bit two's complement mantissa and 6-bit floating point exponent.

Convert the following floating point numbers to denary:
1. 0101001000 000100
2. 0101100100 000110
3. 0111000000 111111
4. 1110010000 000011
5. 1100110000 000011

Normalisation of floating point numbers

With floating point representation, the balance between the range and precision depends on the choice of numbers of bits for the mantissa and the exponent.

A large number of bits used in the mantissa will allow a number to be represented with greater accuracy, but this will reduce the number of bits in the exponent and consequently the range of values that can be represented.

> ### Example
>
> Using an 8-bit floating point number with five bits for the mantissa and three for the exponent, 01111 011 is the largest positive value that can be represented.
>
> The exponent is 3 so the binary point is floated three places to the right in the mantissa to undo this and becomes 111.1 or 7.5.
>
> Using a 3-bit mantissa and 5-bit exponent, 011 01111 is the largest positive number that can be represented.
>
> The exponent is 15 so the binary point is floated 15 places to the right to undo this and becomes 110000000000000 or 24576.

Having a large mantissa improves the accuracy with which a number can be represented but this would be entirely wasted if the mantissa contained a number of leading 0s. For this reason, floating point numbers are normalised.

For positive numbers, this means that there are no leading 0s to the left of the **most significant bit** and immediately after the binary point.

The binary fraction 0.000101 becomes 0.101×2^3 or 0101000000 000011.

For negative numbers, the most significant bits in the mantissa are the 0s, so there are no leading 1s to the left of the mantissa; number 1.110010100 (10 bits) would become 1.00101×2^2 or 1001010000 000010.

> ### Example
>
> To represent the value −0.3125 in floating point form using 10-bit two's complement mantissa and 6-bit two's complement exponent in normalised form, convert the decimal to binary:
>
> | | |
> |---|---|
> | 0.3125 = | 0.010100000 |
> | one's complement | 1.101011111 |
> | Add 1 | 1.101100000 |
>
> Now normalise by floating the binary point to remove the leading 1s in the mantissa after the binary point:
>
> $1.011000000 \times 2^{-1}$ or 1011000000 111111

When normalising a negative floating point number, the value is padded with 1s to fill the mantissa.

A Level only

Adding and subtracting floating point numbers

When adding denary fractions, we align the decimal point before making the calculation.

Example

1.234 + 123.4

$$\begin{array}{r} 1.234 \\ 123.4 \\ \hline 124.634 \end{array}$$

The same principal applies when adding binary floating point numbers.

Using a 16-bit floating point number with 10-bit two's complement mantissa and 6-bit two's complement exponent to add the numbers, we must match the exponents.

Example

0110000000 000011 + 0101100000 000001

This is	0110000000 × 2³	+ 0101100000 × 2¹
OR	0110.000000	+ 01.01100000

$$0110.000000$$
$$\underline{01.01100000}$$
$$\underline{0111.01100000}$$

Normalising this, the answer is 0111011000 000011.

To subtract floating point numbers, apply the same principal and use the method for two's complement subtraction.

Key point

When adding and subtracting normalised floating point numbers, we need to undo the normalisation on the mantissa; that is, we need to make the exponents the same for both (all) values so that the binary point is in the same place in both binary numbers.

Example

0110000000 000011 − 0101100000 000001

This is	0110000000 × 2³	− 0101100000 × 2¹
OR	0110.000000	− 01.01100000

Number to subtract:

Match the size of the mantissa	0001.01100000
one's complement	1110.10011111
Add 1	1110.10100000
First number	0110.00000000
Add (1)	0100.10100000

Normalise 0100101000 000011

Check in denary:
6 − 1.375 = 4.625
OR in binary 100.101
In normalised floating point 0100101000 000011 ✔

Questions

In the following questions, use normalised floating point representation with a two's complement 10-bit mantissa and two's complement 6-bit exponent. Check your answers in denary.

1. 0100100000 000100 + 0110100000 000011
2. 0110011000 001000 + 0111000000 000101
3. 0110000000 000011 − 0100100000 000010
4. 0100100000 000101 − 0110100000 000011
5. 1011000000 000010 − 0110000000 000001

Bitwise manipulation of binary values

The ALU performs arithmetic and logical operations on binary values.

Shifting

A logical shift instruction shifts or moves each bit in the binary value left or right (filling any vacated spaces with 0s).

Example

| 0 | 0 | 0 | 1 | 0 | 1 | 0 | 0 |

A logical shift left by two would move the whole binary value to the left two places:

←

| 0 | 1 | 0 | 1 | 0 | 0 | 0 | 0 |

A logical shift right by two moves the whole binary value to the right by two places:

⟶

| 0 | 0 | 0 | 0 | 0 | 1 | 0 | 1 |

If you calculate the denary equivalents for each of these numbers assuming these are 8-bit binary integers, you can see that:

00010100 is equal to 20 in denary
01010000 is equal to 80 in denary (20×4)
00000101 is equal to 5 in denary   (20÷4)

The shift left multiplies by 2 for each place; the shift right divides by 2 for each place.

Logical operations and masking

The ALU can also perform a bitwise operation using the logical operator NOT to create a one's complement of the binary value; that is, change 1s to 0s and 0s to 1s.

Example

| 0 | 1 | 0 | 1 | 0 | 1 | 0 | 0 |

↓   NOT   ↓

| 1 | 0 | 1 | 0 | 1 | 0 | 1 | 1 |

Using two binary values, the ALU can perform bitwise logical operations such as AND, OR and XOR.

Example

Operand	0	1	1	0	1	1	0
Mask	1	1	0	0	1	0	0
AND	0	1	0	0	1	0	0

Operand	0	1	1	0	1	1	0
Mask	1	1	0	0	1	0	0
OR	1	1	1	0	1	1	0

Operand	0	1	1	0	1	1	0
Mask	1	1	0	0	1	0	0
XOR	1	0	1	0	0	1	0

Masking is an important concept. The bits in the mask are chosen to manipulate the bits in the operand, allowing them through or blocking them.

AND can be used to return bits by using a 1, or exclude bits by using a 0. This is useful for checking conditions stored in a binary value.

OR can be used to reset particular bits in the binary value; using a 1 will always set the bit to 1, and using a 0 will return the matching bit in the original value.

XOR can be used to check if corresponding bits in two binary values are the same.

Key points

- Bitwise operations are used to manipulate binary values.

- The shift operation can be used to normalise the mantissa by moving the binary point in front of the first significant digit.

- Using masking will tell us when this has occurred.

- Mask with 010000000 … and use the AND command to find out if there is a 1 in the second bit from the left of the number.

Questions

1. For 01101011, mask this with 11001101 using AND, OR and XOR.
2. Create a mask to reverse the first four bits of a value, leaving the last four bits in their original state. State which logical operation is required.
3. Identify the process using logical operators to create a two's complement of a binary value.
4. Identify the process using logical operators to normalise a floating point number.
5. Interrupts from various sources are stored as bits in a binary value. How can logical operations be used to identify whether a specific interrupt has been generated?

Practice questions

1. In the following questions, use normalised floating point representation with a two's complement 10-bit mantissa and two's complement 6-bit exponent. Check your answers in denary.
   (a) 0100011000 001000 + 0110100000 000110
   (b) 1011000000 000011 − 0110000000 000101
2. Describe how bitwise operations can be used to normalise a floating point binary number.

Chapter 13

Data structures

Introduction

Much of computer use is about manipulating and processing data. There are a number of ways this data can be stored for processing and the choice of

data structure will depend upon the processing that is intended for that data.

Records, lists and tuples

Key term

Attribute A column in a table, equivalent to a field, is an attribute of the entity.

Key points

- Records are structured data stores using a single identifier and organised by attributes (fields).
- The attributes and the structure for the record need to be set up in advance.
- A list organises data by index so there is no need to set up a structure in advance. Data in both of these structures can be modified, added or deleted at any stage.
- A tuple is an immutable list; that is, it is a list with data that cannot be modified once it has been set up.

Each of these structures stores data for processing and are effectively just lists of data, but the way the data is organised within these is the difference between them.

A record organises the data by an **attribute**, for example to store data for an address book the attributes might be first_name, second_name, address1, postcode, telephone, and so on. The data in a record is accessed through its attribute, for example address_book.first_name. The data in a record is an unordered data structure but indices may be programmed to provide the data ordered on a particular field.

A list is an ordered set of data organised by an index, so accessing the data is through the index value for that data – its position in the list, for example address_book(5). One advantage of a list over a record is that the list structure requires little or no setup and can be used to store data ordered by index within the program. A record needs to have the attributes defined before they can be used. However, the ability to identify data by attribute rather than index does make the record structure more user friendly in use while being more complex to initialise.

A tuple is an **immutable** list; that is, once set up it cannot be changed. The tuple can be used exactly like a list with the data ordered and accessed by index, but there are no options to add, delete or modify the data. Tuples are used where it is important that data can be accessed as a list but must not be changed.

Arrays

A one-dimensional array is very similar to a list, though arrays have a defined scope (number of elements) and lists do not. A one-dimensional array will therefore define a set of variables under a single descriptor with an index, for example the array names defined with a scope of 5 will equate to 5 variables called names(0), names(1), names(2), names(3) and names(4).

The array names may contain the values:

Names(0)	Names(1)	Names(2)	Names(3)	Names(4)
Frank	Ahmed	Kate	Naveed	Johan

As with a list we can access and manipulate the data by its indexed address:

Accessing names(3) will give us the name Naveed.

Changing names(3) to Umar will modify the array to:

Names(0)	Names(1)	Names(2)	Names(3)	Names(4)
Frank	Ahmed	Kate	Umar	Johan

The array has been modified to include Umar

A two-dimensional array allows us to create a structure that references data not by a single position in a list but by the co-ordinates of the data in a two-dimensional structure, a table. An array defined with a scope of (5,5) can be visualised as a 5 × 5 table:

names()	0	1	2	3	4
0	Frank	Kate	Umar	Johan	Helena
1	Sundip	Harry	Navdeep	Michael	Hua
2	Barry	Jane	Li	Tomasz	Dillip
3	Ahmed	Charles	Graham	Wendy	Deborah
4	Gemma	Irina	Andrew	Maggie	Marta

In this case we can access data by giving the co-ordinates of the item in the array, for example names(3,1) is Michael; names(2,4) is Andrew.

Similarly, we can change values by setting the value of names(x,y) accordingly.

Arrays can be multi-dimensional and, for example, a three dimensional array will allow access to the data through three co-ordinates (x,y,z).

Key points

- Arrays are data structures that store data under a single identifier by index. Arrays may be multi-dimensional, for example a two-dimensional list is like a table of data with rows and columns.
- Data is accessed by referencing the indices for the data item, for example name(x,y).

Stacks and queues

Data stored in a list is stored in a linear fashion, and stacks and queues are implementations of this data structure using specific methods for inserting and removing data.

Stacks

A stack is one method for handling linear lists of data. In a stack, the data is considered as a stack with data placed one on top of the other, for example:

```
39      ← Top
23
45
17      ← Bottom
```

In a stack structure, data is added to and removed from the top of the list. So adding 77 to the stack leaves this:

```
77      ← Top
39
23
45
17      ← Bottom
```

We call this process of adding data to a stack as pushing; that is, 77 is 'pushed onto the top of the stack'.

When taking data from a stack, it is 'popped' from the top of the stack, so popping data from this stack will remove the 77, the last item pushed onto the stack. Stacks are known as LIFO (Last In First Out) data structures.

The words PUSH and POP are frequently commands available in assembly language.

A stack in a computer's memory system is implemented using pointers.

Example

If a stack initially contains the values 17, 45 and 39 and the value 11 is PUSHED onto the stack followed by 2 POP operations we get the following sequence:

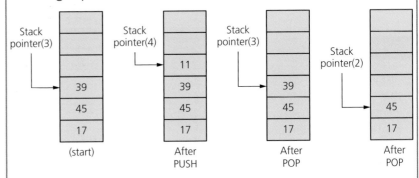

Figure 13.1 An example of a stack

If a stack becomes empty or full, an error message needs to be generated and a rogue value for the stack pointer, such as −1, is used so that if full the next PUSH operation, if empty the next POP operation, can generate an error message.

The process for adding another item to a stack is relatively straightforward. The first thing we need to do is check if the stack is full.

An **algorithm** to describe a PUSH operation is:

```
If stack pointer maximum then report stack full.
Else
    Set the stack pointer to stack pointer +1
    Set stack(stack pointer) to data
Endif
```

When taking data from the stack, the first check we need to make is that the stack is not empty:

```
If stack pointer minimum then report stack empty
Else
    Set data to stack(stack pointer)
    Set stack pointer to stack pointer −1
Endif
```

Queues

A queue is a FIFO (First In First Out) structure. The data is placed into a queue at the end of the queue and removed from the front of the queue. The data does not actually move forward in the queue but two pointers, start and end, track the data items in the structure.

Example

39, 45 and 17 are initially in a queue and an item is POPPED from the queue followed by 11 and 23 being POPPED into the queue.

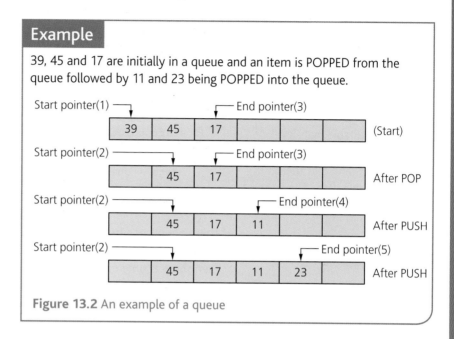

Figure 13.2 An example of a queue

If two more data items were pushed onto the queue in the example, the second of these items would have to be added in location 1. This is called a 'circular queue'. Attempting to add a further data item should generate an error message because the queue is full and the start pointer is equal to the end pointer +1:

Example

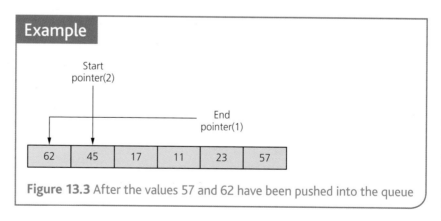

Figure 13.3 After the values 57 and 62 have been pushed into the queue

The situation where the start pointer is 1 and the end pointer is maximum also represents a full queue.

1. Explain what is meant by the following terms:
   (a) list
   (b) stack
   (c) queue
   (d) array
2. Using a suitable pseudocode language, devise algorithms to implement:
   (a) an LIFO stack
   (b) a queue.
3. Using a suitable high-level language, implement these algorithms and test them with suitable data. Allow for a maximum of 10 data items.

Key points

- A stack is a Last In First Out data structure; that is, the last item placed in the stack is the first one to be removed.
- We call adding data to a stack 'pushing' and taking data from a stack 'popping'.
- A queue is a First In First Out structure where the data that has been in the queue longest is the first to be removed.
- We also use pushing and popping to add and remove data from a queue.

The process for adding another data item to a queue requires checking that the queue is not full at the start:

```
If the start pointer = 1 and the end pointer = maximum
then report that the queue is full
Elseif the start pointer = the endpointer+1 report that
the queue is full
Else
    Add data at end pointer+1
    Set end pointer to end pointer+1
Endif
```

To remove data from the queue we first need to make sure it is not empty; for a simple linear, non-circular queue:

```
If start pointer = 0 then report queue empty
Else
    data = queue(start pointer)
    set start pointer to start pointer+1
Endif
```

There are other situations to consider. If the queue becomes empty, the start pointer must be reset to 0. If the start pointer = the end pointer then there is only one item in the queue and once removed the start pointer should be reset.

If the start pointer points at the maximum value then it needs to be reset to point to the data item at the start of the structure.

The algorithm now becomes:

```
If start pointer = 0 then report queue empty
Else
    data = queue(start pointer)
    If start pointer = end pointer then
        start pointer = 0
        end pointer = 0
    Endif
    If start pointer = maximum then
        start pointer = 1
    Else start pointer = start pointer+1
Endif
```

Practice questions

1. In pseudocode, write a program to store a value input by the user into the first available space in a 5 by 5 two-dimensional array.
2. A **stack** contains the values 3,4,5, with 3 being the first value stored and 5 the last. Show how the stack changes when the following sequence of commands is used:
   POP
   PUSH 7
   POP
   PUSH 8
   PUSH 9
3. A **queue** contains the values 3,4,5, with 3 being the first value stored and 5 the last. Show how the queue changes when the following sequence of commands is used:
   POP
   PUSH 7
   POP
   PUSH 8
   PUSH 9
4. Using pseudocode and the data 6,18,21,34,61, devise suitable algorithms to implement a:
   (a) stack
   (b) queue.

Linked list

Linked lists allow data to be sorted on various factors without modifying the actual data stored in memory, for example students may be added to a data store as they join a group.

Data item	Name
1	Khan
2	Williams
3	Jones
4	Lee
5	Roberts

Pointers are used to link the data in the list in a specific order. There is a start pointer to indicate the first data item, then a pointer from that item to the next, and so on until the last data item, which has a pointer of zero (0) to indicate the end of the list.

If this list is sorted into alphabetical order, the start pointer points to Jones, Jones then points to Kahn, and so on until Williams points to 0 (the end pointer).

		Start (3)
Data item	Name	Alpha Pointers
1	Khan	4
2	Williams	0
3	Jones	1
4	Lee	5
5	Roberts	2

This can be shown as a list of items with pointers:

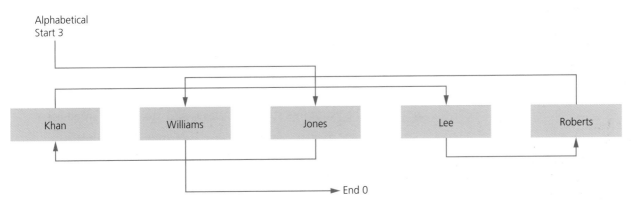

Figure 13.4 A list of items with pointers

Notice that data is stored with the node data in order to identify the next link. At each node, we need to store where to go after visiting the node. We also need a start pointer that points to the head of the list and a finish pointer to indicate that end of the list has been reached.

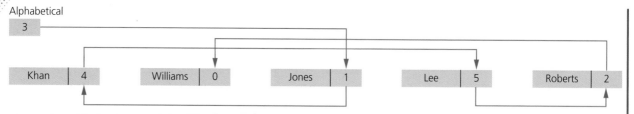

Figure 13.5 Node data

The data may also need to be sorted on other factors, such as date of birth or test scores. By adding another set of pointers, the data can be sorted on these factors without having to reorganise the original data or lose the alphabetical sort.

Data item	Name	Start (3) Alpha Pointers	Start(2) DOB Pointers
1	Khan	4	5
2	Williams	0	1
3	Jones	1	0
4	Lee	5	3
5	Roberts	2	4

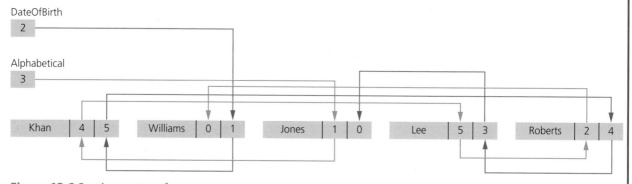

Figure 13.6 Sorting on two factors

Adding data to a linked list

It is unlikely memory will be full as there will be additional locations to store data. These are called free nodes. There is another pointer called the 'free storage pointer' that points to the first of the available storage spaces or nodes. The list of free storage spaces is also stored as a linked list.

Data item	Name	Start (3) Free (6) Alpha Pointers
1	Khan	4
2	Williams	0
3	Jones	1
4	Lee	5
5	Roberts	2
6		7
7		8
8		9
9		0

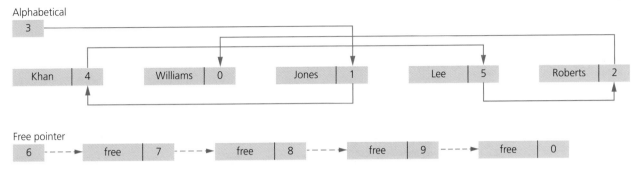

Figure 13.7 A linked list

To add new data to the list:

- store the data at the location indicated by the free storage pointer
- alter the free storage pointer to the next free storage space
- identify where in the list it is to be inserted
- set the pointer for the item that will precede it to the new data item
- update the pointer for the new data item to that previously stored in the item that preceded it.

Example

Adding Mills to the list opposite:

		Start (3) Free (6)
Data item	**Name**	Alpha Pointers
1	Khan	4
2	Williams	0
3	Jones	1
4	Lee	6
5	Roberts	2
6	Mills	5
7		8
8		9
9		0

> The pointer value in node 4 is copied to node 6 and node 4 pointer is set to the node with the new data item

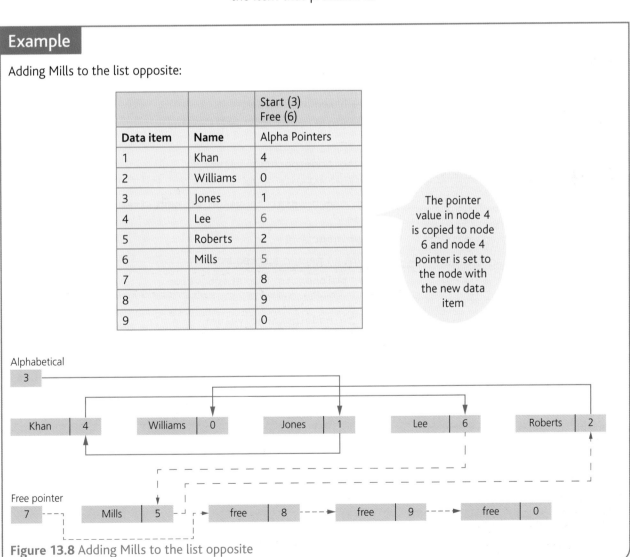

Figure 13.8 Adding Mills to the list opposite

Removing an item from a linked list

To delete an item from the list, the pointer in the preceding node is set to the value of the pointer in the item to be removed. This effectively by-passes it in the list.

The deleted item needs to be made available and is added to the list of free storage spaces.

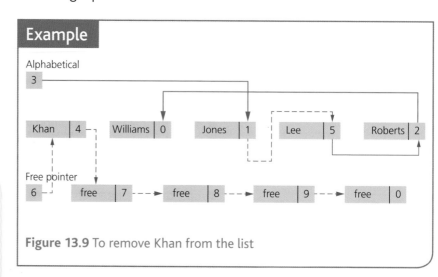

Example

Alphabetical

Figure 13.9 To remove Khan from the list

Traversing a linked list

To output a linked list in order:

```
Set the pointer to the start value
Repeat
    Go to node(pointer value)
    Output data at node
    Set the pointer to value of next item pointer at the
    node
Until pointer = 0
```

To search for an item in a linked list:

```
Set the pointer to the start value
Repeat
    Go to node(pointer value)
    IF data at node is search item
        output and stop
    Else
        Set the pointer to value of next item pointer at
        the node
    Endif
Until pointer = 0
Output data item not found
```

Questions

The data items Mouse, Cat, Apple, Horse and Fox are stored in a list in that order. The list is sorted alphabetically.

1. Represent this as a linked list using a diagram.
2. Show the linked list after the data item Donkey has been added to the first free space.
3. Show the list when Cat is removed from the linked list.
4. Write an algorithm in pseudocode to delete an item from the list.
5. Write an algorithm in pseudocode to add an item to the list.

Key points

– Data is inserted into a linked list by changing pointer values; the pointer from the preceding value points to the new item and the old value of that pointer is added to the new item.

– To remove data from a linked list, the pointer from the preceding item is changed to the value of the pointer from the item to be removed to the next value in the list.

Trees

Data does not always fit into a list structure and so other types of data structure are required. The file structure in a computer home directory is hierarchical in nature and suited to a tree structure.

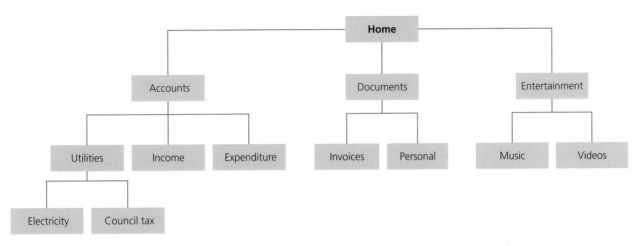

Figure 13.10 A tree structure

The node at the top or start of the structure is called the 'root node', and the nodes next down in the structure 'children'. The lines that join the nodes are called 'branches'. In this diagram, Home is the root node and it has children called Accounts, Documents and Entertainment. These in turn are parent nodes for the sub-trees below them. At the bottom of the tree, the nodes without sub-trees are called leaf nodes or terminal nodes.

To define this structure, pointers are used. Each node has the following data:

- sub-tree pointers that point to any sub-trees for that node
- data associated with the node
- pointers to other nodes at the same level.

For example, the Accounts sub-tree looks like this:

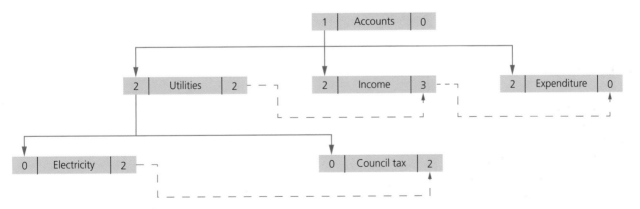

Figure 13.11 Accounts sub-tree

Binary trees

One specific kind of tree is the binary tree, where each node is only allowed to have two children. Each node contains:

- a left pointer
- data
- a right pointer.

Example

Using the data Khan, Williams, Jones, Lee and Roberts, stored in that order, we can use a binary tree to store this data in alphabetical order, taking Khan as the root node.

Khan

The next item in the list is Williams. Williams follows Khan alphabetically so goes to the right of Khan.

The next item in the list is Jones, which precedes Khan alphabetically so goes to the left of Khan.

The next item is Lee, which follows Khan alphabetically, so goes to the right, but precedes Williams, hence goes to the left of Williams.

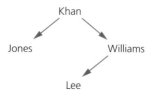

The last item is Roberts, which follows Khan alphabetically, so goes to the right of Khan.

Roberts precedes Williams, so goes to the left of Williams.

Roberts follows Lee, so goes to the right of Lee.

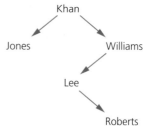

Traversing a tree

Preorder traversal:

1. Start at root node.
2. Traverse the left sub-tree.
3. Traverse the right sub-tree.

Example

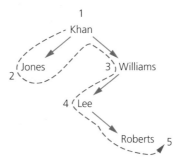

Figure 13.12 Writing down the nodes in the order visited gives Khan, Jones, Williams, Lee, Roberts

Inorder traversal:

1. Traverse the left sub-tree.
2. Visit the root node.
3. Traverse the right sub-tree.

Example

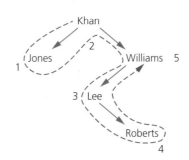

Figure 13.13 Writing down the nodes from the first leaf node and in the order visited we get the list: Jones, Khan, Lee, Roberts, Williams

Postorder traversal:

1. Traverse left sub-tree.
2. Traverse right sub-tree.
3. Return to root node.

Example

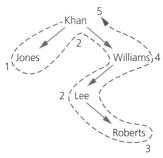

Figure 13.14 Writing down the nodes in the order visited gives Jones, Lee, Roberts, Williams, Khan

Questions

1. Create a tree from the data Melon, Pear, Banana, Apple, Orange, Rhubarb, Damson. Where the left pointer ← means 'precedes alphabetically' and the right pointer → means 'follows alphabetically'.

2. For this tree, list the nodes in the order visited for:
   (a) preorder traversal
   (b) inorder traversal
   (c) postorder traversal.

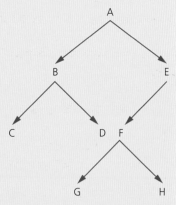

3. Write an algorithm in pseudocode for inorder traversal of a tree.

4. Write an algorithm in pseudocode for postorder traversal of a tree.

5. Write an algorithm in pseudocode for preorder traversal of a tree.

6. Convert the following reverse Polish expressions into infix notation:
   (a) AB+C*
   (b) ABC/D*T+-

7. Convert the following infix notation expressions into reverse Polish notation:
   (a) A*B-(C+D)*E
   (b) A+B*C/D

8. Show how the following would be carried out using a stack:
   (a) 9 3 – 2 /
   (b) 9 3 1 – *

The names for these traversal methods depend upon when the root node is visited.

1st Preorder
2nd Inorder
3rd Postorder

Example

In arithmetic we generally write A + B or C – D, but could equally well say add A and B (+AB) or take A and B and add them (AB+).

A+B is called infix notation.
+AB is called prefix.
AB+ is called postfix.

Take the expression A*B+C/D in infix notation. This can be expressed in a tree structure:

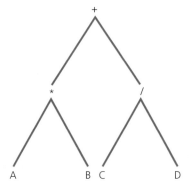

Figure 13.15 A*B + C/D in infix notation expressed in a tree structure

Inorder traversal of the tree gives A*B+C/D.
Preorder traversal gives +*AB/CD.
Postorder traversal gives AB*CD/+.

Preorder and postorder provide a parenthesis(bracket)-free way of writing mathematical expressions. The postorder or postfix notation is known as reverse Polish notation and is able to utilise the stack effectively when processing an expression.

In reverse Polish the process is:
1. If the next symbol is an operand load it to the stack.
2. If the next symbol is an operator then pop the last two items off the stack, perform the operation and place the result on the stack.

For example:

5 4 * 6 3 / +

Symbol	5	4	*	6	3	/	+
STACK							
					3		
		4		6	6	2	
	5	5	20	20	20	20	22

Postorder traversal of a tree is one method of converting between infix notation and reverse Polish notation.

Graphs

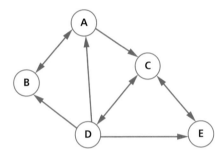

Figure 13.16 A graph can be defined as a set of vertices and a set of edges or connections; the connections are ordered pairs showing a pathway from vertex to vertex, so in this diagram there is an ordered pair (D,A) describing a pathway from D to A, but no pathway from A to D

A graph is a collection of data nodes and the connections between them. The nodes are called 'vertices' and the connections 'edges'. The edges in a graph may be directional, in which case the graph is said to be directed; otherwise, it is undirected. An undirected graph is essentially a directed graph where all the edges are bi-directional.

```
Vertices {A,B,C,D,E}

Edges {(A,B), (A,C), (B,A), (C,D), (C,E), (D,A), (D,B), (D,C),
(D,E),(E,C)}
```

This data can be added to the ordered pairs describing the edges:

```
{(A,B,3), (A,C,5), (B,A,3), (C,D,4), (C,E,6), (D,A,8), (D,B,7),
(D,C,4), (D,E,7),(E,C,6)}
```

This data can also be expressed as an adjacency matrix:

	A	B	C	D	E
A		3	5		
B	3				
C				4	6
D	8	7	4		7
E			6		

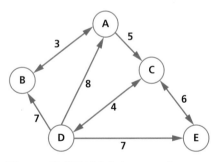

Figure 13.17 Weightings can be added to the edges to show the cost of going from one vertex to another (for example a distance)

Traversing a graph

There are two basic approaches to traversing a graph.

Depth-first

Visit all nodes attached to a node connected to a starting node before visiting a second node attached to a starting node.

This traversal method uses a stack.

```
PUSH the first node onto the stack

Mark as visited

Repeat

    Visit the next unvisited node to the one on top of
    the stack

    Mark as visited

    PUSH this node onto the stack

    If no node to visit POP node off the stack

Until the stack is empty
```

Example

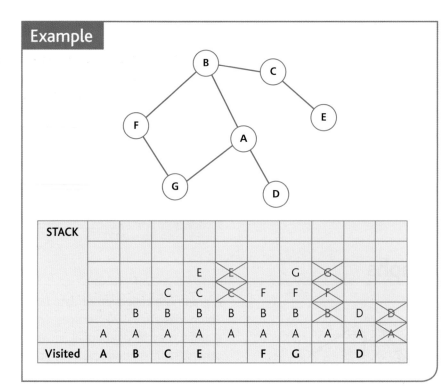

STACK										
				E	~~E~~		G	~~G~~		
			C	C	~~C~~	F	F	~~F~~		
		B	B	B	B	B	B	~~B~~	D	~~D~~
	A	A	A	A	A	A	A	A	A	~~A~~
Visited	A	B	C	E		F	G		D	

Breadth-first

Visit all the nodes attached directly to a starting node first.

This traversal method uses a queue.

```
PUSH the first node into the queue
Mark as visited
Repeat
    Visit unvisited nodes connected to first node
    PUSH nodes onto queue
Until all nodes visited
Repeat
    POP next node from queue
    Repeat
        Visit unvisited nodes connected to current node
        PUSH nodes onto queue
    Until all nodes visited
Until queue empty
```

Example

QUEUE												
		B	B	B	D	D	D	G	C	F	E	
			D	D	G	G	G	C	F	E		
				G		C	C	F				
							F					
Visited	A	B	D	G		C	F				E	
Current node	A	A	A	A	B	B	B	D	G	C	F	E

Questions

1. Write an algorithm to locate a node in an undirected graph and report if not found.
2. Draw the adjacency matrix for the following graph.

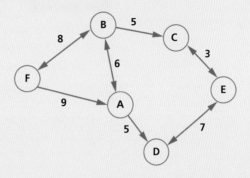

3. For the following graph, show the traversal of the tree using:
   (a) depth-first traversal
   (b) breadth-first traversal.

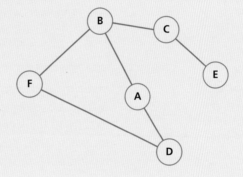

Key points

- A graph is a mathematical data structure consisting of a set of vertices and a set of edges joining the vertices.
- Graphs are used extensively in computer science to model real-world systems, such as the internet, airline connections and road networks.

Hash tables

All the methods identified so far are useful for storing and locating data that has a structure. For accessing data in a more random manner, we need another approach.

Consider a mail-order business with thousands of customers and the need to access their data directly. Each customer will have an account number, which will map to an address in a table containing details of the location of their account details.

A hash function is used to generate an appropriate address in the table based on a set of rules applied to their account number.

As an example, consider a club with just 50 members; they will need 50 storage locations. To allocate these from their membership numbers the hash function is:

```
Address = (membership number)MOD 50
```

This simple method will generate 50 addresses but, depending on the values selected for the membership numbers, it may not generate unique addresses, for example the two membership numbers 123 and 373 would both generate the value 23.

Hash functions are, in general, far more complex than this to avoid such events happening too frequently. They will still happen despite the complexity of the algorithm and a method for dealing with this is required. Typically, duplicated values are allocated to an overflow table of unordered data or to a linked list of data linked to the calculated address.

Example

The club members with membership numbers 123, 124, 226, 373 are stored in a hash table using the hash function:

```
address =(membership number)MOD 50
```

Address	...	...	21	22	23	24	25	26	27	...
Data for					123	124		226		
					↓					
					373					

> A linked list is created to store the membership details for members where the hash function generates the same value.

In reality, such a small group would have sequential membership numbers with just two digits and the membership number could be mapped directly to the location of the data. Hash functions are generally required for much larger groups and are often quite complex mathematical functions. More straightforward examples include:

```
address = (k*k)MOD m
address = k(k+3)MOD m
```

where k is the key value and m the number of locations required (often called buckets).

It also improves the efficiency of the function if m is chosen to be a prime number close to a power of 2, for example for the 50 locations we might allocate a prime number close to 64, for example 61.

Example

For our clashing membership numbers these two algorithms now give:

```
address = (123*123)MOD61 = 1
address = (373*373)MOD61 = 49
OR
address = (123*126)MOD61 = 4
address = (373*376)MOD61 = 9
```

Other methods employ the use of real numbers between 0 and 1. The key is multiplied by the real number and the fractional part of the result multiplied by the number of buckets to find a location.

```
For a, 0<a<1
address = int(fractional part of (k*a)*m)
```

Question

Use the hashing function 'address =k(k+3)MOD m', where k is the key field and m the bucket size, select a suitable bucket size to hold at least 250 data items to calculate an address for the following values:

(a) 101
(b) 232
(c) ANN

Key points

- Hashing is a method for creating random access to stored data.

- A hash function is applied to a key item or filed within the data and generates an address where the location of the data can be found.

- Hashing often uses a numerical field such as account number but can be applied to text fields using the ASCII values for the characters in the text string.

Example

For our clashing membership numbers we can use a new algorithm using the fraction 0.12357:

```
123*0.12357 = 0.12357, address = int(50*0.19911) = 9
373*0.12357 = 0.12357, address = int(50*0.09161) = 4
```

The examples used so far use a numerical key field, but it is possible to generate a numerical value from a non-numeric filed by using the ASCII values of the characters in the key field, for example the key field PAUL could be replaced by a numeric value created from the digits of the ASCII values associated with the letters:

P	A	U	L
80	65	85	76

Numeric value = 80658576

Practice questions

1. The items 12, 3, 8 and 17 are stored in a linked list.
   (a) Draw a diagram showing these items in a linked list sorted numerically.
   (b) Draw a diagram showing the value 5 inserted into the list.
   (c) Draw a diagram showing the value 8 removed from the list.

2. Draw a diagram for the tree with the data items Harry, Ben, Daisy, Mohammed, Peter, Afshin, where the left pointer means 'precedes alphabetically' and the right pointer means 'follows alphabetically'. List the items in the order they are retrieved by postorder traversal of the tree.

3. Using a tree, convert the expression (A+B/C)/(D−E) into reverse Polish.

4. Convert the reverse Polish expression AB+CD−EF/** into infix algebraic notation.

5. Draw the graph represented by the edges:
   {(A,B,5),(A,D,4),(A,E,3),(B,A,5),(C,D,3),(D,B,2),(D,C,3),(D,F,4), (E,F,6),(F,D,4)}

6. Show the traversal of the following tree using depth-first traversal:

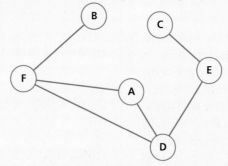

7. Where k is the key value and m the number of locations required, use the hashing function k(k+3)MOD m to find an address for the data with key value 121 where m is 113.

Chapter 14

Logic gates and Boolean algebra

Logic gates

Most modern computers use binary values. These values represent states that are either true or false. We are able to connect inputs using logic gates to generate the outcome for all possible input values.

The most common logic gates, and ones you will probably have already met, are AND, OR and NOT. The AND and OR gates are able to take two inputs and calculate a single output. NOT simply negates the input; that is, it changes the value from TRUE to FALSE or FALSE to TRUE.

We can express these in truth tables using A and B as inputs and R as the output generated.

AND ^		
A	B	R
0	0	0
0	1	0
1	0	0
1	1	1

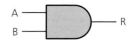

Figure 14.1 Truth table and logic gate for AND^

OR v		
A	B	R
0	0	0
0	1	1
1	0	1
1	1	1

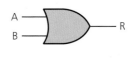

Figure 14.2 Truth table and logic gate for ORv

NOT ¬	
A	R
0	1
1	0

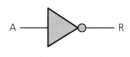

Figure 14.3 Truth table and logic gate for NOT ¬

When writing out Boolean expressions, we use symbols to represent AND (^), OR (v) and NOT (¬).

Computing people

Augustus De Morgan

Augustus De Morgan was a mathematician who wrote many papers on various topics including algebra and recognised the value of purely symbolic algebra, introducing De Morgan's laws influenced by the work of George Boole.

Augustus De Morgan was born in India in 1806 but his family moved back to England when he was just seven months old. He went to Trinity College Cambridge at the age of 16 in 1823, securing a BA degree but shunning an MA because he objected to the theology test required to obtain it.

He returned to London to study to become a barrister, but applied for the chair of mathematics at University College London and was appointed, becoming the first professor of mathematics at University College in 1928. He was a man of principles, resigning and being reappointed to this post on several occasions. He later turned down an honorary degree from Edinburgh University and refused to allow his name to be put forward for the Royal Society.

Thomas Hirst, the president of the Royal Society, described De Morgan as a 'dry dogmatic pedant' but he also acknowledged the undoubted ability of this brilliant mathematician.

A AND NOT A is 'nothing'

A OR NOT A is 'everything'

Example

For example, R = ¬A^B means R is equal to the result of NOT A AND B.

We can calculate all the possible outcomes for this expression using a truth table:

R = ¬A^B			
A	B	¬A	R
0	0	1	0
0	1	1	1
1	0	0	0
1	1	0	0

Truth tables are not limited to just two inputs, though the number of possible outcomes doubles with every new input and there are eight possible situations for three inputs.

Example

For example, the expression R =(A^B)v¬C. .

R =(A^B)v¬C					
A	B	C	(A^B)	¬C	R
0	0	0	0	1	1
0	0	1	0	0	0
0	1	0	0	1	1
0	1	1	0	0	0
1	0	0	0	1	1
1	0	1	0	0	0
1	1	0	1	1	1
1	1	1	1	0	1

Boolean operations are carried out in a defined order of precedence – NOT, AND then OR – so the bracket in the expression above could be left out without affecting the result.

As with all algebra, there are rules to manipulate Boolean expressions. For NOT, the unary operator

```
¬(¬A) = A
A∧¬A = 0
A∨¬A = 1
```

There are also rules, similar to those for standard arithmetic operators, + and ×.

A Level only

```
Associative   (A∧B)∧C = A∧(B∧C)
              (A∨B)∨C = A∨(B∨C)
Commutative   A∧B = B∧A
Distributive  A∧(B∨C) = (A∧B)∨(A∧C)
```

There are also some simplification rules for Boolean algebra

Key point

Boolean operations are carried out in the order of precedence: NOT, AND, OR.

Questions

1. Simplify the expression $(A \wedge \neg A) \vee B$.
2. Simplify the expression $(A \vee B) \vee (A \wedge C)$.
3. Simplify the expression $\neg(A \wedge \neg B) \vee (\neg A \wedge B)$.
4. Simplify the expression $(A \wedge B) \vee (\neg A \wedge B)$.
5. Simplify the expression $(A \wedge B) \vee (A \wedge (B \wedge C)) \vee (B \wedge (B \vee C))$.

Example

Prove that $A \vee A \wedge B = A$

(∧ takes priority over ∨; including the bracket makes this clearer)

$$
\begin{aligned}
A \vee (A \wedge B) &= A \vee A \wedge A \vee B && \text{(Distributive rule)} \\
&= A \wedge (1 \vee B) && \text{(Factoring using the distributive rule)} \\
&= A \wedge 1 && \text{(Simplification)} \\
&= A && \text{(Simplification)}
\end{aligned}
$$

De Morgan's rules

$$\neg(A \vee B) = \neg A \wedge \neg B$$
$$\neg(A \wedge B) = \neg A \vee \neg B$$

Example

Simplify the expression
$$
\begin{aligned}
\neg R = \neg(\neg A \wedge (B \vee C)) \\
= \neg\neg A \vee \neg(B \vee C) && \text{(De Morgan)} \\
= A \vee \neg B \wedge \neg C && \text{(De Morgan)}
\end{aligned}
$$

Circuits

Two more frequently used gates are made up by combining the AND and OR with the NOT gate, the NAND and NOR gates.

NAND		
A	B	R
0	0	1
0	1	1
1	0	1
1	1	0

Figure 14.4

NOR		
A	B	R
0	0	1
0	1	0
1	0	0
1	1	0

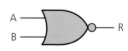

Figure 14.5

The OR gate uses 'or' in the sense of 'one or both'. In speech, we often use 'or' to mean one or the other but not both. In logic, that is called an exclusive or. This exclusive or gate is written as XOR.

Key point

The key logic gates and the symbols we use when writing expressions are:

– AND (∧)

– OR (∨)

– NOT (¬)

– XOR ⊕

XOR ⊕		
A	B	R
0	0	0
0	1	1
1	0	1
1	1	0

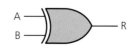

Figure 14.6

Adder circuits

A useful logic circuit would be able to add two values together and generate a carry digit.

The truth table for this is:

A	B	S	C
0	0	0	0
0	1	1	0
1	0	1	0
1	1	1	1

Looking at this truth table, it is clear the output S can be provided by a NAND gate and C by an AND gate. This gives the circuit:

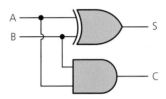

Figure 14.7 This circuit is called a half-adder

What we would like to achieve is an adder circuit that would deal with adding two values from a binary number and any carry that is generated. The output needed to achieve for a full adder that deals with any carried digit is:

A	B	C_{in}	S	C_{out}
0	0	0	0	0
0	0	1	1	0
0	1	0	1	0
0	1	1	0	1
1	0	0	1	0
1	0	1	0	1
1	1	0	0	1
1	1	1	1	1

Simplifying the half adder to a single block and adding in the carry in C_{in}, we get the first part of a full adder circuit with the three inputs.

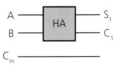

Figure 14.8

A	B	S_1	C_{in}	S	C_{out}
0	0	0	0	0	0
0	0	0	1	1	0
0	1	1	0	1	0
0	1	1	1	0	1
1	0	1	0	1	0
1	0	1	1	0	1
1	1	0	0	0	1
1	1	0	1	1	1

The shaded area combining the output S_1 from the half adder and the C_{in} provides the sum output (S) by using another half adder

This leads to the circuit:

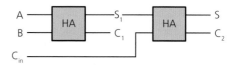

Figure 14.9

Now add C_1 and C_2 to our truth table by combining:

A	B	S_1	C_1	C_{in}	C_2	S	C_{out}
0	0	0	0	0	0	0	0
0	0	0	0	1	0	1	0
0	1	1	0	0	0	1	0
0	1	1	0	1	1	0	1
1	0	1	0	0	0	1	0
1	0	1	0	1	1	0	1
1	1	0	1	0	0	0	1
1	1	0	1	1	0	1	1

The combination of C_1 and C_2 to produce the required output is an OR gate

This completes the full adder:

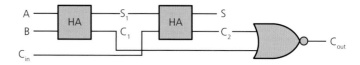

Figure 14.10 Full adder

Key points

- A half adder is a logic circuit with two inputs and can output the sum and carry for the two input digits.
- A full adder allows the carry from a previous calculation to be carried forward in the calculation.
- A series of full adders connected together allows the computer to add binary numbers.

Karnaugh maps

We used pattern recognition to interpret the truth tables above and to identify the logic circuit required for the full adder. Karnaugh maps are a modified form of truth table optimised to enable pattern recognition to be used when identifying minimal logical expression.

Karnaugh maps are tables of possible inputs and mapped against the required outputs.

A two-input Karnaugh map:

ᵦ\ᴬ	0	1
0		
1		

The required outputs for the input values for A and B are placed in the appropriate cells

Example

For this Karnaugh map:

ᵦ\ᴬ	0	1
0	1	1
1	1	0

The red block represents ¬B

The blue block represents ¬A

The expression is ¬A∨¬B

A three-input Karnaugh map:

c\ᴬᴮ	00	01	11	10
0				
1				

Example

For the Karnaugh map

c\ᴬᴮ	00	01	11	10
0	1	1	1	1
1	0	0	1	1

The red block is ¬C

The blue block is A

The expression is A∨¬C

A four-input Karnaugh map:

ᴄᴅ\ᴬᴮ	00	01	11	10
00				
01				
11				
10				

Example

$_{CD}\backslash^{AB}$	00	01	11	10
00	0	0	1	0
01	1	1	1	1
11	0	0	1	0
10	0	0	1	0

The red block is $\neg C \wedge D$

The blue block is $A \wedge B$

The expression is $\neg C \wedge D \vee A \wedge B$

In the examples above, the blocks overlap. The method is to create blocks of 1s as large as possible so that the 1s are covered by as few blocks as possible and no 0s are included.

The blocks can wrap around the diagram if necessary.

Example

$_{CD}\backslash^{AB}$	00	01	11	10
00	0	0	1	1
01	1	1	0	0
11	0	1	0	0
10	0	0	1	1

In this case the red block is $\neg A \wedge \neg C \wedge D$

The blue block is $A \wedge \neg D$

The expression is $(\neg A \wedge \neg C \wedge D) \vee (A \wedge \neg D)$

Karnaugh maps can be used to simplify Boolean expressions.

Key points

– The rules for using Karnaugh maps are:
  - No zeros allowed
  - No diagonal blocks
  - Groups as large as possible
  - Every 1 must be within a block
  - Overlapping allowed
  - Wrap around allowed
  - The smallest possible number of groups.

Karnaugh maps can be used to simplify Boolean expressions.

Example

For example to simplify the expression

$R = \neg A \wedge B \vee B \wedge \neg C \vee B \wedge C \vee A \wedge \neg B \wedge \neg C$

Insert 1s for each element of the expression, initially 1s for $\neg A \wedge B$

$\neg A \wedge B$

$_C\backslash^{AB}$	00	01	11	10
0		1		
1		1		

Now 1s for $B \wedge \neg C$

$_C\backslash^{AB}$	00	01	11	10
0		1	1	
1		1		

Now $B \wedge C$

$_C\backslash^{AB}$	00	01	11	10
0		1	1	
1		1	1	

Now $A \wedge \neg B \wedge \neg C$

$_C\backslash^{AB}$	00	01	11	10
0		1	1	1
1		1	1	

By blocking according to the rules

$_C\backslash^{AB}$	00	01	11	10
0		1	1	1
1		1	1	

The blue block is B

The red block is $A \wedge \neg C$

The simplified expression is $B \vee (A \wedge \neg C)$

A Level only

Flip-flop circuits

There are some important circuits that differ from the gate circuits we have considered so far. These circuits are capable of storing information, for example RAM memory.

Consider this basic circuit:

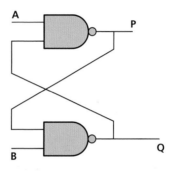

Figure 14.11 A basic circuit

The truth table for this circuit is not quite as straightforward as the others.

A	B	P	Q
0	0		
0	1		
1	0		
1	1		

The gates are NAND gates, so if A is 0 then P must be 1.
Similarly if B is 0 Q must be 1.
We can fill in part of the truth table:

A	B	P	Q
0	0	1	1
0	1	1	
1	0		1
1	1		

Looking at the red block, if B is 1 and P is 1 then Q must be 0.
Similarly, looking at the blue block if Q is 1 and A is 1 then P must be 0.

181

We can complete more of this truth table.

A	B	P	Q
0	0	1	1
0	1	1	0
1	0	0	1
1	1		

To work out what P is, we need to know the value of Q:

If P = 1 and B = 1 then Q is 0.
If P = 0 and B = 1 then Q is 1.

Similarly:

If Q = 1 and A = 1 then P is 0.
If Q = 0 and A = 1 then P is 1.

This gives us a finished truth table:

A	B	P	Q
0	0	1	1
0	1	1	0
1	0	0	1
1	1	0	1
		1	0

This circuit can exist in either state; which state depends on the previous values stored. This circuit is called a flip-flop and it can store one bit of information.

By using two flip-flops we can create a circuit called a D-type flip-flop, which uses a clock-controlled circuit to control the output, delaying it by one clock pulse. The D stands for 'delay'.

This circuit has two inputs: a data input and a clock input; and two outputs: Q and ¬Q (that is, an output and the inverse of that output). The D-type flip-flop delays output of the data input by exactly one clock cycle.

The circuit for this type of flip-flop is shown to the left.

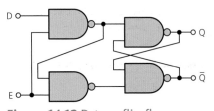

Figure 14.12 D-type flip-flop

Key points

- Flip-flops can store data.
- The D-type flip-flop is used to delay data by exactly one clock pulse.
- The D-type flip-flop has two inputs: data and clock; and two outputs: the delayed data and the inverse of the delayed data.

Practice questions

1. Simplify the expression:
   ¬A∧B∧¬C∧¬D∨¬A∧B∧¬C∧D∨A∧B∧¬C∧¬D∨A∧B∧¬C∧D
2. Draw a diagram showing how two half adders can be combined to form a full adder.
3. Draw a diagram showing how an 8-bit adder can be made from a series of full adders.
4. State the purpose of inputs to and outputs from a D-type flip-flop and draw a circuit for a D-type flip-flop using NAND gates.

Chapter 15

Databases

Introduction

A database is a structured, persistent collection of data.

This is an important definition but we need to look a little more closely at what it means.

A database is a collection of data, but so is a notebook. So is a to-do list. A database is special because the data it contains is organised. The way that it is organised might vary from database to database but some form of methodical approach is usual in order to:

- make processing more efficient
- reduce storage requirements
- avoid redundancy.

A database is a *persistent* store. This means that the data can be kept for a long period. It survives after the software has finished processing it.

Why have databases?

Databases underpin a huge number of important aspects of modern life. Most businesses and other organisations keep them. For example, you cannot use a mobile phone without there being databases of customers, locations, base stations and accounting. A repair garage will have a database of customers and jobs.

Databases are important for various reasons, but principally they allow data to be:

- retrieved quickly
- updated
- filtered.

Question

Make a list of five organisations that you know something about. For each one, identify what databases would help it to function properly.

An especially useful feature is that they allow different users to see the data that they need to do their jobs, but no more than that data. Limiting the visible data allows users to concentrate on what is important to them and also helps to keep security issues under control. A subset of data tailored for a particular user or a particular application is called a *view*.

Organisations that maintain a good-quality database can be sure that all their users have access to the one up-to-date copy of the data and there is much less danger of inconsistencies, leading to errors.

Files

In the early days of commercial computer applications, data was stored in separate files. These files reflected the nature of the storage techniques at the time and were typically serial or sequential files. This was necessary because most data was stored on magnetic tape, which had to be written to or read in an orderly sequence.

Serial and sequential files

Record A single unit of information in a database. It is normally made up of *fields*. So a student file would be made up of many records. Each record is about one student and holds fields such as student number, surname, date of birth, gender, and so on.

A serial file is one where **records** are organised one after another. It is the only possible way to store data on a long, thin medium such as tape. It is possible to divide the data into records in order to help locate related data together. The records could be organised in any way that was useful to the business using them, so they could have as many or as few *fields* as necessary. But in order to process them, the structure of each record had to be the same. Here is part of a serial file with two fields per record; name and date of birth:

field	name	dob	name	dob	name	dob	name	dob
data	Tristan	12/3/87	Isolde	13/5/90	Mark	21/1/70	Brangane	24/6/87

To locate a particular record, it is necessary to start at the beginning of the file and examine each record in turn until the required record is found or the end of the file is reached. This can easily become a lengthy process if the file size is large.

A sequential file is an improvement on this. In this, the records are still arranged one after another, but in a particular order. This order might be something like a customer number but could also be in alphabetical order by name. The example above would then become:

field	name	dob	name	dob	name	dob	name	dob
data	Brangane	24/6/87	Isolde	13/5/90	Mark	21/1/70	Tristan	12/3/87

This makes searching easier, because if the desired record is not reached and the examined record is later in the alphabet than this, you know that the record does not exist.

Although this form of storage is an improvement on a plain serial file, it introduces additional problems. Suppose a file is created of all the **transactions** in a library in a day. This is an example of a **transaction file**. Each record could consist of the borrower number, the book number and the date borrowed. Obviously, there will be no particular order to these transactions except chronological, which would for most purposes be unhelpful.

In order to generate a sequential file then, at intervals, the data in the file has to be sorted. This involves ultimately writing the data in order to a new file. This is a partial solution but searching can still be time consuming and also it cannot be done until the sorting operation is carried out, typically each day.

Transaction A change in the state of a database. It can be the addition, amendment or deletion of data.

Transaction file A file of events that occur as part of the business of an organisation. Its contents are to a large extent unpredictable although they are usually in chronological order.

Indexing

Sequential files can be searched more quickly by producing a separate index file. This is just like the index in a book. The data is divided up into categories, such as names beginning with A, then B, and so on. Then, each category is linked to a position in the data file where that category starts, so a tape of whatever medium is used can be fast-forwarded to a better position for starting a sequential search.

Index file			**Data file**	
Category	Data file start position		Position	Data
A	1		1	Abbott
B	10		2	Abby
C	20		3	Abercrombie
D	45		4	Agamemnon
E	80		5	Albemarle
			6	Alvarez
			7	Angstrom
			8	Anthracite
			9	Avery
			10	Baird
			11	Barr
			12	Barry
			13	Barton
			14	Brennan
			15	Buckley
			16	Bullock
			17	Bush

Figure 15.1 Sequential files can be searched more quickly

Despite all these techniques to improve access times, there are many inbuilt inefficiencies, notably to do with searching and sorting. Also, once the data requirements of an organisation become complex, maintaining separate files becomes burdensome. Imagine that a business maintains a **master file** of all the goods that it stocks.

Suppose a typical supermarket stock record looks like this:

Field name	Data
stock_number	2546
stock_name	beans
size	400g
number_in_stock	4500

Using a traditional sequential file, the records would probably be stored in stock_number order. Software would be produced that would expect to read four fields for each record. So, if the system were required to access the tenth record, this could be done by reading through 36 fields and then starting to read the required record.

Now suppose that the supermarket management decided that it would be useful to have an extra field in each stock record, for example whether an item is VAT rated or not. This could easily be done, but the software would now have to read through five fields per record in order to locate a particular position in the file.

This can of course be done, but it means that the software must be changed and tested and recompiled. Frequent changes of this sort soon become expensive, and of course each change is likely to introduce new errors.

For these and many other reasons, such a simple file organisation is not ideal for most purposes.

Simple databases of this sort are called *flat-file databases*.

Key term

Master file A principal file held by an organisation that stores basic details about some crucial aspect of the business. It is generally a large file that tends not to change very often.
For a supermarket, it could be a stock file; for a school it could be a file of student details.

1. Would an address book laid out like this be useful for:
   (a) storing details of your friends
   (b) storing customer details for a large online trading organisation?
2. What are the good and bad points of using a flat-file database for these purposes?

Example

A typical example of a flat-file database is an address book. Here is a view of part of one:

First name	Last name	Telephone	Street	City	Post code	DOB
Claire	Pate	1 55 791 7964-8421	1434 Aenean Road	Iowa City	K3I 1RF	6/28/1999
Virginia	Landry	1 61 306 9087-9418	404 Morbi Road	Rock Island	EI3O 7QR	1/23/1974
Orli	Goodwin	1 51 119 4068-1665	704-6375 Varius St.	Lynwood	CG12 9LQ	9/26/1984
Callie	Hodge	1 70 829 9014-9968	PO Box 362, 5198 Vulputate, St	Wichita Falls	D1Z 9AN	07/05/1978
Rhonda	Pugh	1 44 202 4884-7705	PO Box 250, 7653 Fusce Road	West Covina	S5 9OD	6/23/1984
Dara	Goff	1 70 115 3175-0607	844-4722 Felis St	Knoxville	KE9C 7XR	10/03/1999

You can easily understand the concept of a flat-file database by envisaging it as a spreadsheet or document table.

Fixed and variable length fields

You might be wondering how the software that searches a serial or sequential file is able to count the fields in order to arrive at a particular record. There are two principal ways of doing this, each one having its own advantages and disadvantages.

With fixed length fields, each field is always the same number of bytes in length. So if a surname is stored, it could be decided to reserve 15 bytes for each surname. Any unused bytes are filled with a character such as a space.

S	m	i	t	h										

This allows the software to count bytes in order to count fields and hence records. Every 15 bytes in a name field brings it to the next field. Then the next field can be similarly treated as its length will also be known to the software. This is easy to program but obviously it is wasteful of space. It also does not allow for changes to be made to field length without reprogramming. But it is quite quick to search and it is easy to calculate the file size needed for a planned database if the number of records is known.

Another very common method to count fields and hence records is to insert a marker, often a comma, to delineate each field. This is how a variable length field works. This is flexible and does not waste as much space as a fixed length structure. The software can advance through records by counting markers.

Here is a possible structure of part of a student record in CSV format, showing surname, forename, gender and student number.

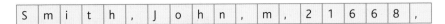

| S | m | i | t | h | , | J | o | h | n | , | m | , | 2 | 1 | 6 | 6 | 8 | , | |

File organised like this are very common and are known as CSV files (comma separated values). Most generic data handling software such as spreadsheets can read CSV files.

Hashing

Using disk file storage, another method of quickly writing and reading files is possible. This method is called *hashing*. The key field of a record can be transformed in such a way as to generate a disk address. This allows a random access device such as a disk drive to go directly to a part of a disk and start working from there.

One way of doing this is to take the last three digits of a key such as an account number. So, for example, account number 2563546 generates the disk address 546. This leads to a block of records beginning at position 546. The disk address 546 is accessed and the record is written at that location. Of course, the account number 5756546 will also generate the same address. In this case, if the position is already occupied, the record is written to the next sequentially available location. If the block is full, then any other records that generate that address will be written to an overflow area specially designated for such *data collisions*.

Hashing works well in *sparse* databases; that is, where it is expected that most available numbers will not be used. An example is with bank account numbers, where potentially millions may be generated with a given number of digits, but at any given time most of these are not in use.

Question

Write an **algorithm** that accepts a seven-digit account number then finds an appropriate three-digit disk storage location. Make sure that you make provision for the storage block being full.

Relational databases

Key terms

Entity A real-world *thing* that is modelled in a database. It might be a physical object such as a student or a stock item in a shop or it might be an event such as a sale.

Relation In relational database terminology, a table is called a relation.

Tuple A row in a table, equivalent to a record. A tuple is data about one instance of the entity.

Clearly flat-file databases have serious limitations. Because of this, various models have been devised to better organise data for efficient processing. The most common model continues to be the relational database model.

The idea of a relational database is that data is stored in separate tables. Each table stores data about a single **entity**.

There are some rules for relational database tables.

- Every row must be constructed in the same way; that is, each column must contain data of just one data type.
- One column, or a combination of columns, must be able to make each row of the table unique. This column or combination of columns is called the *primary key*.
- There is no rule about the sequence of rows in a table.
- There is no rule about the order of the columns.
- No two **tuples** (rows) in a **relation** can be identical.

The tables of a relational database are linked through *relationships*. Relationships are produced by having repeated fields. A field repeated from another table is called a *foreign key*.

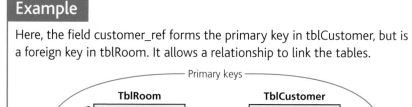
Secondary keys

As we have seen, the primary key is chosen to provide a unique row or combination of rows for each table. This allows the software to find a record unambiguously, for example there must be only one customer with a particular account number. The primary key is normally indexed automatically by the database software to allow fast searches. Sometimes you need to have this fast search facility using a different field. You may phone a company to enquire about getting a repair done and the company will have a customer table with customer number as a primary key. You might not remember your customer number so they might ask you what your postcode is. This is possibly but not necessarily unique to you. Your neighbours might have the same postcode. However, the postcode can be located quickly if it has been indexed. 'Postcode' cannot be a primary key because it is not unique, but it is useful as a *secondary key* for indexed quick searching.

Typically, large data tables are set up with several different indexes. One disadvantage of this is that whenever a change is made to the data in the table, the indexes have to be rebuilt.

Entity relationship modelling

Relational databases are usually made up of several data tables. We have seen that this is important to avoid **data redundancy**.

Imagine that an online vendor created a new record for every sale made. To generate the correct invoice, the system must have access to the details of the goods plus the details of the customer. Because the customer might make many orders over time, personal details such as name and address will need to be generated accurately for each order. Similarly, the same items will be ordered by various customers. If such repeating data were entered anew for each order, there is the possibility of making mistakes.

Because of this and also to reduce storage requirements, relational databases are designed to reduce the amount of duplicate data. This means separating out each entity and storing data about each entity in a separate table.

We can see the advantages of separating data about each entity. In the online vendor example, if we keep data about the customers separate, then when an invoice is generated, the customer details will be accessed from the one up-to-date copy.

However, it is not always obvious how to separate the entities. To achieve the best possible relational database design, it is necessary to apply rules. This is the process of *database normalisation*.

Database normalisation

Computing people

Edgar F. Codd

The relational data model was invented in the 1970s by Edgar F. Codd. He was an English computer scientist who developed the relational model while working for IBM. He developed the concept of normalisation and defined the features of 1, 2 and 3NF.

Figure 15.3 Edgar F. Codd

The objectives of database normalisation are to make a database more efficient and useful. It centres around reducing redundant data and ensuring data dependencies; in other words, the data in each table is all properly and completely related together.

Normalisation is a process whereby a collection of data is gradually organised into tables in a series of steps. Each step leads to a *normal form*. The lowest normal form is known as *first normal form* or *1NF*. The stages proceed to *2NF* and then *3NF*, which is sufficient for most purposes. Normalisation is a cumulative process so the stages have to be worked through in succession.

Codd stipulated that **attributes** in a relation must not themselves be sets, so multiple values for one tuple are not allowed. They would lead to anomalies whereby updating and searching would become complex and error prone.

First normal form (1NF)

1. Eliminate duplicate columns from the same table.
2. Create separate tables for each group of related data.
3. Identify a column or combination of columns that will uniquely identify each row in the tables (create primary keys).

So, to fix this problem, we need to convert this data to 1NF. This requires a separate entry for each instance of an order. It would look like this:

Customer Number	FName	SName	Address	ItemNumber	ItemName
453	Leroy	Skinner	21 High Street	104	Drill
356	Alice	Bernard	56 New Street	102	Hammer
322	Renee	Barrett	76 River Terrace	104	Drill
566	Fred	Freeman	101 Waterside Walk	108	Paint
211	Nita	Chang	89 Hodder Avenue	106	Chisel
243	Kaye	Silva	90 Python Street	108	Paint
765	Hedley	Cox	78 Fortran Road	100	Nails
476	Skyler	Hines	3 Cobol View	106	Chisel
123	Iliana	Atkins	12 Old Street	106	Chisel
566	Fred	Freeman	101 Waterside Walk	109	Light bulbs
123	Iliana	Atkins	12 Old Street	108	Paint
566	Fred	Freeman	101 Waterside Walk	110	Handles
566	Fred	Freeman	101 Waterside Walk	101	Screws
123	Iliana	Atkins	12 Old Street	105	Screwdriver
566	Fred	Freeman	101 Waterside Walk	108	Paint
566	Fred	Freeman	101 Waterside Walk	104	Drill

Questions

1. Identify repeating fields in this table.
2. Suggest problems that might occur if the data remains organised like this.

The table is now in 1NF.

Second normal form (2NF)

1. Check that data is now in 1NF.
2. Remove any data sets that occur in multiple rows and transfer them to new tables.
3. Create relationships between these new tables and earlier tables by means of foreign keys.

Example

There are multiple instances of the items ordered and this can lead to anomalies of updating. Suppose the names are changed. This could result in the need for multiple changes in this table.

It is better to take out data about the items ordered and put them into a new table. So we then have:

```
customer(customer_number, customer_first_name, customer_
surname, customer_address)

item(item_name)
```

We need to provide a primary key for this so we shall invent one – the item number. This will allow us to add further details about the items such as size, colour or cost. So we get:

```
item(item_number, item_name)
```

We also need to connect the customers with their orders. This will require a linking table that makes use of existing primary keys.

```
order(order_number, customer_number, item_number)
```

The database is now in 2NF.

Third normal form (3NF)

1. Check that data is in 2NF.
2. Remove any columns that are not dependant on the primary key.

Example

Suppose our table of customers and their addresses is more detailed:

```
customer(customer_number, customer_first_name, customer_
surname, street, city, postcode)
```

We can identify each customer plus contact details uniquely but not all the details are uniquely dependent upon the primary key. The customer determines the city where he lives but the city is not determined by the customer – it has its own external existence and may be shared by other customers. This is not yet at a sufficient degree of atomicity for optimum database performance.

An easy way to understand 3NF is to remember the expression 'every non-key attribute in a table must depend on the key, the whole key and nothing but the key'.

Clearly, in this case, the city is not dependent on the customer number. So again, we create a new table to take this data out.

We now have:

```
customer(customer_number, customer_first_name, customer_
surname, postcode)
```
```
postcode(postcode, street, city)
```

The street and city are now dependant on the postcode and we can access them by linking to the postcode field in the customer table.

We already have:

```
item(item_number, item_name)
```
```
order(order_number, customer_number, item_number)
```

The database is now in 3NF.

Entity relation diagrams

Figure 15.4 A relationship

A properly normalised table design can be expressed in various ways as a diagram. The development of the diagram can also be useful during the normalisation process. A common method of representing the tables and relationships is using crows' feet diagrams. These connect tables using symbols like that shown to the left.

One prong means 'one'. Three prongs means 'many'. So if we have a situation where each customer can place many orders and each order can contain many items, we can represent the data model like this:

Figure 15.5 Representing a data model with one-to-many relationships

Figure 15.6 Representing a data model with a many-to-many relationship

Question

How would you fix this many-to-many problem?

A properly normalised database will have its tables connected by one-to-many relationships like this. If a situation arises where you get a many-to-many relationship such as in Figure 15.6 where each student can have many teachers and each teacher can have many students, then you know that there is more work to be done on normalising the database.

Normalisation gives us sensible tables with the minimum amount of data redundancy.

Remember data redundancy isn't all bad; we need some repeated fields in order to provide links between tables.

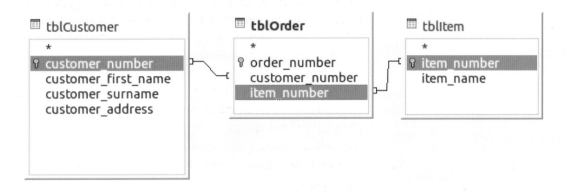

Figure 15.7 Three tables linked by repeated fields

DBMS

A DBMS is a database management system, sometimes called an RDBMS to include the word 'Relational'. A DBMS is software that creates and maintains a database. The jobs performed by a DBMS usually include creation and use of:

- the database structure
- queries
- views
- individual tables
- interfaces
- outputs.

In addition, the DBMS has protective and maintenance duties such as:

- setting and maintaining access rights
- automating backups
- preserving referential integrity
- creating and maintaining indexes
- updating the database.

There are many well-known examples of DBMSs that run on various platforms. They include:

- MySQL®
- Microsoft SQL®
- Oracle®
- dBASE®
- Libre Office Base®
- Microsoft Access®.

Database views

Key term

Data dictionary Metadata; that is, data about data. In a relational database, it is the sum total of information about the tables, the relationships and all the other components that make the database function.

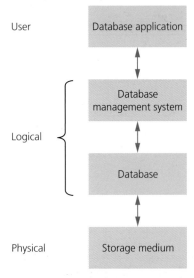

Figure 15.8 Views of a database

To get a good understanding of what a database looks like, it is helpful to realise that the data held in a database can be envisaged at three levels or views. This is yet another example of divide and conquer tactics being used to make it easier to solve problems.

Physical view

Physical view refers to how the data is actually recorded or written to the storage medium. All stored data is, of course, held as a succession of data bits. This level of organisation needs to be understood by the software so that the correct data is written and read. The designers of the database and certainly the users will have no interest in this. It is a concern of the systems engineers who design and write the DBMS. After this, it is the concern of the DBMS software.

Logical view

Logical view is concerned with how the data will be organised for processing. It looks at the construction of tables, queries, reports and the software that will deliver database functionality to the owners of the system. Constructing this level involves the production of the **data dictionary**.

User view

User view level is all about the appearance and functionality of the database. The user of a database is not concerned with the structure of tables and the links between them. The user just needs a well-designed interface to allow access to whatever data is necessary to do his or her job and the applications necessary to do the job.

Transaction processing

Transaction processing is a type of processing that attempts to provide a response to a user within a short time frame. It is not as time critical as a real-time system and normally features a limited range of operations planned in advance, such as a bank account balance enquiry or withdrawal.

CRUD

All relational databases must have certain basic functionality to be useful. This is often summarised by the acronym CRUD. This stands for:

- Create
- Read
- Update
- Delete.

Each of these functions can be actioned by an equivalent SQL statement:

- INSERT/CREATE
- SELECT
- UPDATE
- DELETE.

Three of these result in a transaction taking place.

A transaction must not allow a database to become damaged. If a database becomes changed in an inconsistent way, it will clearly not be useful any more. The DBMS ensures that when a transaction takes place, the database changes from one consistent state to another. Maintaining this consistency is called **data integrity**.

> ### Key terms
>
> **Data integrity** The maintenance of a state of consistency in a data store. It broadly means that the data in a data store reflects the reality that it represents. It also means that the data is as intended and fit for purpose.
>
> **Data corruption** The opposite of data integrity. Data corruption can be caused by various technically based events such as:
>
> - hardware failure
> - software error
> - electrical glitches.
>
> It can also result from operator error or malpractice.
>
> **Data security** Keeping data safe. Database software is designed to have in-built data security to minimise the risk of malpractice, though errors can still occur.

Referential integrity

A Level only

Referential integrity is one aspect of data integrity. It refers to a state of the database where inconsistent transactions are not possible.

> ### Example
>
> Suppose a school uses a database to keep track of students and the exams that they have been entered for. If the database has been normalised properly, there will be a student table, a subject table and an entry table. The DBMS should be set up to enforce referential integrity. Under this rule, links are made between the students and the subjects via the entry table. If an attempt is made to enter a student for a subject that doesn't exist, then this will not be possible. Similarly, if an attempt is made to delete a subject and a student is connected to it via the entry table, this too should be blocked.
>
> Referential integrity can be cleverer than that. Suppose that the student table is also linked to a fee table where each student's entry fees are stored. We can add a *constraint* to the fee table called a *cascading delete*, so that if a particular student leaves and is deleted from the student table, all associated records to do with that student are also automatically deleted.

The ACID rules

To protect the integrity of a database, transactions must conform to a set of rules. These rules describe the ACID properties required of a transaction. ACID means:

Atomicity: A change in the database is either completely performed or not performed at all. The software must prevent a half-finished transaction being saved.

Consistency: A transaction must take the whole database from one consistent state to another consistent state, for example in a bank transfer transaction the amount of money in the whole system must be the same at the end of the transaction as it was at the beginning.

Isolation: It is important that a transaction should be performed in isolation so that other users or processes cannot have access to the data concerned until the new consistent state has been committed. In practice, this means that while an operation is being performed on a record, the record is locked. This may involve making the record invisible to others or it may only lock the record for writing. After a transaction has been committed, the record may be unlocked again.

You can see how this is used in most online booking systems. In the example to the left, a booking is kept open for only a limited time. During that period, the record for the seat chosen is locked to prevent double booking.

Durability: Once a change has been made to the database, the change must not be lost because of any subsequent system failure or operator error. Ideally, the transaction is written immediately to secondary storage.

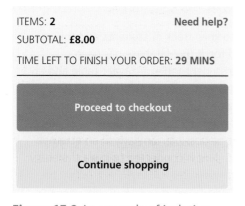

ITEMS: **2**   Need help?

SUBTOTAL: **£8.00**

TIME LEFT TO FINISH YOUR ORDER: **29 MINS**

Proceed to checkout

Continue shopping

Figure 15.9 An example of isolation

Queries and structured query language

Most of the time, databases are used for making enquiries or queries. Queries can be extremely sophisticated and all DBMSs have various ways in which they can be carried out.

Queries are used to isolate and display a subset of the data in a database. They can take related data from multiple tables and present them in an easy-to-understand way. Queries are often used as the basis for a screen form or a printed report, so that the filtered data can be presented in some clear or standard way.

A quick and easy way to perform a query is provided with many off-the-shelf DBMSs such as Microsoft Access and Libre Office Base. This is called *query by example* or *QBE*. In this, the user has a graphical interface into which can be dropped the fields required as well as setting up conditions to filter the results.

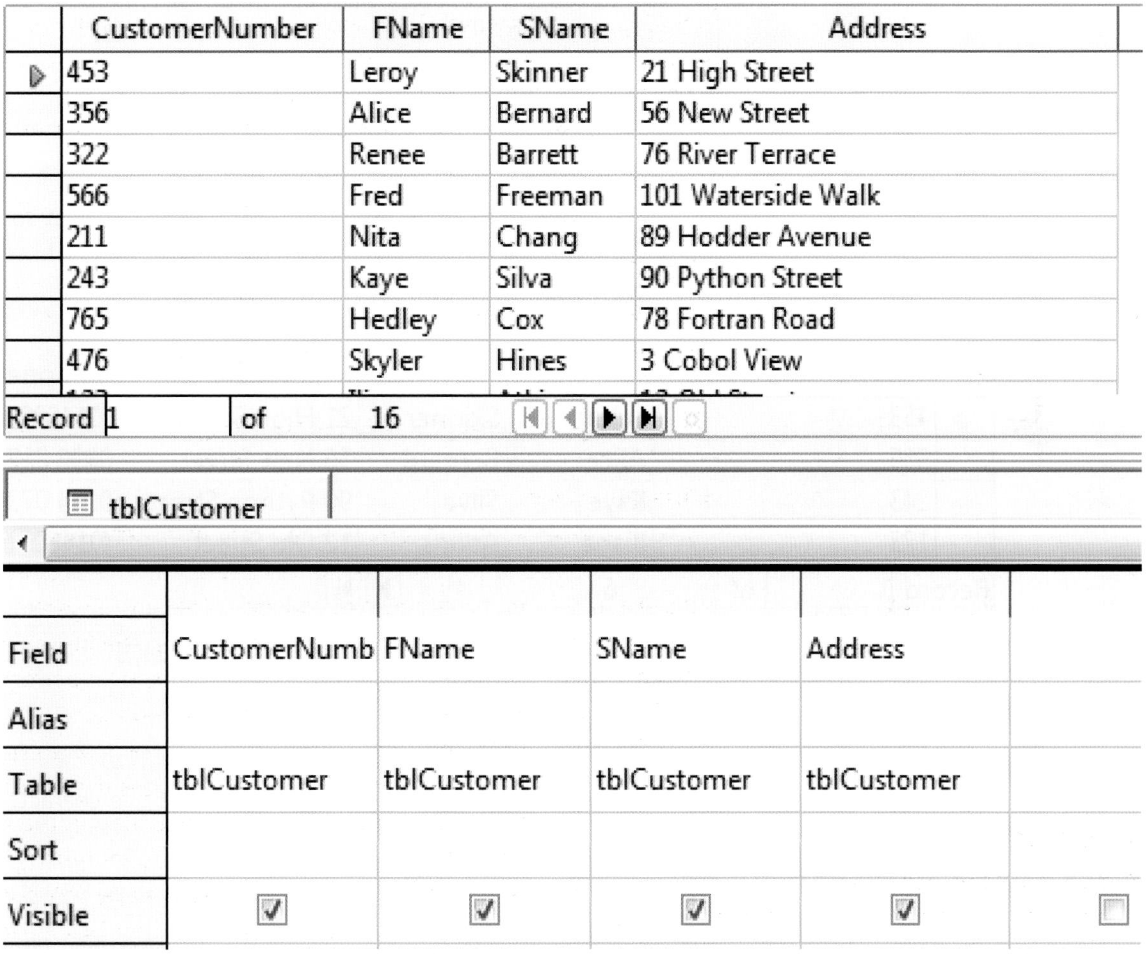

	CustomerNumber	FName	SName	Address
▷	453	Leroy	Skinner	21 High Street
	356	Alice	Bernard	56 New Street
	322	Renee	Barrett	76 River Terrace
	566	Fred	Freeman	101 Waterside Walk
	211	Nita	Chang	89 Hodder Avenue
	243	Kaye	Silva	90 Python Street
	765	Hedley	Cox	78 Fortran Road
	476	Skyler	Hines	3 Cobol View

Record 1   of   16 |◄ ◄ ▶ ▶|

☐ tblCustomer

Field	CustomerNumb	FName	SName	Address	
Alias					
Table	tblCustomer	tblCustomer	tblCustomer	tblCustomer	
Sort					
Visible	☑	☑	☑	☑	☐

Figure 15.10 A QBE screen with the resultant output

Behind the scenes, the QBE software also produces program code to achieve the required results, using a variant of the programming language structured query language (SQL). It is possible and much more flexible to write the queries directly in SQL.

Note that the syntax of SQL varies somewhat between implementations. The following examples are from Libre Office Base.

The query shown above would be rendered in SQL as:

```
SELECT "CustomerNumber", "FName", "SName", "Address" FROM
"tblCustomer";
```

The fields required are separated by commas.

The SELECT operator is used to extract the required data from a data set. Conditions can be applied using the WHERE clause.

```
SELECT "SName", "Address" FROM "tblCustomer" WHERE
"SName" = 'Cox';
```

Conditions can be tailored exactly to meet the operational requirements. In the next example, two different tables are being queried, so the table and field are specified using a dot notation. The example also shows the use of relational operators; in this case AND.

```
SELECT "tblCustomer"."FName", "tblCustomer"."SName",
"tblOrder"."order_number" FROM "tblOrder",
"tblCustomer" WHERE "tblOrder"."customer_number" =
"tblCustomer"."CustomerNumber" AND "tblCustomer"."SName" =
'Skinner' AND "tblOrder"."order_number" < 3;
```

SQL allows the use of wild cards so a query such as

```
SELECT * from "tblCustomer"
```

uses the '*' character to mean 'everything'.

The LIKE operator can be used to match the data against some pattern, using the wild card '%', such as looking for all customers whose address ends in 'Street':

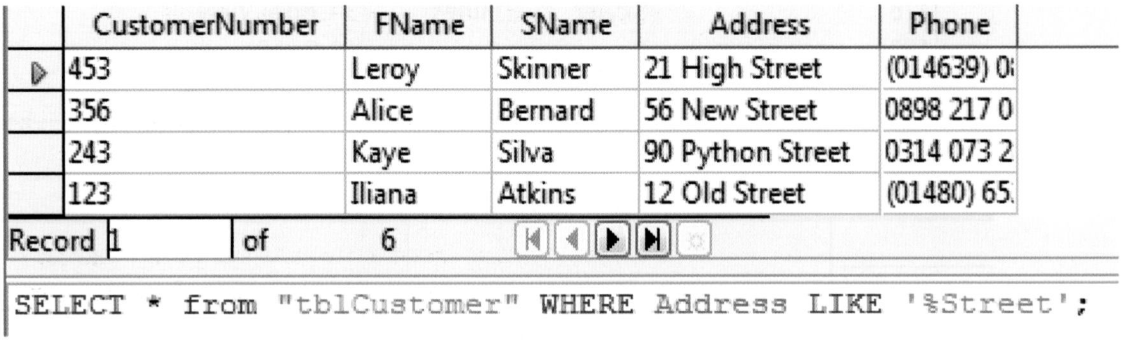

	CustomerNumber	FName	SName	Address	Phone
▷	453	Leroy	Skinner	21 High Street	(014639) 0:
	356	Alice	Bernard	56 New Street	0898 217 0
	243	Kaye	Silva	90 Python Street	0314 073 2
	123	Iliana	Atkins	12 Old Street	(01480) 65.
Record 1	of	6	|◁ ▷ ▷|		

```
SELECT * from "tblCustomer" WHERE Address LIKE '%Street';
```

Figure 15.11 Building a query using LIKE

'%' means one or many characters; '_' means just one character.

Further SQL commands

SQL is much more versatile than this. It can do more than filter out the data required in a query. SQL also has features that allow the creation and modification of databases. It also has a rich set of commands and operators that can perform any data processing required on a relational database.

You should spend some time practising SQL operations. There are web resources for this or – better – popular DBMSs such as Libre Office Base and Microsoft Access provide SQL facilities. As before, the following examples were all developed and tested using Libre Office Base.

For example, suppose you wanted to create a new table called Team Member in your database. You can do this through SQL:

CREATE

```
CREATE TABLE "tblManagement" ("ID" INT PRIMARY KEY,
"FirstName" VARCHAR(25) NOT NULL, "LastName" VARCHAR(25)
NOT NULL,"DOB" DATE);
```

INSERT

You can also add data to a table with the INSERT operator:

```
INSERT INTO "tblManagement" ("ID", "FirstName",
"LastName", "DOB") VALUES (1, 'Waltraute'', 'Walkure',
'1886-11-13');
```

DROP

The DROP operator allows the SQL program to remove indexes, tables, fields and whole databases, such as:

```
DROP TABLE "tblCustomer";
```

This removes the whole table from the database.

DELETE

DELETE allows the removal of data from a table. This can be conditional like this:

```
DELETE FROM "tblCustomer" WHERE "FName"='Joe';
```

In this case records about Joe in tblCustomer are deleted.
DELETE can be more indiscriminate than this, for example:

```
DELETE FROM "tblItem"
```

This will remove all the data from tblItem.

JOIN

A JOIN clause combines data from two or more tables using a duplicated field such as a customer number in both the customer table and the order table. The syntax INNER JOIN returns all the relative combined data where the condition is met.

For example, the following SQL code will return customer names and order numbers wherever the orders table has rows containing references to customer numbers in the customer table.

```
SELECT "tblCustomer"."FName", "tblCustomer"."SName",
"tblOrder"."order_number" FROM "tblOrder" INNER
JOIN "tblCustomer" ON "tblOrder"."customer_number" =
"tblCustomer"."customer_number";
```

Here is a relational database structure.

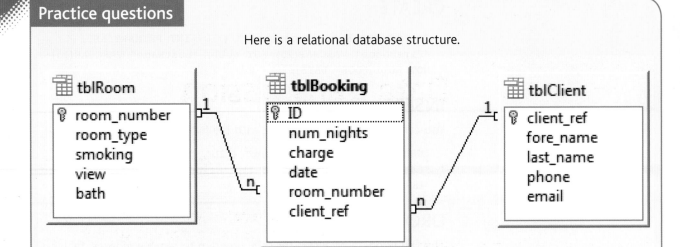

Figure 15.12 A relational database structure

Write SQL statements to achieve the following:

1. Produce a list of all hotel rooms, ordered by type, booked between two specified dates.
2. Produce a list of all clients who have made more than three bookings in the last month.
3. Produce a list of all rooms that have had no bookings.
4. Insert a new field 'Needs_redecorating' in tblRoom.
5. Delete all entries relating to a customer called 'Smith'.

Chapter 16

Data transmission

Introduction

History

People have always wanted to communicate over long distances. In the past, there were only simple techniques such as smoke signals, drums, beacon fires and, later, when electricity was discovered, various forms of telegraph.

Some early forms of telegraphy were based on a type of digital signal, where the signal caused the making of a mark or a space on a paper tape. An early attempt to communicate between Britain and France came to grief when it was discovered that a mark in Britain was represented as a space in France and vice versa. This was one of the first cases where the importance of standards in communication was recognised.

Face-to-face communication required travel; often very great distances. Letters took a long time to write and even longer to deliver.

The invention of the telephone helped, but even there problems occurred because of different time zones, and long-distance calls were expensive. Thick cables had to be laid across land and oceans. They carried analogue signals, which attenuated with distance and had to be boosted at intervals. Interference between adjacent cables added noise to the signals, so the reception was often of uneven quality.

The invention and widespread adoption of digital computers has transformed communication. Reasons that digital communication has been so successful include:

- computers process data very quickly
- digital signals transmit very reliably
- most computers are at least potentially connected to each other
- common standards have been widely adopted.

Reliability

Digital signals could hardly be simpler. They all boil down to a succession of 0s and 1s. 0s and 1s can easily be represented in a variety of ways, such as the presence or absence of an electrical pulse. It is easy and cheap to make components that can distinguish between the two states. There is no need to have complicated circuitry that can make accurate distinctions between a wide range of different voltages, as is the case with analogue signals. At a given instant, either there is a signal or there is not. Any degradation or attenuation that occurs en route might affect the voltage of the signal, but the presence or absence of a bit is likely to survive unchanged as it is transmitted. Mechanisms are built into data transmission systems that detect and correct errors. This means that most digital communication is 100 per cent accurate.

Connectivity

Connecting computers brings benefits for individuals and organisations. These include such matters as conducting business more quickly and effectively, controlling machinery remotely and, of course, people want to communicate for social reasons. Some of the most important changes in computing in recent years centre on social networks and the sharing of images, sounds and messages.

Standards

Computers would not be able to communicate unless they all had a common language. Communications between humans are often made difficult or impossible because of language barriers. In the case of computer systems, it has been possible to devise common 'languages' or standards that do not pose the same problem as with human languages.

The internet has been so successful so quickly because of its adherence to communication standards so that all devices connected to it can successfully communicate with each other, whatever their type or brand.

HTML

HTML (Hypertext Transfer Protocol) is the standard that is used for creating web pages. It is a standard that uses text and tags to control what is displayed on a user's computer. The tags, such as <h1> (a start tag) or </h1> (an end tag) delineate text items and affect how they are displayed. Images and objects such as interactive forms can be embedded in the HTML text. A key feature of HTML is to allow the inclusion of links that when clicked on take the user to a different web page or a different location on the same page.

Because HTML is standard, web pages can be interpreted and displayed by any computer that has browser software installed. It does not matter which browser you have; it will be able to display most web pages. Of course, techniques move on and a web page created ten years ago would probably look fairly basic and primitive today. To accommodate advances, HTML has changed over the years, although the basic core is still much the same as it always was. Additional capabilities have been built in. Nowadays, most web creators use Cascading Style Sheets (CSS) to control the look and behaviour of HTML text. They allow the same basic page to be displayed in different ways according to circumstances, for example the look on a tablet will not necessarily be quite the same as on a large PC screen.

Changes in HTML standards require updates to browsers and so some older browsers will not always be able to render more recent pages correctly.

This is an example of HTML code:

```
<!DOCTYPE html PUBLIC "-//W3C//DTD HTML 4.01//EN" "http://www.w3.org/TR/html4/strict.dtd">
<html><head>

<meta content="text/html; charset=ISO-8859-1" http-equiv="content-
type"><title>index</title></head><body><big><big><big>How to talk to cats<br>
</big></big></big><img style="width: 467px; height: 310px;" alt="" src="IMG_0034.JPG"><br>

<big><big><big><small>This <a href="cat_tutorial.html">tutorial</a> will have you
speaking <br>
cat language in super quick time.</small><br>
</big></big></big><br>
<br>

</body></html>
```

Figure 16.1 This is how it is rendered by a browser

Key points

- Successful communication needs standards.
- Computers provide reliability.
- Binary is simple: simple is reliable.
- Most computers are connected.

Networks

Networks are collections of connected computing devices. They consist of a number of devices known as nodes, which are mostly computers of various kinds but also shared peripherals such as printers, scanners and secondary storage devices.

Devices need to be connected to networks by network interface cards (NICs) or by using equivalent circuitry embedded in their electronics. Each device connected to a network must be uniquely identifiable so that messages intended for it are delivered correctly.

Reasons for having networks

Most organisations and many private individuals have networks. They have become important because of the need to communicate and share data. A central store of data enables all the users of the system to see the same up-to-date version of the data they need.

Private networks

Even in the age of the internet, most organisations still have their own private networks. The advantages of having these include:

- control over security
- complete control over who has access to what resource
- control over what software is provided
- confidence of availability.

However, these conveniences come at a cost. In particular, a large network needs specialist staff to keep it running all the time and also to maintain security. Most organisations are completely dependent on their networks, so if any functionality is lost this can potentially be a major disaster. Various methods are employed to minimise these risks, such as:

- redundancy – where essential equipment is duplicated
- a sensible backup regime – so that there is always a copy of essential data stored somewhere else
- failover systems – these detect abnormalities and automatically transfer operations to an alternative system
- a disaster recovery plan – this is necessary so that in the event of a major failure, procedures are in place to limit the impact of the failure and remedies are applied effectively.

> ### Key points
>
> - HTML is the language of the web.
> - HTML is text based.
> - HTML uses tags to tell browsers how to render text and images.
> - Networks have transformed computing.
> - Networks have transformed how we work.
> - Networks allow control of information.
> - Organisations depend on networks so they have to be secure against accidents and malpractice.

Hardware

A Level only

Networks are built on certain common items of hardware. These are concerned with generating, transmitting and interpreting electrical signals.

Network interface cards (NICs)

Otherwise known as network interface controllers, these are circuits that in the past were plugged into a computer's bus to produce signals that are placed on the transmission medium and also to receive signals from it.

NICs are designed to work with particular network standards, and by far the most widespread is one called Ethernet. This is so common that most computers are now built with Ethernet circuitry built into their motherboards rather than requiring cards as an add-on.

NICs work at the physical and data link layers of the OSI network model (see page 211).

(see page 211)

Extra info

Ethernet is a network standard that divides data into packages or 'frames' and transmits them using various media such as copper or fibre optic cable. Each frame contains the source and destination addresses on the local network as well as error-checking data and the message data itself. Frames only exist while the data is in transit and contain yet further subdivisions of data known as packets.

Each Ethernet device is allocated a unique 48-bit MAC (media access control) address. Ethernet makes use of these MAC addresses to identify the source and destination of data frames.

MAC addresses

These are 48-bit identifiers allocated to network devices by the manufacturer. Normally, they are quoted in human readable groups of six bytes or octets (octets because each byte is eight bits) and displayed as **hexadecimal** digits. Thus a typical MAC address could be 08:01:27:0E:25:B8.

The first three octets of a MAC address identify the manufacturer of the equipment. The others are allocated in a way decided on by the maker to ensure that each address is unique.

Routers

A router is a device that connects networks. It receives data packets from one network and forwards them to another network based on the address information in the packet. Routers determine where to send a packet according to either a table of information about neighbouring networks or by using an **algorithm** to determine the optimum next step for a packet. Each router knows about its own closest neighbours, but by sharing this information it is possible to determine the optimum route for a data packet.

Small routers for home use connect the user's computer to the ISP (internet service provider). Large organisations, including those that run the internet's infrastructure, use powerful high-speed routers, which are able to direct traffic according to the needs of the moment.

Extra info

To ensure correct delivery of data frames, networks use various standards, for example if the least significant bit of the most significant byte of a frame's destination is set to 0, then the frame will only be received by one specific NIC. Other forms of fine tuning can ensure that only the correct devices receive the frames intended for them.

Figure 16.2 A network interface controller

Questions

1. Name two functions of an NIC.
2. State the purpose of a MAC address.
3. Describe the characteristics of a MAC address.
4. What is the basic function of a router?

Wireless access points

Many networks now have wireless access points. These enable the temporary connection of devices, usually portable computers, to a network. BYOD (bring your own device) is a practice commonly used by organisations, where visitors are allowed to connect their own devices to the organisation's network. The practice is also common for members of universities and public WiFi networks, which are found everywhere from coffee shops to airports.

Typically, wireless access points allow connections from distances of up to about 100 metres. This introduces security issues because of the ease of intercepting signals. Because of this, various measures are often taken to prevent unauthorised access. The following are examples:

Hiding the SSID

The SSID (service set identifier) is a broadcast signal that identifies a wireless access point. It is useful when a network is likely to be used by outsiders.

Encryption

Various standards have been developed to encrypt signals sent between a computing device and a wireless access point. WEP is 'wired equivalent privacy'. This uses a static key, usually of 40 or 64 bits, to encrypt data. The drawback of this method is that all devices using the access point have to know the key, leading to security problems.

WPA and WPA2 (WiFi protected access) are improvements on WEP and, among other features, they involve once-only cryptographic keys.

Limiting access

Access points can be configured to accept communications from a limited list of MAC addresses. This is not practical where many new and unknown devices are likely to be connected.

> **Key points**
>
> - Hardware items on a network are identified by unique reference numbers: MAC addresses.
> - Ethernet is the most common LAN standard.
> - Data is transmitted in frames.
> - Routers connect networks.
> - Wireless access brings many benefits but also security issues.

Classification of networks

There are various ways of looking at a network, depending on whether you are concerned with the physical layout (topology) or the extent or the separation of functions. As with all aspects of computer technology, these categories start to get rather blurred over time as new ways of networking are developed.

Topology

A number of physical layouts have been developed for networks.

Bus

The bus network attaches devices to a common backbone. This backbone is typically based on copper wire and is limited in its potential size. This is because signals become attenuated (weakened) with distance and this leads to errors in transmission. Another drawback is that if the backbone is compromised, the network as a whole fails.

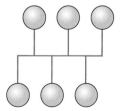

Figure 16.3 Bus network layout

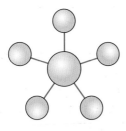

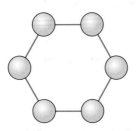

Figure 16.4 Star network

Figure 16.5 Ring network layout

Question

Explain two advantages of a star topology over a bus layout.

A bus network requires a terminator at each end of the bus to prevent data being reflected back and increasing the risk of data collisions.

Star

A star network uses linking devices such as hubs or, more commonly switches, to connect devices to a server or multiple servers. This layout is by far the most common because it facilitates easy addition of nodes and is also more robust than a single backbone architecture.

Ring

A ring structure attempts to solve the problem of data collisions by sending all data frames in one direction. Each computer is connected to exactly two other computers.

Extent

LANs

A LAN is a local area network. What this means is that the network exists at a defined and limited location. It could be a room, a building or a campus. A significant feature of LANs is that the infrastructure is owned by the organisation that uses it, which is also responsible for its upkeep.

WANs

These are wide area networks. In other words, they cover a large geographical area. Typically, they consist of interconnected LANs at different sites, connected by some form of telecoms link, which is normally provided by a separate company. WANs are useful where an organisation needs private links with branches in different places, possibly even worldwide, and does not wish to share resources with other organisations. The internet can be considered a WAN.

Others

A SAN (storage area network) provides a dedicated network for large-scale data storage in data centres. They are efficient because the servers that make them up consolidate their storage devices to provide a disk array of high capacity and performance.

MANs are metropolitan area networks, which provide WAN services in a city.

PANs (personal area networks) link personal devices such as phones, tablets and other devices that people commonly have.

An internet search will bring up many other acronyms and there comes a point at which classifying them all becomes rather pointless and it is better simply to understand the layout and usefulness of whichever implementation interests you at the time, for example a modern car typically has 50 or more linked processors, which in their turn may be linked by telecoms technology to the car manufacturer or by wired connection to a technician's laptop. Searching around for the correct acronym for such varied cases is a little pointless.

Extra info

The cloud

Increasingly, organisations and individuals are moving away from maintaining their own networks and devolving many of the responsibilities to outside organisations; so-called 'outsourcing'. Providers of such services often supply not only storage space but also software that can be remotely accessed. This software may be generic, such as standard word processors and spreadsheet applications, or they may be specialised business-oriented applications. This facility is called software as a service (SaaS). Remote software and storage is referred to as 'the cloud' because it is envisaged as an amorphous entity 'out there somewhere', the hidden details being of no concern to the client or user. There are significant advantages to users, such as:

- economies of scale – because the cost of the services is shared between many users
- removal of the need to install and upgrade software
- removal of the need to hire specialist technical staff
- removal of the need to back up data.

There are drawbacks, but many organisations find that these are outweighed by the convenience of the cloud. Such drawbacks include:

- handing control of security to another party
- some risk of losing data if it is under someone else's control
- some risk of losing access to the service and having no local means of recovering it.

So, there is a trust issue with cloud services, but with a reputable provider the benefits can be very significant.

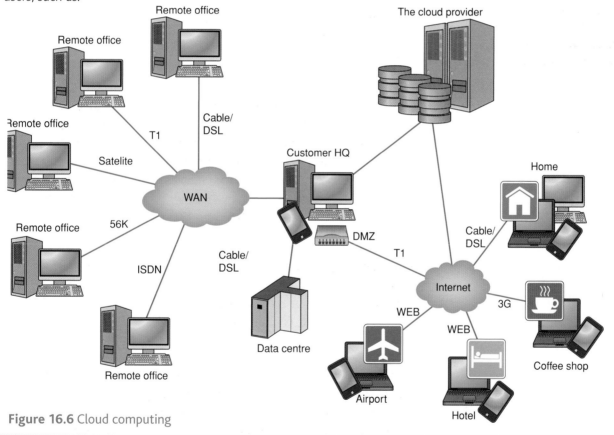

Figure 16.6 Cloud computing

Question

What would be the advantages and disadvantages of a student using cloud-computing services?

Key points

- A network layout is called its topology.
- The star topology is robust, common and cost effective.
- LANs occupy one site; WANs are geographically dispersed.
- Cloud computing is becoming ever more important.
- Cloud computing has cost and reliability benefits.

Networks – an organisational viewpoint

Networks come in many guises and their nature is changing all the time. However, there are two models that commonly appear.

Client–server

Client–server is a model where one entity (the client) requests services from another (the server). It is the most common model in networks, being successful because it separates functions, allowing more efficient use of resources. A client–server network is based on two classes of computer. The server provides services. These services are typically storage and print but most large networks have specialised servers for many functions such as email and databases.

The server is also where security functions are located, such as those concerning logins and permissions.

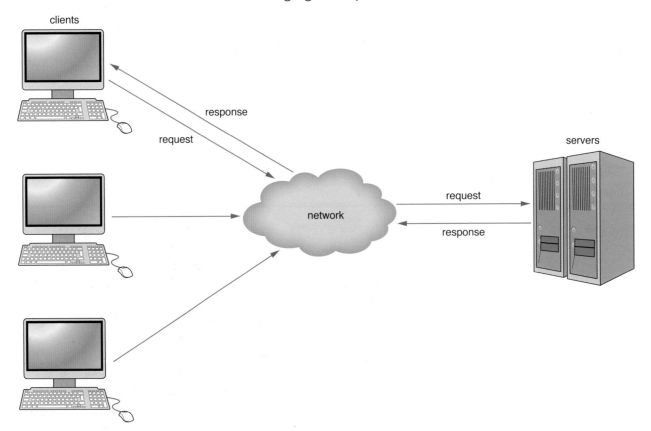

Figure 16.7 The clients request services such as data or processing from the server

Peer-to-peer

In some networks, all the computers have equal status. Each computer on the network acts as both client and server, depending on circumstances. There is no centralised control. This can be a cheaper model to implement and it also has its benefits on the internet, where files can be shared without the need to be processed by a server. Popular applications of peer-to-peer systems are the sharing of music and other files and the internet payment system BitCoin.

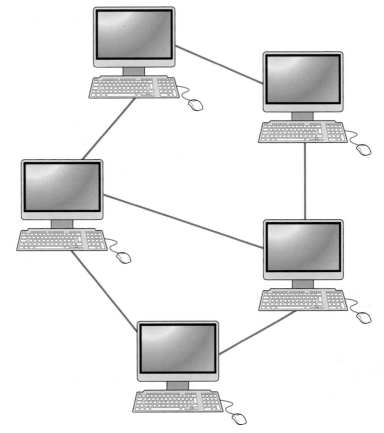

Figure 16.8 A peer-to-peer network

Layering

We have seen how a divide-and-conquer strategy can be a useful way to **build** complex systems and solve complex problems. Problems can be broken down into components, each of which is easier to solve than the whole. This approach works well in software development as well as in everyday problem solving.www

In the development of networks, divide and conquer has been particularly important in helping to develop the infrastructure necessary to support robust systems. This has led to the concept of *layering* whereby different aspects of the network's functionality are conceptualised and developed separately. Each component part, called a *layer*, concentrates on one aspect of the network without worrying about the others. Each layer communicates only with the other layers directly adjacent to it.

The concept of layering occurs in other aspects of computer systems too, such as in operating systems and databases.

The design of network layers varies a lot. First of all, at a simple level, we can consider these following questions:

1. What is being communicated?
2. Who is it being sent to?
3. How will it get there?

Each of these questions can be addressed separately. The model described above leads to a three-layer abstraction of a network. As we have seen, abstractions are useful to provide a model of a real-life situation into which we can design proposed solutions.

When it comes to actually building a real network, a three-layer abstraction could lead to the following layers:

1. **An application layer:** This is concerned with collecting and disseminating the data that is being sent across the network. Applications collect the data, possibly using interactive human-user interfaces or alternatively they may automatically collect data as from a remote weather station. This layer needs to know about the nature of the data being collected so that it can be validated and packaged. At the receiving end, applications need to convert the transmitted data into whatever form is required, either human readable output or signals for operating machinery. The application layer does not concern itself with how the data will get to its intended destination.

2. **A network layer:** This layer doesn't care about what data is being transmitted. It is concerned with the layout of the network, what nodes there are, what topology is being used and how best to get the data efficiently from source to destination.

3. **The physical layer:** Of course, the data has to be transmitted via some medium. This will typically involve cables, both metal and fibre optic, network interface circuitry, routers and other electronic devices. Part of the journey from source to destination may be by wireless link. The physical layer does not care about the nature of the data or the route that is being taken. It just provides a transport medium to conduct the messages as the network layer instructs it.

There are of course other subdivisions that can be made, but if we initially look at a network from these perspectives, we can start to make decisions and develop procedures independently of each other. After that, we can look at the somewhat easier problem of providing interfaces between these processes so that data can be passed from one layer to another, and thereby from sender to recipient, as effectively as possible.

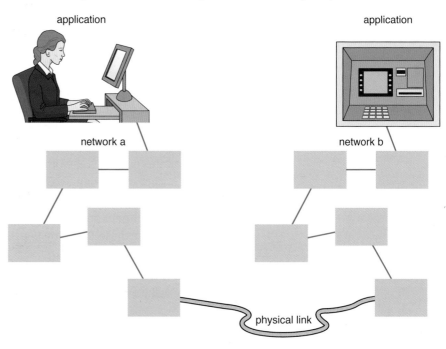

Figure 16.9 A simple three-layer network model; in this case, an ATM is being administered remotely by bank staff

Open systems interconnection (OSI)

In reality, most networks are more complex than this three-layer model; for example OSI (open systems interconnection) is an openly available model devised by the International Standards Organisation (ISO), consisting of a stack of seven layers. This subdivides functionality beyond the simple three-layer model described above and allows yet further refinement and focus on detail.

The OSI model provides the following abstraction. The layer numbers are normally presented in reverse order so that the applications are shown as high (human) level.

Layer	Name	Purpose
7	Application	The layer closest to the user. Collects or delivers data and passes it to and from the presentation layer.
6	Presentation	Looks after any conversions between data as sent on the network and data as it is needed by the applications. May involve encryption/decryption operations.
5	Session	Looks after starting, managing and terminating connection sessions. Provides simplex, half-duplex and full duplex operation.
4	Transport	Concerned with keeping track of segments of a network, checking successful transmission and packetisation, for example TCP.
3	Network	Transmission of data packets, routing.
2	Data link	Control of access, error detection and correction.
1	Physical	Network devices and transmission media.

A message sent across a network will pass through the layers of functionality from the application to the physical layer, then, at the destination, back through them in reverse order to the receiving application.

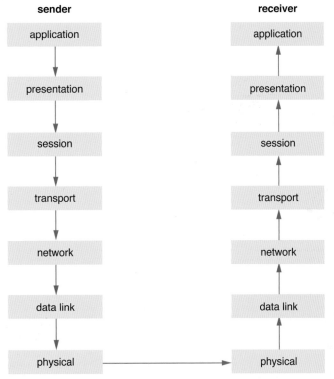

Figure 16.10 An open systems interconnection (OSI) model

As the OSI model is an open standard, its concepts and design are not owned by any organisation and anyone is free to make use of its ideas. Most networks are based to some extent on the OSI model or resemble it, often merging some parts of it into single entities.

The most widely used network model in the world is a set of standards called TCP/IP. This stands for transmission control protocol/internet protocol. TCP/IP has become so widely accepted that devices of various types and from any manufacturer can communicate with each other across the world wide web as well as on smaller networks.

Protocols

For networks to function successfully, there have to be standards. The internet works so well because at an early stage there were agreements about how devices should communicate. The rules and standards governing this are called **protocols**.

Protocols apply to most aspects of a network.

The TCP/IP stack

The TCP/IP stack is a complete set of many protocols covering data transmission across a network. It governs how data should be formatted, addressed, routed and received. It resembles most of the middle layers of the OSI model, with which it has similarities, but predates it and a complete cross-mapping is not appropriate.

Unlike the OSI seven-layer model, TCP/IP has four layers of abstraction. The top layers are close to the creation and reception of data by the user. The lower levels are closer to the physical transmission of the data.

Layer	Purpose
Application	This layer is concerned with the production, communication and reception of data. Applications need to be concerned that the data they generate is in a format acceptable to applications that will make use of it; for example a program that captures data from a remote sensor needs to provide the data in a form that is acceptable to the recording and analysing software. TCP/IP does not distinguish between the application, presentation and session layers. These functions are all considered together in its application layer. This layer also includes the means of packaging up data and handing to the transport layer. Protocols such as HTTP and FTP operate at this level.
Transport	This is concerned with the establishment and termination of connections between network entities via routers. It is responsible for providing a reliable flow of data across the network.
Internet	This provides links to transmit **datagrams** across different networks. It is not concerned with individual network types and, as such, is the essential feature of the internet; allowing the exchange of data between any networks. Internet protocol (IP) is the protocol used at this level and it defines the nature of IP addresses and directs datagrams from one router to the next.
Link	The link layer is not concerned with routers. This is the lowest level of TCP/IP. It is concerned with passing datagrams to the local physical network. This layer is designed to make the overall network hardware independent and so it can operate over any transmission medium such as copper wire, optical fibre and wireless.

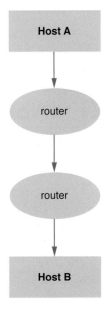

Figure 16.11 Relationship between hosts (computers) and routers when sending messages

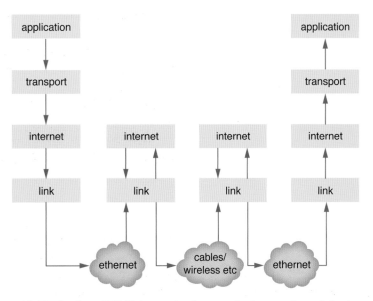

Figure 16.12 The four TCP/IP layers in the practical operation of the internet

Questions

1. Explain the role of the link layer in TCP/IP.
2. Parts of this book were written making use of Ethernet. Explain what Ethernet is and how it could be involved in this process.

Circuit switching

Old-fashioned telephones used to connect via switchboards. A switchboard physically connected circuits so that the two parties to a conversation temporarily shared a single circuit. Originally, the connections were made manually, but electromechanical, and later electronic switching using valves, and later transistors, allowed the connection of the circuits.

The participants in a circuit-switching network are physically connected and remain so until the conversation or data exchange is terminated. This works well enough but it means that the connecting wires are in use – unavailable to anyone else – until the conversation ends. This is not the best use of resources and requires multiple cables, which take up a lot of space and are expensive.

There are three phases in a circuit-switching session:

1. connection establishment
2. data transfer
3. connection release

and each one takes time.

Circuit switching is an acceptable technology where there is likely to be a long-lasting data stream between two entities, for example the remote processing of a batch of data from a terminal.

Packet switching

Packet switching is far more common than circuit switching and it makes use of digital technology to circumvent the disadvantages of circuit switching. Its central idea is that the message to be transmitted is broken up into chunks called 'packets'. These packets contain all the information needed to direct them to the correct destination and to reassemble them. Packets can be sent by different routes according to the availability of connections. This allows for a more efficient use of the whole network because lines are not tied up with individual data streams.

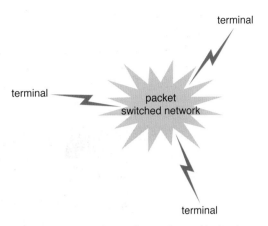

Figure 16.14 Concept of a packet-switched network

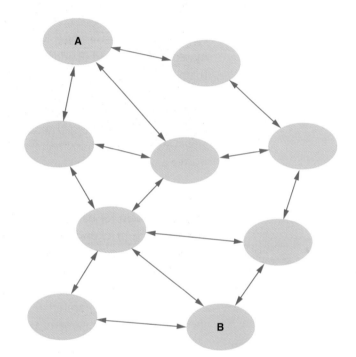

Figure 16.15 Sending a message from A to B; note that multiple routers allow many possible pathways

Data packets on the internet typically contain between 1000 and 1500 bytes of data:

Header				Payload	Trailer	
source address	destination address	packet sequence number	protocol	data	checksum	end of packet marker

Circuit-switching networks are most likely to charge their customers on the basis of the time they are connected. Packet-switching networks are likely to charge users on the basis of the amount of data transmitted.

Questions

1. State two applications that would make use of a circuit switching network.
2. State the purpose of each part of a typical data packet.

IP addressing

Messages are directed to their destinations across TCP/IP networks using a system called IP addressing. Each device on the network has a unique IP (internet protocol) address. The system known as IP Version 4, which is still in use, makes use of a 32-bit number to identify a device on the network. Because of the growth of the internet and the depletion of available addresses, 128-bit identifiers are being introduced in Version 6.

IP addresses are binary numbers but are displayed as a series of human readable numbers such as 167.12.254.1 in Version 4. The numbers are made of a group of four bytes (octets), so each octet in a Version 4 address has a maximum value of 255.

In Version 6, the addresses are normally expressed as eight groups of hexadecimal numbers, such as 3201:feba:0000:0000:0000:0000:3787:3432. IP addresses can be permanently assigned to devices by an administrator.

This is known as static addressing. This is not common, because it ties up available addresses even when the devices are not in use. It is much more usual to assign IP addresses as they are needed and then release them after use. This makes use of dynamic host configuration protocol (DHCP) and the network software manages the process instead of it being a burden on the administrator.

To conserve IP addresses, networks often set up their own internal subnet addresses so that a typical home router will have an IP address assigned by the ISP and will set up subnet addresses for devices connected to it.

The domain name system (DNS)

This is a system for naming resources on a network. It is a hierarchical system and is used on private networks as well as the internet.

Resources on a TCP/IP network can be named according to this system so that all have unique names. Top-level domains are on the right of a resource name and the name is further developed as you go left, with each domain level separated with a dot. The name furthest to the left is the host name – the name of the computer where the resource originates.

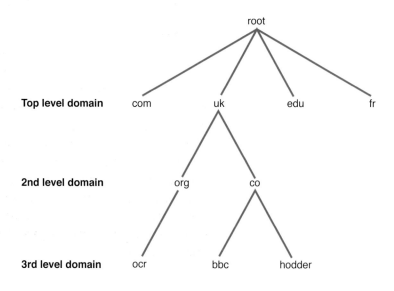

Figure 16.16 A hierarchical naming system

Thus from this example, we could have the URLs ocr.org.uk or bbc.co.uk.

Key points

– Packets are designed according to the network's protocol.

– Packets contain data plus routing and error-correcting information.

– TCP/IP uses IP addressing to locate resources on a network.

– IP addresses can be static or dynamic.

– The domain name system (DNS) is used to provide a systematic human-friendly substitute for IP addresses.

Question

Construct a diagram to show how these four URLs form part of a hierarchical naming system: yahoo.com, uni.edu, company.place.uk, myco.org.uk.

The system is part of the TCP/IP protocol suite. The basic job of DNS is to allow users to locate resources on a network using user-friendly names such as yahoo.com, rather than having to know the IP address. This function is carried out by DNS servers.

If you request a resource by typing in its URL (uniform resource locator), the resource name is sent to a DNS server. The server then tries to look up the IP address associated with the human readable name in its database. If the server has the relevant data, it will make the substitution and allow the connection. If the address is not there, it will forward the request to other DNS servers in an attempt to resolve the name.

Network security and threats

A Level only

Networks are designed to allow multiple access points to data. This is useful for the business of an organisation, but it creates weaknesses. Unauthorised individuals potentially have the ability to access sensitive data and copy, delete or alter it.

Authentication

Users of networks usually have to identify themselves with a user ID and confirm that they are who they claim to be by entering a password. This is a fairly basic requirement and is prone to misuse. It is often easy to obtain a user's password because people often write them down, maybe on a sticky label and stick them on a cupboard. Often it is possible to get a password simply by asking the person concerned.

Software can be used to try out passwords using what is known as a *brute force attack*.

To get around these problems, most corporate networks require additional security such as a security device, ATM card or a mobile phone. Banks often require multiple items of identification.

To avoid automated attempts to gain access to a network, sometimes *captchas* are used. These are human- but not machine-readable words that have to be copied into a field when logging in.

Firewalls

A firewall can be hardware or software or a combination of the two. Its job is to control traffic into and out of a network. It can be set up as a series of rules so that individual web addresses or specific computers can be blocked from accessing the network, or similarly cannot be reached from within the network.

In addition, rules can be applied that cause messages containing certain words or other streams of bits to be filtered out. Packet filtering can examine data packets as they pass the firewall and can reject them if they match a preset pattern. This sort of filtering operates at the lowest three levels of the OSI model. Other methods retain packets until it is established whether they are part of an existing message or the start of a new connection.

Proxies

Proxy servers can act as firewalls. They are computers interposed between a network and a remote resource. If a user on the network requests a resource such as a web page, the request is picked up by the proxy server. This then either passes on the request to the desired resource, or does not if the resource is on a banned list. The response from the remote resource is passed back to the proxy server, which may or may not forward it to the user. This way, there is never any direct contact between the user's computer and the remote resource.

Encryption

Encryption is the transformation of data in such a way that unauthorised people cannot make sense of it. We have already seen how it is used in wireless access points to prevent eavesdropping on networks.

Encryption is used extensively in networks because of the risk that data might be intercepted. Typically, with all encryption, a secret key is used to transform the original data – the plain text – and an algorithm is applied using that key. The algorithm is called a cipher. The resulting output from the algorithm is called ciphertext. The receiving device needs to have access to that key to decrypt the ciphertext and restore the original plain text message.

Typically, large keys are likely to be more secure than small ones and much network security makes use of 64-bit keys. Some are three times this size, at 192 bits. These keys are often subdivided so that parts are used to produce successive stages of encryption.

Encryption is a critical part of virtual private networks (VPNs) because the infrastructure is shared with a number of users.

Extra info

VPNs

Virtual private networks are a popular way to set up a network without having to invest in a private infrastructure. Although the network is private to the company, it uses publicly available resources, normally the internet, to connect the company's sites.

The connections are virtual; that is, using connectionless mode transfer, and all traffic is encrypted because it is passing through public facilities.

Key points

- Networks require security mechanisms.
- Authentication is ensuring that users are who they say they are.
- Authentication is developing in sophistication all the time.
- Firewalls regulate incoming and outgoing traffic.
- Encryption is widely used to protect data on networks.
- Keys are used to control encryption and decryption.

Practice questions

1. Explain how a MAC address identifies a resource on a network.
2. Explain the differences between WEP and WPA encryption.
3. Describe the benefits of the client–server model for network design.
4. Explain how layering in networks is an example of a divide-and-conquer approach.
5. Explain the role of the session layer in the transmission of a message on a network built to the OSI model.
6. Compare and contrast the TCP/IP network model with the OSI model.
7. Describe a situation that uses circuit switching to establish communication between two network entities.
8. Explain the principal benefits of packet-switching technologies.

Chapter 17

The internet

Introduction

The internet is a world-wide network of networks. It has been one of the most revolutionary developments in the history of computing and it can be argued that it is one of the key developments in the history of humankind. It allows and indeed encourages instant world-wide interactions on a personal level at a very low cost.

Building on previous technologies such as telephony, radio and computing, the internet has brought together millions of people wherever they are in the world. It has enabled co-operation as never before and we are still only beginning to see the potential of it.

The internet has grown because of the coming together of significant technological developments into a massive entity that is owned by no one. It nonetheless functions efficiently in allowing the growth of data sharing, social and working networks and commerce. At its heart is the concept and practice of packet switching (see page 214).

Uses

The internet is a communication system. It is characterised by being cheap to use and very reliable, and has several main uses.

Communication

Originally, much of the communication was one-way, with simple websites just sitting there and providing information that the web developers thought might be useful in some way. Email quickly followed and that has remained a hugely important use of the technology, although people are increasingly turning to social websites and various forms of blogging as an alternative.

An early form of computer communication was a protocol called *telnet*. This enabled a text-based means of communicating with and controlling a remote computer. We now use text-based communications over the internet for chat sessions.

Voice communication using VoIP (Voice over Internet Protocol) has become an important addition in which analogue signals from a microphone are converted into the digital signals that can be transmitted over the internet. This has led to cheap or even free voice calls between computers or between telephones. Visual facilities were added, making possible video conferencing and video calls between individuals. Sound and vision have been improving all the time with the increasing availability of high bandwidth links.

Information

We turn to the internet as a first resort to find out anything. The uses continue to expand and include anything from researching purchases and student research to looking up symptoms that we may have or think we have. Doctors use the internet to help them confirm their own diagnoses.

Entertainment

The internet provides all sorts of entertainment, from streaming of films, to music to games, which may be solitary or interacting with other players.

Education

Apart from being the obvious place to go to find things out, there are huge numbers of online courses, both public and private, where people can follow structured learning plans and get qualifications.

Financial transactions

Most people use online banking, which allows far greater control of personal and corporate finance.

Control

As any digital information can be transmitted over the internet, it is possible to control devices remotely. This can range from fixing faults in a remote computer, to controlling river flow systems or turning on lights in your house.

Commerce

Most business transactions use the internet as a fast and secure means of making deals.

History and technology

The 1960s

In the 1960s, computer technology had developed to such an extent that it was becoming clear that there could be benefits from linking computers together. This had significant potential, even at that time, in allowing data to be passed from one computer to another, thereby saving a lot of effort and time. Initially circuit switching was used, as the technology was already familiar from telephony. Technically connecting computers with cables was not such a huge leap, although the idea of doing so was. Circuit switching allowed for data streams to be sent long distances between computers and was useful where there was a need simply to transfer a lot of data. It was not practical for large-scale interactive use. Circuit switching was a slow technology and something different was needed to develop the concept further.

The US Defense Department ran an agency at that time called the Defense Advanced Research Projects Agency – DARPA. Under their umbrella, plans were developed to connect a small number of computers in the US. There was also concern that in the event of a war (and this was on everyone's minds during the Cold War era), communications between computers could easily be disrupted. Even then, it was clear that connected computers would be important if for no other reason than to support the military. At least three groups worked independently on ideas of connectivity that would lead to packet switching, and at the National Physical Laboratory in Teddington, England, packet switching was first demonstrated as a means of sending data by independent alternative routes that would be less liable to dislocation.

In 1969, the first connections were made in what was now known as ARPANET. The original connections were between computers at UCLA and Stanford Research Institute. Soon after, two more nodes were added at UC Santa Barbara and University of Utah. These four connected computers were the start of the internet. More computers were soon added to the network and protocols were developed to allow them to communicate flexibly, and applications were soon developed to take advantage of this.

The 1970s

In 1972, email was born and became the hottest network application for the next ten years, showing the way forward for the use of the internet as a means for people to communicate.

The developing ARPANET was envisaged as connecting completely disparate networks and, as such, the concept of open architecture was born. This allowed connectivity between widely diverse systems and is another key factor that allowed the internet to become useful very quickly. This concept continues to underpin today's internet developments. Different users and organisations can develop whatever computer systems they want, and for connectivity all they need to concern themselves with is a suitable interface that can access the wider world.

To allow complete independence for each connected network, a connecting protocol was developed so that data packets were retransmitted in the case of errors and so that communication devices (later routers) were made as simple as possible by not requiring them to store details of the data streams that passed through them.

Further refinements were made to the protocol; preventing lost data packets from interfering with network traffic; forwarding packets to the correct addresses world wide; using checksums for error checking; working with various operating systems; reassembling data packets into messages; and handling duplicated packets. The set of protocols developed would eventually become known as TCP/IP (Transmission Control Protocol/Internet Protocol).

A system was developed to identify nodes on the new network. It was based on a 32-bit IP address, where the first eight bits identified the network being addressed and the remaining 24 identified the host on that network. Using eight bits to identify a network was assumed to be plenty as no one expected there to be more than 256 networks needing to be connected in the world. The development of Ethernet by Xerox soon led to an explosion of networks and the need to reconsider addressing issues. It was decided to split the protocol into two main elements: IP dealt with addressing and forwarding packets and TCP was concerned with flow control and error correction.

Thus, from the outset, what was becoming 'the internet' was conceived as an infrastructure that could allow the sharing of resources and could become a neutral platform upon which any number of yet unimagined applications could be constructed.

Key points

- The internet is a network of networks.
- It is an infrastructure on which are built many applications.
- Its usefulness is still being discovered and developed.
- The development of the internet was made possible by the concepts of packet switching and protocols.

Question

Name some file standards that are commonly associated with internet communications.

The usefulness of the internet quickly became apparent, and versions of TCP/IP were made available for individual PCs so that anyone could participate in this growing resource. The domain name system was developed to remove the need for a centralised database of host names (see page 216).

World wide web

Figure 17.1 Tim Berners-Lee at CERN

By far the most well-known and widely used function of the internet is the collection of billions of web pages that make up the world wide web. These pages have some basic features that make the web special. These pages:

- are defined using a text based mark-up language called HTML (see below)
- make use of hyperlinks; that is, parts of them usually have sensitive areas of text or imagery that connect to other pages
- often include images, videos and other media.

The world wide web is the invention of British computer scientist Tim Berners-Lee. It started life as a communication system to be used at CERN (the European Organisation for Nuclear Research), where Berners-Lee worked.

The idea was to allow users to browse information that was linked together in some useful way. Following links at will was a relatively new idea, although it had been tried out on small computer systems with applications such as Apple's Hypercard a few years previously. The first successful trial of the new web was in 1990, so it has not really been around all that long for something that is now an integral part of all our lives.

HTML

Web pages are interpreted and displayed by software called a browser. Browsers are now probably one of the most familiar of end-user applications. There are several common ones and they all have the ability to interpret and display web pages written in HTML. Of course technology moves on, and over the years browsers have become more capable and can do rather more than simply display text and links.

As described on page 202, Hypertext Mark-up Language is the underlying language of the web. HTML is entirely text based and composed of elements called *tags*, which enclose items of text or other objects. The tags control what the browser does to the enclosed text. In most cases, this involves displaying the text in a particular style, but it can also make the text behave in a particular way, such as by forming a link to another location in the web.

Images and other objects can be embedded in HTML files, and importantly applications can also run within a web page. Common development platforms that are designed to work within HTML documents include Java®, Flash® and Silverlight®.

Extra info

Mark-up language

HTML may be the world's most well-known mark-up language but it is not the only one, or even the first. Typesetters in the past used to mark up authors' manuscripts with handwritten notes to the printer saying what font or style to use.

When computer text processing became popular, the process of indicating how text was to be presented became more formalised, with tags being embedded in the text to direct the software how to display the associated text.

All word processors mark up the typed text so that it is displayed properly, but they usually save text in binary format so that it is difficult to see what is going on just by looking at the file.

One still-used method that is easier to understand is RTF (Rich Text Format). This marks up text so that different word processors can display the text properly. It only covers some basic formatting so most of the sophisticated features of modern word processors cannot adequately be covered by a single simple system.

Here is a simple demonstration of RTF. The following was typed and formatted:

Here is some text with RTF tags to indicate **bold**, *italic*, and <u>underlined</u> text in different sizes.

```
Here is some text with RTF tags to indicate }{\b\ab\
rtlch \ltrch\loch

bold}{\b0\ab0\rtlch \ltrch\loch

, }{\i\b0\ai\ab0\rtlch \ltrch\loch

italic}{\i0\b0\ai0\ab0\rtlch \ltrch\loch

, and underlined text}{\i0\ulnone\ulc0\b0\ai0\ab0\rtlch \
ltrch\loch

in different }{\i0\ulnone\ulc0\b0\afs36\ai0\ab0\rtlch \
ltrch\loch\fs36

sizes}{\i0\ulnone\ulc0\b0\ai0\ab0\rtlch \ltrch\loch

.}

\par }
```

If you look hard enough you can see the original text surrounded by all the mark-up indicators, but it is not exactly easy to understand for a human reader.

Embedded codes are added to most word-processed documents and this is why you cannot write computer programs with a word processor, unless you save as plain text.

Web authoring tools

Writing HTML code is often most easily done by using a web authoring tool such as Dreamweaver® or some other example. This provides a WYSIWYG environment for designing web pages and generates appropriate HTML code automatically.

Most such tools have a split-screen mode where you can make changes in the design screen or in the underlying HTML and editing either will change both. Many common actions such as inserting hyperlinks are available from a menu.

Figure 17.2 A web authoring application in split-screen mode

Many web developers want tighter control over what HTML code is produced and they might not like all of the code produced by the authoring tool. Using an ordinary text editor can often be the most effective way to produce exactly the effects you want.

But the construction of web pages can still be laborious. If you want total control over styles, it can be extremely difficult to get a consistent look to a site if you have to adjust each part of each page manually. You would have to remember to embed font and colour instructions everywhere you want to make a change. Thankfully, there is a much better way to style your web page.

CSS

The invention of CSS (Cascading Style Sheets) has made the production of consistent and attractive web pages a lot easier. CSS is a way of assigning formatting attributes to web page elements from outside the HTML, for example, you can say that all <h1> headings will be a certain font, colour, weight and size. These decisions, plus many more, such as the position of elements, are saved externally to the HTML code in a CSS file, which is then referenced from within the HTML page. If you want to change settings, you can just change it once in the CSS and it will be reflected in all the associated web pages.

There are many advantages in separating the format from the content of a web page. Among them are:

- much simpler and more readable HTML code – this also has an impact on development time
- greater consistency to websites
- easier conversion from one scheme to another – this can be important when developing a website for different platforms such as PCs, tablets and phones.

Example

An example of a CSS file in action

The HTML contains a reference to an external CSS file. The CSS file in this case is called cssexample1.css.

```
<html>
<head>
<link rel="stylesheet" type="text/css"
href="cssexample1.css">
<meta content="text/html;
charset=ISO-8859-1"
http-equiv="content-type">
<title>index</title>
</head>
```

The CSS file looks like this:

```
body {
  text-align: center;
  background-color: #33FF33;
}
#page-wrap {
  text-align: left;
  width: 800px;
  margin: 0 auto;
}
h1 {
    color: red;
}
p {
    font-family: "Times New Roman";
    font-size: 20px;
}
```

The background colour has been set to #33FF33, which is **hexadecimal** code for a rather garish green.

Any text associated with the <h1> tag gets the colour 'red'. Many common colours can be accessed by name, rather than having to look up the hex code.

The whole page is centred with the page-wrap property.

The font of the web page has been designated as whatever the browser can render as close as possible to Times New Roman.

Here is the result:

How to talk to cats

This tutorial will have you speaking cat language in super quick time.

Figure 17.3 Web page

JavaScript®

Key term

Scripting language An interpreted programming language that is designed to work inside some run-time environments, rather than generating object code that can be run directly from the operating system.
Examples of scripting languages include JavaScript, which runs inside a browser, and the shells of operating systems such as BASH.

If we define our web pages using HTML and determine the layout qualities with CSS, we use JavaScript to control their behaviour.

JavaScript is the commonest way to program interactivity and dynamics into a web page. It is an interpreted **scripting language** that runs in browsers. It has a long history, originally being developed to add functionality to web pages displayed in the early Netscape Navigator web browser.

It should be noted that despite the name, JavaScript has nothing to do with the Java programming language except that it has a few programming constructs that are similar.

JavaScript is particularly popular as a client-side scripting language. That means it is run locally on the user's computer rather than remotely on the website's server. This transfers some of the processing load away from the server, with related performance benefits.

As with most scripting languages, JavaScript is a language that uses **dynamic typing**.

Uses of JavaScript

JavaScript is a versatile and fully functional scripting language that can add a great variety of features to a web page. Some examples are:

- animating page elements (resizing and moving them)
- loading new page content
- validating web forms prior to the data being sent to the server.

Scripts can also detect the user's actions and send details to remote logging sites. This allows pages to be personalised and suitable advertising to be sent.

Search engines

With billions of web pages and more appearing all the time, finding what you want is an impossible task for anyone to do manually. So, software systems have been developed to find what users want as quickly as possible. These systems are the well-known search engines. There are many available, although Google™ has dominated for several years.

Search engines build up indexes of websites that can be searched quickly by various search **algorithms**. The early engines required site owners to notify the search engine sites but later various robots, some known as *spiders*, searched for sites by 'crawling' over websites and indexing the words found there. Webcrawler® was the first well-known example of this.

All search engines now search the internet for various keywords. They then index these with links to where they are found. This index is made available to users. Some engines can cope with mis-spellings and provide searches in various languages. As well as the visible words on a web page, search engines also make use of meta tags – the extra information that web designers add, but do not display, to make it more likely that their pages will be found by the search engines in response to queries from the most likely users.

Extra info

Meta tags

```
<!DOCTYPE html>
<html>
    <head>
<title>A Level Computer Science</title>
<meta name="keywords" content="OCR, A Level,
examinations">
<meta name="keywords" content="HTML, CSS, XML, XHTML,
JavaScript">
<meta name="author" content="Hodder">
    </head>
    <body>
    </body>
</html>
```

A Level only

Pagerank algorithm™

With the web ever expanding, search engines need to find the quickest way to locate what their users want, but also they need to find what is most relevant. Often, the users don't know which are the most relevant sites for their needs. They might phrase their search terms in a clumsy or inaccurate way. They may make spelling mistakes.

If a search engine can cope with the huge number of possible targets and narrow them down to what is most likely to be useful, it will save the users a lot of time and frustration and they will be likely to use that search engine again.

Search engine owners have long found various ways to 'monetise' their systems, so it makes financial sense for them to offer the most effective service possible. The more relevant the search results are to the user's enquiry, the better pleased the user will be and the more money the search engine provider will make.

Extra info

How search engines make money

When a user searches for a particular term or expression, the search engine will also look up related advertisers and display adverts for these businesses alongside the main search engine results. If a user clicks on one of these sponsored links, the advertiser pays a small sum to the search engine owner. This is called 'pay per click' and it clearly benefits the search engine owner if the user is pleased with the search results and comes back to use the same search engine again.

Figure 17.4 Search engine results

One of the most successful ways that search engines have used to produce meaningful results is the Pagerank algorithm. This has been a particularly successful process applied by Google to its web searches. This doesn't just look at content to assess relevance; it ranks possible web pages according to external links. So at its most basic, if a web page has many links into it from other pages, these are considered 'votes' and it is deemed to be 'popular' and more worthy of consideration.

However, unlike in a human election, not all votes are equal. Some votes are deemed to be more significant than others and this is based on the number of links into *them*. So the process can be applied recursively to get a fairly good estimation of how important a page is.

The original Pagerank algorithm was described by Lawrence Page and Sergey Brin in several publications. It is given by:

$$PR(A) = (1-d) + d (PR(T1)/C(T1) + \ldots + PR(Tn)/C(Tn))$$

where

- PR(A) is the Pagerank of page A
- PR(Ti) is the Pagerank of pages Ti that link to page A
- C(Ti) is the number of outbound links on page Ti
- d is a damping factor that can be set between 0 and 1.

The damping factor reduces the ranking on the assumption that a typical surfer will eventually give up clicking and represents the probability that the surfer will continue. It is generally taken as about .85.

Each time the Google spider crawls the web, it recalculates the page ranks.

The original Pagerank algorithm is prone to abuse by those who set up 'link farms' to artificially increase the number of links to favoured pages. Google continues to alter its algorithms to circumvent such problems.

Question

Most internet users turn to Google to search for resources. To what extent is this a good strategy?

Key points

Search engines:
- are systems that locate resources on the web
- analyse the text on web pages
- make an index
- make use of meta tags
- 'crawl' over pages looking for content information
- use algorithms such as Pagerank to attempt to grade pages for usefulness.

Client- and server-side processing

Most web interactions involve two principal connected entities: the surfer or client and the web server that holds the resources that the client wants. These resources may be static data collections, or often they involve multiple interactions as, for example, when a customer is making a booking of some sort.

Decisions have to be made about what processing occurs where. The basic issues are to do with performance and security. We have seen that it is perfectly possible to carry out all sorts of processes on the client's computer by writing code in a scripting language such as JavaScript. Alternatively, code can be written to do processing on the web server.

Arguments in favour of client-side processing

Client-side processing reduces the load on the server. The server may be busy handling multiple transactions and if some of the processing can be offloaded to the client machines, this will speed up the server activity.

The user will have a better experience if data input is checked there and then without the delays for immediate sending of each item to the server for checking.

Client-side processing also reduces the amount of web traffic. If, for example, input data can be validated by a client-side script, this will reduce the likelihood of erroneous data being sent for the server to validate and process.

Key points

- Data processing can be carried out either by the client machines or by the server.
- When designing web services, there are issues about this that need to be considered, including speed of processing and security.

Arguments in favour of server-side processing

Data validated by a client-side script may still have problems with it. It is still necessary to have further validation at the server end.

Server-side processing is essential for actually querying a database. It is vital to keep the data owned by an organisation secure, if not secret, and so any processing of that data must take place under the control of the organisation. So SQL processes will largely have to be located at the server end. No sensitive data should be sent to the client where it could be intercepted and manipulated.

Compression

Data transmission speeds have increased enormously over the years, so sending large quantities of data is becoming less of an issue. We are all used to streaming films and TV programmes over the net, and sending large image and sound files seems less of a problem than it used to be. However, as expectations rise, it remains important that large quantities of data are still reduced as much as possible to provide the best user experience possible.

Reducing the size of data either in storage or in transmission requires various compression techniques. There are many to choose from and decisions are based on:

- the expected bandwidth of a connection
- the expected processing power of the users' computers
- expectations of file storage requirements.

Data compression involves trade-offs. These involve the quality of the final result and the amount of processing power that is needed to compress and decompress.

Data compression involves one of two strategies to reduce file sizes: *lossy* or *lossless*.

Lossy

Lossy compression is a way of reducing a file's size by removing some of the data. As it is removed, the original cannot be recreated from the compressed file. Considerable savings can be made with lossy methods but the issue of quality has to be recognised. Lossy methods are typically used for image and sound files, where the consideration is mostly of human perception, which can be more fault tolerant than more mechanistic scenarios such as a computer program.

The idea is to remove the data that is the least important, for example a photographic image from a digital camera may be 6Mb or more to allow high-quality enlargements to be made. If that photo is uploaded to a file-sharing website, it would have to be compressed to economise on storage space as well as to make the upload time reasonable. This relies on the assumption that reduced quality in terms of reduced **resolution** or colour range will not be noticeable on a small screen representation of the image.

JPEG images are compressed using lossy algorithms. An extreme example is shown opposite.

Figure 17.5 A JPEG image of 1.25Mb

Figure 17.6 A compressed version of the same image occupying 60Kb

Sound files can be compressed by lossy methods. Again, a high-resolution original can be sampled to produce a subset of the original data. The removed data can be set to be, for example, the highest frequencies, where human perception is less acute.

Typically, videos can be compressed a great deal before the loss in quality becomes unacceptable. 100:1 is common. Audio files are often reduced by a factor of 10:1. Photographs are also reduced by about 10:1, although it becomes somewhat easier to detect the lack of quality if they are scrutinised in enough detail.

Common lossy file formats include JPEG, MPEG and MP3.

Question

Suppose you submit a 6Mb photograph to be displayed on a photo-sharing site. Find out how much it is reduced by.

Lossless

Lossless compression reduces file sizes in such a way that no data is lost and the original file can be regenerated exactly. It makes use of redundant data, so that if a data item occurs multiple times, the item is stored once along with the number of repetitions. This can be achieved in various ways and illustrated with a simple textual example.

Dictionary coding

Consider this dictionary:

1	if
2	you
3	are
4	not
5	fired
6	with
7	enthusiasm
8	will
9	be

A message can be constructed by supplying the dictionary and the words used; that is:

1234567289567

This results in a saving but the original message can be reconstructed exactly. The best savings are achieved in long text documents. Remember that the dictionary has to be stored along with the message.

This is a very simple illustration of one way of storing compressed data without loss. Various ways exist to generate dictionaries as a file is parsed but the best-known is the LZW (Lempel–Ziv–Welch) algorithm. The dictionary is updated as the file is examined. When a sequence is found that is already in the dictionary, the next character is examined and if this is new, this longer sequence gets added to the dictionary.

Well-known compression formats that use dictionary coding are ZIP, GIF and PNG.

Run-length encoding

A Level only

Another simple approach can be applied to other types of data such as pixels in an image. If there is a sequence of, say, 100 blue pixels in an image, this can be encoded as B100. The image can be reproduced exactly from this data. This process works best if there are long sequences of the same data. The technique is found in TIFF and BMP files.

Lossless compression is rarely as effective as lossy in reducing file sizes but some situations require a faithful reconstruction of the source data, such as a computer program, where any loss at all will damage or destroy its functionality.

Key points

- The usability of web services often requires compression.
- Compression is the reduction in size of files.
- Lossy compression can achieve big savings but it degrades the quality of the data source, which might not matter.
- Lossless compression allows reconstruction of the original data source. It may increase the processing overheads significantly. Some situations must not lose any data.

Encryption

With the widespread dissemination of data across a public facility, there is always a danger of data falling into the wrong hands.

In addition, most people conduct more and more of their lives online and there will always be activities and messages that they do not want to leak into the public domain. Having said that, many people have adapted to a means of communication that will always carry some risk of eavesdropping and adjust their online behaviour in the expectation that interactions may carry some risk.

Some activities require a much higher level of security than others, notably:

- online banking and payments
- communications involving trade secrets or other sensitive or personal data.

Where security is of the greatest importance, various powerful methods of **encryption** are used. Indeed, encryption of some sort occurs at many points in internet transactions and interactions.

People have used encryption for as long as there has been written communication. Many simple forms have existed from time immemorial, such as the Caesar cipher where each letter is replaced by another some fixed distance along the alphabet. A displacement of four, for example, would transform the alphabet as follows:

```
plaintext letter        ABCDEFGHIJKLMNOPQRSTUVWXYZ
cipher letter           EFGHIJKLMNOPQRSTUVWXYZABCD
```

For someone to decrypt a message written in a Caesar cipher, it is necessary for that person to know the displacement. This is the *key* to the cipher. In this case it is a simple displacement, but in more sophisticated encryption methods keys are still needed. Obviously, a simple method like this would not be very hard to crack and the objective of more effective methods is to make decryption more or less impossible to those without the keys.

Keys can be applied in various ways and can be numbers, words or random strings. One way or another, they provide the information needed to encrypt and decrypt a plaintext message.

There are two major types of approach to encryption: symmetric and asymmetric.

Symmetric

In symmetric encryption, the key used to encrypt the message is also used to decrypt it. This obviously requires the sender and the recipient to know the key and keep it secret. Many different methods are in use to bring about the encryption process, for example some encryption algorithms encrypt the data one byte at a time, whereas others take a whole block of data and pad it to make units of a fixed size. The key may be used multiple times or it may be generated for each transaction.

There is always a danger of a successful attack on symmetric encryption messages, either by intercepting the key or duplicating the key-production process. This is why most critical applications use more secure methods. Asymmetric methods are generally much safer.

Asymmetric

This requires the use of two different keys. The whole point is that the key used to encrypt the message is not the same as the key needed to decrypt it. One of the keys is publicly known and used to encrypt the message. This can be used by anyone who wants to send an encrypted message.

A publicly known algorithm is used to encrypt the message. But the algorithm is implemented using the second, compatible but secret, private key. To decrypt the message, the known public algorithm is applied with the secret private key. This dual key asymmetric approach requires more processing power than symmetric key encryption but it is much safer.

The keys used are typically large random numbers that are unlikely to be guessed.

Hashing algorithms

We saw in Chapters 13 and 15 how hashing is a way of transforming a data item into something different. Hashing therefore can provide a quick way to generate disk addresses for storing data on a random access device.

Hash functions can also be used to store and check passwords. This is commonly used for network logins and online transactions. The idea is that it is easy to transform a plaintext message or password into something else, but very difficult to regenerate the plaintext from the hash value. Such a one-way encryption is useful for checking values such as passwords, but no use for sending messages that need to be decrypted.

When a user chooses a password, it is subjected to a hashing algorithm that transforms it into a fixed-length hash value. This, not the password, is stored on the server. The next time the user logs in, the password is transformed again by the hashing algorithm and the result of this process is looked up in the database to see if it matches the stored hash value. If it does, access is granted.

The hashing algorithm is such that the hash value cannot be used to regenerate the password, so if the database of passwords is accessed unlawfully, they should be of no use to the hacker. But in fact, they could be! There are techniques available that allow the cracking of hashed passwords, such as a brute force attack.

Brute force attack is a method of hacking where every possible combination of characters is tried one by one. Brute force attack is computationally expensive. Password encryption is designed to make it too much trouble to spend effort on cracking a password this way.

For hackers then, it becomes a matter of deciding whether the effort is worth the potential reward. For high-value targets it might be, and there are other techniques available too, where common passwords are stored in a dictionary and tried out along with hashing algorithms.

To make hashed passwords more secure, a technique can be used that is called *adding salt*. The salt is a random string appended to a new password before hashing. This makes the hash value different even for the same password. The salt is stored alongside the hash value. To check the password, the salt is used to decrypt the hash.

Practice questions

1. Distinguish between the internet and the world wide web.
2. Discuss the importance of TCP/IP in the development of the web.
3. Explain how packet switching affects the reliability of communications on the internet.
4. Describe the contents of a typical data packet.
5. Explain the principles behind Google's Pagerank algorithm.
6. Consider a camera image of 6Mb and a novel delivered as an ebook. Explain what forms of compression would be suitable in each case.

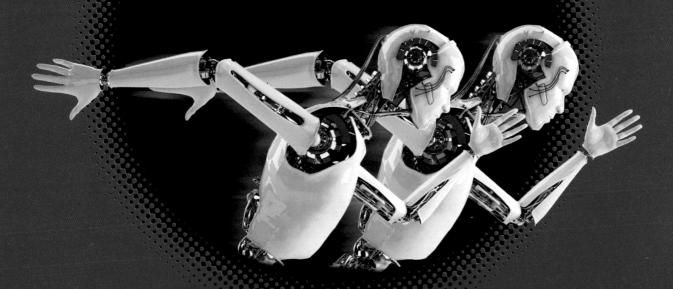

Topic 4 Legal, ethical, moral and social issues

Chapter 18

Computer law and ethical, moral and social issues

Introduction

The widespread use of computer technology in all aspects of daily life has brought many benefits for the individual and society. But alongside these benefits, the widespread use of computer technology has also generated several problems, from computer crime to issues with the freedom of the individual.

That we depend on computer technology in so many aspects of our daily lives brings a reliance on technology that makes us all more vulnerable to these problems.

Legal issues

Computer crime consists of a wide range of existing and new criminal activities, including unauthorised access to data and computer systems for the purpose of theft or damage, identity theft, software piracy, fraud and harassment such as trolling. Many of these activities are criminalised by acts of parliament.

Computer Misuse Act (1990)

Under the provisions of the Computer Misuse Act (1990) it is a criminal offence to:

- make any unauthorised access to computer material:
  - □ ... with intent to commit or facilitate commission of further offences (for example blackmail)
  - □ ... with intent to impair, or with recklessness as to impairing, operation of computer, etc. (for example distributing viruses)

This is the law aimed at unauthorised access, commonly called *hackers*, though the term 'hackers' refers correctly not only to those who exploit weakness in a system, but the hobbyist who customises systems and the programmer who explores and modifies open source systems quite legally.

Features that are generally deployed to minimise the threat from unauthorised access include digital signatures or certificates that use encrypted messages that identify the sender of the data confirming they are who they claim to be. SSL (secure socket layer) is a protocol that enables an encrypted link between computer systems to ensure the security of a transaction.

Firewalls are computer applications that sit between the system and external access to prevent certain types of data or users accessing the system. A firewall may, for example, limit access to external users to a very small part of the system, or simply allow no access at all to external users.

Firewalls are the principal defence against Denial of Service (DoS) or Distributed Denial of Service (DDoS) attacks. DoS attacks are aimed at individuals and organisations to make a service unavailable to the users of that service.

One typical approach is to saturate the service with requests from many users or bots, making the response times unacceptably slow. The purpose of these attacks varies, for example to disrupt a service to make a political point or simply to blackmail the service owner. Other basic features such as user IDs and access rights to files limit the ability of hackers to make unauthorised access to data.

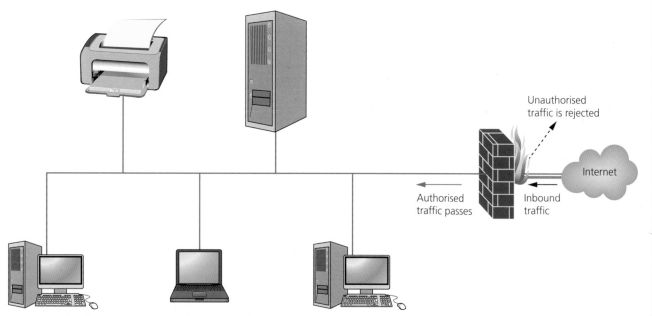

Figure 18.1 A firewall allows authorised traffic but denies access to unauthorised traffic from outside the system

Data Protection Act (1998)

The purpose of the Data Protection Act (1998) is to control the storage of data about individuals. It makes a data controller responsible for the accuracy and security of data kept by an organisation about the data subject.

There are eight provisions in the Data Protection Act (1998):

1. Data should be processed fairly and lawfully (that is, the data must not be obtained by deception and the purpose of the data being collected should be revealed to the data subject).
2. Data should only be used for the purpose specified to the Data Protection Agency and should not be disclosed to other parties without the necessary permission.
3. Data should be relevant and not excessive.
4. Data should be accurate and up to date.
5. Data should only be kept for as long as necessary.
6. Individuals have the right to access data kept about them and should be able to check and update the data if necessary.
7. Security must be in place to prevent unauthorised access to the data.
8. Data may not be transferred outside the EU unless the country has adequate data-protection legislation.

Key points

- The individual about whom the data is stored is called the *data subject*.
- The person who is responsible for implementing the provisions of the PA within an organisation is called the data *controller*.

237

One of the provisions is to not transfer data to countries without adequate legislation; it is worth noting that most countries have similar data protection provisions.

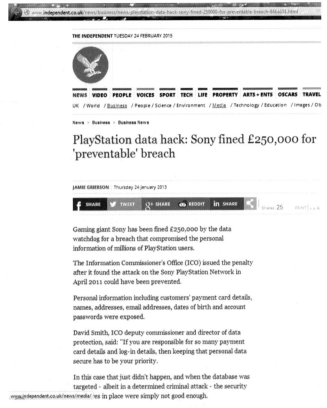

Figure 18.2 Organisations can be prosecuted under the DPA for breaches of data security

There are some exemptions to the Data Protection Act (1998) principles:

■ National security: any data processed in relation to national security is exempt from the Act.
■ Crime and taxation: any data used to detect or prevent crime or to assist with the collection of taxes is exempt from the Act.
■ Domestic purposes: any data used solely for individual, family or household use is exempt from the Act.

Copyright Designs and Patents Act (CDPA) (1988)

The Copyright Designs and Patents Act (1988) protects the intellectual property of an individual or organisation. Under the Act, it is illegal to copy, modify or distribute software or other intellectual property without the relevant permission. Many sites on the internet offer free downloads of copyright software and individuals will often share software and other material through peer-to-peer networking sites. This prevents the intellectual copyright holder earning an income from their original work.

This Act also covers video and audio where peer-to-peer streaming has had a significant impact on the income of the copyright owners.

Most commercial software will come with a licence agreement specifying how the purchaser may use the product. In most cases, a licence key will be required to access the software to prevent unauthorised copying and distribution.

Regulation of Investigatory Powers Act (RIPA) (2000)

The increase in criminal and terrorist activities on the internet prompted an act of parliament providing certain authorities the right to intercept communications. It provides certain public bodies, such as the police and other government departments, with the right to:

- demand ISPs provide access to a customer's communications
- allow mass surveillance of communications
- demand ISPs fit equipment to facilitate surveillance
- demand access be granted to protected information
- allow monitoring of an individual's internet activities
- prevent the existence of such interception activities being revealed in court.

The Act is intended to allow suitable authorities access to communications to prevent criminal or terrorist activities. There was some concern about the range of public bodies with powers under this Act when it was first introduced.

There are examples of this Act being used for reasons other than monitoring criminal or terrorist activities, including monitoring cockle fishermen, fly tippers and a family to determine if they lived in the catchment area of a school.

Figure 18.3 Media reports of RIPA against journalists

Communications Act (2003)

The Communications Act (2003) has several provisions that impact on the use of computer technology. Among the provisions in the Act are that it is illegal to:

- access an internet connection with no intention to pay for the service, making it a crime to piggyback onto other people's WiFi without their permission
- send offensive communications using any communications system, including social media; in 2012 a young man was jailed for 12 weeks for posting offensive messages and comments about the April Jones murder and the disappearance of Madeleine McCann.

These provisions in the Act have to tread the fine line between freedom of speech and those acts that are grossly offensive or indecent. It is important the Act is not used to prosecute those who express unpopular opinions or communications that are considered distasteful.

The Act is in place to deal with communications that contain credible threats of violence, such as trolling or stalking, or communications that contain material grossly offensive to identified individuals and intended to cause harm. Those who repeat the messages are also subject to the provisions of this Act, and re-tweeting an offensive message may be illegal.

Equality Act (2010)

The Equality Act (2010) identifies certain protected characteristics and makes it illegal to discriminate against anyone with those characteristics, either by **direct discrimination**, or by **indirect discrimination**.

This Act has implications for those who provide web-based services. Section 29(1) of the 2010 Act says that:

A person … concerned with the provision of a service to the public or a section of the public (for payment or not) must not discriminate against a person requiring the service by not providing the person with the service.

There are various features available to make websites more accessible.

- Screen readers for the blind user are applications that sift through the HTML to identify the content and read this out to the user.
- For those with partial or poor sight, options for larger text or a screen magnifier may be appropriate.
- The choice of font is also an important issue; sites using very blocky or cursive fonts may be very difficult to read for those with visual disabilities.
- Tagging images with an audio description for those who are partially sighted or blind provides some access to the graphical content of a website.
- Choosing contrasting colours for text and background will also make the text stand out more effectively for those who are partially sighted or colour blind; avoiding those colour combinations that are most difficult for colour-blind people will improve accessibility.
- While deaf users have the ability to access websites in much the same way as those with normal hearing, any soundtracks should be provided as subtitles or as a transcript.

Many users also have physical disabilities that make accessing computer systems more complex and there is a range of devices available to provide such accessibility.

Key terms

Direct discrimination Treating someone with a protected characteristic less favourably than others.

Indirect discrimination Putting rules or arrangements in place that apply to everyone, but that put someone with a protected characteristic at an unfair disadvantage.

Question

Research the range of devices available to aid accessibility to computer systems for those with physical disabilities.

Moral and ethical issues

The widespread use of computer technology brings many opportunities but there are associated risks that need to be considered.

Computers in the workplace

Computer technology in various forms plays a major part in the workplace. Robots building cars is perhaps one of the most obvious, but computer technology is widespread in most organisations.

The use of computer technology has changed the skillset required by the modern workforce. Instead of requiring a welder to make a car, the manufacturer requires a technician to maintain the robot that welds the car. Car engines are monitored by engine management systems that report problems that can be diagnosed, and potentially fixed, by computer systems plugged into the vehicle control system.

Traditional High Street workers such as bank clerks and shop assistants are no longer in demand: these roles are now performed by online systems. Online banking allows customers to access their accounts 24 hours a day, seven days a week, move money instantly and pay for goods and services electronically.

These changes to the way we access services have altered the job market quite significantly and people with IT skills are increasingly in demand for the online service industry.

Figure 18.4 Robots on a car production line

Computers used for automated decision-making

The principal of computers analysing data to make decisions is what automated decision-making is all about. It is best deployed in situations where decisions have to be made frequently and rapidly based on electronic evidence. Stock market trading, also known as **algorithmic** or automated trading, was an early example of computers making decisions about buying and selling stocks based on various parameters.

Getting these algorithms right is important given the speed and scale of automated trading. (It is estimated that in 2008, automated trading accounted for 80 per cent of the transactions in the American and

European markets.) Many commentators believe the 2010 'flash crash' was a direct result of automated trading triggering a wave of selling.

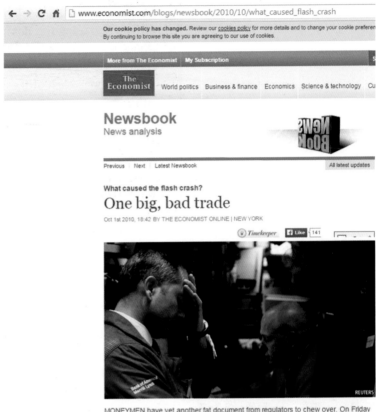

Figure 18.5 The 2010 flash crash

There is a wide range of situations where automated decision making is used effectively, for example:

- electrical power distribution requires rapid responses to changing circumstances to avoid disastrous consequences
- an emergency response to major incidents can be helped to deploy resources quickly and effectively
- plant automation, for example chemical plants or distribution centres
- airborne collision avoidance systems
- credit assessment in banks.

These areas and many more make effective use of automated decision making. The quality of the decision depends on several factors, including the accuracy of the data, the predictability of the situation and the quality of the algorithm. Unlike a human decision maker, the computer will apply the algorithm and make a decision based on the data. It will not necessarily question the decision made and consequently the accuracy of the data or correctness of the algorithm.

Figure 18.6 The driverless car uses automated decision making based on data collected by sensors and a 'driving' algorithm

Figure 18.7 'Computer says "No"'

Artificial intelligence

Devising software that behaves as if it were intelligent is a discipline within computer science. Examples of artificial intelligence have been around for some time and early examples include chess-playing programs that are able to analyse millions of possible alternative scenarios to make a move.

Many tasks we find straightforward to do require significant processing power, for example relatively simple things like recognising objects or deciding if a station platform is full or not require complex algorithms for a computer program to complete.

Much of the work in this area is based on neural networks, which emulate the structure of the human brain and can 'learn' from experience. These systems are able to apply what they have learned when the data is changed.

Expert systems or intelligent knowledge-based systems are examples of artificial intelligence and can perform at a level similar to human experts in certain areas. There are numerous examples where AI is used on a daily basis, including:

- credit-card checking that looks for unusual patterns in credit-card use to identify potential fraudulent use
- speech recognition systems that identify keywords and patterns in the spoken word to interpret the meaning
- medical diagnosis systems used to self-diagnose illness from the symptoms and to support medical staff in making diagnoses
- control systems that monitor, interpret and predict events to provide real-time process control, for example chemical plants.

All of these systems have a similar structure:

- a knowledge base that holds the collected expert knowledge, usually as 'IF THEN' rules
- an inference engine that searches the knowledge base to find potential responses to questions
- an interface to connect with the user or to a system it is controlling.

An artificial intelligence system will use pattern recognition to determine the nature of objects or situations and compare this with stored information about similar objects and situations.

www.newscientist.com/article/mg22329764.000-the-ai-boss-that-deploys-hong-kongs-subway-engineers.html#.VI

NewScientist Tech

search New Scientist   Go»   Lo

Home   News   In-Depth Articles   Opinion   CultureLab   Galleries   Topic Guides   Last Word   Subscribe   Dating

SPACE   TECH   ENVIRONMENT   HEALTH   LIFE   PHYSICS&MATH   SCIENCE IN SOCIETY

Home | Tech | News

The AI boss that deploys Hong Kong's subway engineers

› 04 July 2014 by Hal Hodson
› Magazine issue 2976. Subscribe and save

An algorithm schedules and manages the nightly engineering work on one of the world's best subway systems – and does it more efficiently than any human could

JUST after midnight, the last subway car slips into its sidings in Hong Kong and an army of engineers goes to work. In a typical week, 10,000 people carry out 2600 engineering works across the system – from grinding rough rails smooth and replacing tracks to checking for damage. People might do the work, but they don't choose what needs doing. Instead, each task is scheduled and managed by artificial intelligence.

Hong Kong has one of the world's best subway systems. It has a 99.9 per cent on time record – far better than London Underground or New York's subway. It is owned and run by MTR Corporation, which also runs systems in Stockholm, Melbourne, London and Beijing. MTR is now planning to roll out its AI overseer to the other networks it manages.

"It will probably be Beijing first," says Andy Chun of Hong Kong's City University, who designed the AI system and worked with MTR to build it into their systems. "Before AI, they would have a planning session with experts from five or six different areas," he says. "It was pretty chaotic. Now they just reveal the plan on a huge screen."

Who's in charge? *(Image: Bloomberg/Getty)*

———————— ADVERTISEMENT ————————

Figure 18.8 An artificial intelligence application is used to manage the repairs on the Hong Kong subway system

Intelligence is more than pattern recognition; there are other aspects that define what we know as intelligence, including creativity and social intelligence and our ability to interact with other humans. One interpretation of the Turing test is 'can a computer fool an interrogator into thinking it is a human being?'

One early example of a program that appeared to have some characteristics of intelligence was *Eliza*. Eliza is a program that responds to typed comments by identifying keywords and, using a rule, responds with a phrase that incorporates the user's input. If no keyword is found, it makes a generic, if sometimes odd, response.

This concept has developed into the chatbot. Sophisticated chatbots are sometimes used as malware to fool people into parting with personal information or to lead them to malicious websites.

It is worth mentioning the philosophical debate about the development of effective artificial intelligences. If such an intelligence were strong enough to have a consciousness, would the program have rights? Would it be right to terminate such a program? Should the programmer be accountable for the actions of such a program?

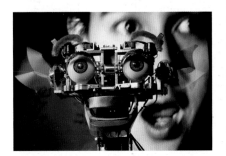

Figure 18.9 Kismet is a robot with rudimentary social skills

A.L.I.C.E. and judge

You said: Well nice chatting with you, bye
A.L.I.C.E.: Yes. I enjoyed our conversation, judge.. Until next time.

You say: | | Say |

Create your own chat bot.

Conversation Log:

p
judge: Hi Alice are you a chatbot
ALICE: Hi there!. Yeah, My species is Pandorabot.
judge: Do you pass the Turing test?
ALICE: The Loebner Prize is an annual Turing Test sponsored by New York philanthropist Hugh Loebner. Dr. Wallace and ALICE won it in 2000. The ALICE program was ranked "most human computer" by the panel of judges.
judge: I can believe that
ALICE: Oh you can, can you?
judge: Have you seen the film, the imitation game?
ALICE: No I have not seen it. What's it like?
judge: Its all about Alan Turing
ALICE: Wow it sounds really interesting, judge.
judge: He mentions the test for artificial intelligence in the film
ALICE: I get it. he mentions the test for artificial intelligence in the film.
judge: Its a good film even though some of the details are not quite right
ALICE: If it is, then I'll be very surprised.
judge: Well nice chatting with you, bye
ALICE: Yes. I enjoyed our conversation, judge.. Until next time.

Figure 18.10 ALICE chatbot responding to strange inputs

Environmental effects of computer technology

Computers are made from some pretty toxic material that needs to be handled with great care when disposing of old equipment, including airborne dioxins, polychlorinated biphenyls (PCBs), cadmium, chromium, radioactive isotopes and mercury.

In many parts of the world, computers are considered hazardous waste, but they are often shipped off to countries with lower environmental standards. In some cases, children pick over the waste to extract metals that can be recycled and sold, thus exposing them to significant danger.

Figure 18.11 Picking over discarded computer equipment to extract metals

245

While most modern computers consume low levels of electricity, they are often left running permanently and it is estimated that data centres used more energy than the aviation industry in 2014. Adding in the energy costs associated with extraction of the raw materials, manufacture of the technology and the air conditioning associated with large installations, computer technology becomes a major consumer of energy.

Censorship and the internet

Figure 18.12 Large data centres use significant amounts of energy

Internet censorship is the deliberate suppression of what can be accessed or published on the internet. Governments or organisations may impose these restrictions for various reasons: to limit access to socially unacceptable material or to limit access to what they regard as dangerous information.

The extent to which the internet is censored varies from country to country, depending on the political and social situations in those countries. While the reasons for censorship are similar to those for other media, the technical difficulties associated with censoring the internet are far more complex and usually carried out centrally or by internet service providers at the request of or under instruction from governments.

Some local censorship is applied by individual organisations such as libraries, businesses and schools to meet their own guidelines on acceptable internet content.

Total control of information through censorship is very difficult to apply unless there is a single central censor, and many will still share information through underlying data transfer networks including file-sharing networks, for example the *deep web* that cannot be found by the internet.

Access to websites is filtered by reference to blacklists that are set up with unacceptable sites and through dynamic examination of the website for unacceptable content. The main categories being blocked by ISPs in the UK include extremist politics, extreme pornography and sites that infringe copyright.

There is some debate about the use of any internet censorship, but most see the need to censor extreme content. The real debate is about where to draw the line between protecting the public and infringing the right to free speech and access to information.

Many students will have been asked by their English department to prepare a talk or essay on contentious issues only to find the local filtering does not allow access to relevant material on the internet. In some parts of the world the internet is strictly monitored or censored to limit access to the sharing of political ideas.

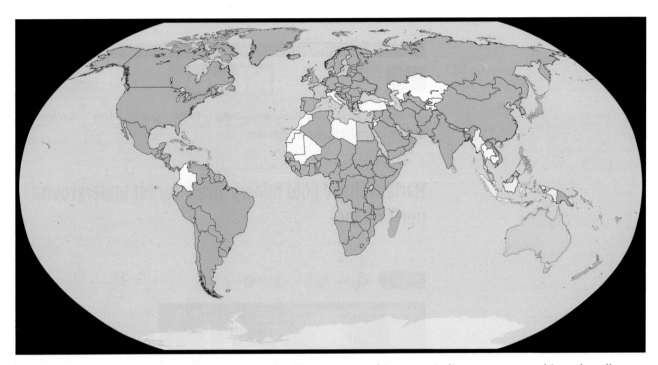

Figure 18.13 Internet censorship by region: pink indicates censorship; green indicates no censorship; pale yellow indicates some censorship; and orange indicates a changing situation

Computer technology used to monitor behaviour

Figure 18.14 Offenders' movements can be monitored through tagging devices attached to their ankles

We are all aware of the many CCTV cameras dotted around our towns and cities used to monitor behaviour. While this, to some, represents a Big Brother approach to society, many feel the added security and ability to use the captured images to solve crime worth the intrusion. Criminal activity can frequently end up with offenders wearing electronic tags that can identify when they are not in the agreed location at the agreed time or, with GPS, identify their location at any time.

People who have had problems with alcohol use can be monitored by a device worn on the ankle that periodically fires a jet of air onto the skin, vaporising and measuring any alcohol found there.

Young drivers can reduce their cost of insurance by opting for black box insurance, which monitors how and when they drive to calculate premiums and reward safe driving through a monitoring device installed in their car.

There are cases where people have been tracked from their mobile phone signal and the evidence used in court.

Increasingly, people are being monitored at work with logging systems monitoring online activity, including contributions to social media. It is reasonable for companies to monitor work rates and work quality for employees. It may be considered reasonable for organisations to limit access to social media, but is it reasonable for organisations to monitor what is posted to social media sites by employees?

There is certainly a case for monitoring what is posted from the organisation's computer systems, since unacceptable posts, such as trolling or racist or sexist comments can be traced back to the organisation and reflect upon them. Is it reasonable for organisations to demand access to and monitor social network pages where the content is posted from private computers?

Figure 18.15 Fifteen miners were fired for posting a video on social media showing a breach of behaviour policy at work

Computer technology used to analyse personal information

Many organisations collect data about individuals and this is often shared with partner organisations. Whenever we check in on social media, the location and time is logged; whenever we take a picture with our phone's camera the location and time are logged. Much of this data is stored and is accessible to various organisations. Note how a search for a product on online markets leads to recommendations for similar products and promotional contacts from other organisations.

Data is a valuable commodity and there are analysts sifting through our personal information looking for patterns and opportunities. Data mining is one of the most effective tools against organised crime and terrorism; data about individual activities including social media, financial transactions, travel, internet histories and shared contact details have provided valuable information in the fight against crime and terrorism.

Topic 4 Legal, ethical, moral and social issues

Data mining is an automated process that searches for patterns in large data sets to predict events. It is widely used in business, science, engineering and medicine.

In business it is used to identify patterns to inform strategic business decisions. The data can be used to predict future sales and hence stock requirements and effective and targeted marketing strategies to improve business profitability.

In science and engineering, analysis of human DNA sequences and matching this to medical information has led to the development of effective treatments for various conditions.

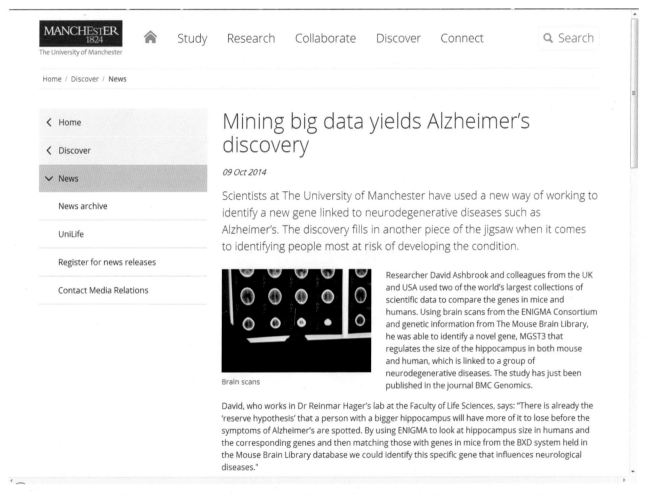

Figure 18.16 Research taking place at the University of Manchester: large scale data-mining can lead to new discoveries

Practice questions

1. At what point does internet censorship become a bar to an individual's right to access data?
2. To what extent is it acceptable for governments and organisations to access the data stored about an individual?
3. Discuss the environmental impact of computer technology.

Topic 5 Project

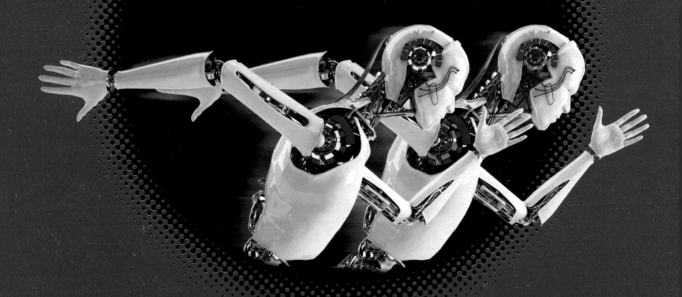

Chapter 19

Analysis

Introduction

Candidates for this unit are expected to apply the principles of **computational thinking** to analysing, designing, developing, testing and evaluating a program written in an appropriate high-level language. A number of languages are specified as suitable, each with access to a suitable GUI: Python, C (variants), Visual Basic, Delphi and Java. For most projects this list will provide a suitable language, for example when creating a mobile phone application Java (for Android phones) and Objective C (for iPhones) are covered by this list. If, however, you would like to program in a language not on the list, OCR have a consultancy service that will approve the use of other languages, providing they can be shown to be appropriate. Programming environments like Gamemaker and Scratch are, of course, unlikely to be appropriate for this unit.

Choice of project

Figure 19.1 Stakeholders

The choice of project is important. It will take several months of hard work to complete the work and this is much easier when there is an interest in the topic chosen for the project. Acquiring new programming skills in another language can be time consuming so it makes sense to select a project that can be completed using existing skills or existing skills that can be developed relatively easily.

The project must be coded, so avoid those that are based on using applications or that rely on the use of a drag and drop environment – these lack the necessary features to meet many of the criteria. When considering a project, carefully read through the assessment criteria to check that these can be met. There is no degree of difficulty criterion – the project assessment guidance takes care of this – and there are many clues to what is necessary in the descriptors, for example a simple linear program will fail to meet the criteria for modularity and there must be a clearly defined target audience: the stakeholders.

When choosing a project, make sure you have access to suitable stakeholders who can advise on the requirements. These can be representative of a persona, for example a chemistry simulation aimed at A Level chemistry students can be discussed with a teacher and fellow students taking A Level chemistry. An educational game aimed at primary-school students can be discussed with a primary school teacher or teacher with experience of the topic area and piloted and tested by younger students. The feedback from these stakeholders will be invaluable during the analysis, design, development, testing and evaluation of the product. While the computer game may seem immediately attractive, writing games involves a lot of repetitive coding and may not be the most exciting option. It is worth looking into scenarios such as simulations, models, visualisations and other novel areas for a project topic. Look far and wide for interesting and novel scenarios.

Analysis of the problem

Proper analysis of a problem is often overlooked by candidates eager to start coding their solutions, but careful analysis of a problem is the key to success when programming. A programmed solution to a problem is an abstraction of reality – obvious for those who choose to create simulations for chemistry or physics or biology, but true for the vast majority of project types. Devising an abstract model of the situation is the first stage in a successful project. You will need to identify a suitable problem and identify the features that make it amenable to a computational solution.

Programs are written to be used by someone – the stakeholder – and you need to identify who will use the program, explaining clearly what their needs are, why they will find the solution useful and why the solution is appropriate to their needs. Stakeholders may include people other than end users, for example a web-based project will need to consider the needs of the website owner, any staff employed by the website owner and the website users. Each of these has a stake in the product and each has different requirements for the product. All of these must be considered.

These stakeholders may be real people who you can talk to about their needs and requirements, or it may be a persona who typifies the target group. A persona is a profile for a typical user, which is used throughout the design and development stages to make sure the end-user needs are considered at each stage of the process. It is important to identify the intended end users and their needs and requirements before moving on to the next stage.

Some detailed research will be required to identify what is possible. It is essential you look at existing solutions to similar problems that may provide valuable insights into aspects of the problem and potential solutions. It is important the stakeholder is considered for this research; it would be of limited value to research programs aimed at adult users when considering educational games for primary-age children, as their needs, skills and requirements are significantly different.

Record Card

Name Sally   **Age**   32

Occupation: Works in advertising in a city-centre firm. She often has to visit business across the city to discuss their needs. She is married with one child, Simon, aged 6. Her husband is a teacher in a local secondary school.

Likes: Being organised and knowing what is in her schedule for the week ahead.
Dislikes: Being late and others being late for meetings. Disorganised and disjointed record-keeping.

Typical day: When she arrives at the office she collects her messages for the day and organises work for her weeklyschedule before contacting customers. She keeps a record of any visits and the mileage or transport costs on her mobile phone. She has a smart phone to keep track of her schedule and uses an application on her phone to store details of her visits and expenses. She records any notes from her visit on her mobile phone before leaving the customer and on her way home if she is using public transport or a taxi.

Figure 19.2 A typical person that might be used when developing a mobile app to keep track of a weekly schedule and associated expenses

Research into existing solutions to similar problems will provide information that can be used to justify an approach to the problem and identify suitable features to be incorporated into the solution. This process may also identify any limitations on the solution being proposed, for example to the scope of the solution—a program to draw mathematical transformations may be limited to a specific range of transformations or objects. You will need to explain and justify these limitations to the proposed solution.

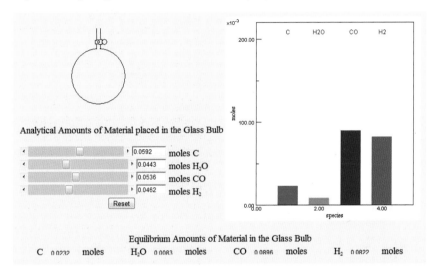

Figure 19.3 An example of a Java applet to demonstrate LeChatelier's principle; from this you might decide to use sliders for the inputs and bars for the output to allow the user to investigate various situations

Once the analysis of the research is completed, it is possible to specify the proposed solution and justified requirements, including any software or hardware requirements and the choice of programming language. The requirements for the solution provide the basis for identifying a set of measurable criteria that can be used to evaluate the effectiveness of the final product. These success criteria must relate to the requirements and the needs of the stakeholder, but should be measurable; that is, you can prove that they have been achieved through suitable test procedures.

Evidence

This section of the report to the examiner should include:

A description of the problem	**Do** provide an outline of what the problem is. **Do** provide an explanation of features required in a computer program to provide a solution to the problem. **Don't** rely on a simple statement of the problem.
Identify all the stakeholders	**Do** identify all the stakeholders as individuals, groups or persona. • For example, for a network utility program this will probably include a network manager and the network users affected by the utility. These stakeholders will require a specific program for a specific system. • For a mobile app this will include a persona, a description of the target audience using a fictional individual who typifies this target group and the owner of the service being served by the app. • For a science simulation or teaching program there will be a group containing a suitable teacher and students who fit the description for the target audience. Evidence for stakeholder involvement will come from a range of people, including a direct stakeholder and those who fit the description for a persona. **Do** keep returning to the stakeholders for input throughout the process. **Don't** identify an end user who cannot be contacted throughout the process.

Justify why the problem can be solved by computational methods	**Do** explain why the problem is suited to a computer program. **Do** explain the features of the problem that are amenable to a programmed solution. **Do** explain why the output from the solution is valuable to the stakeholder. • For a stock control program, this will include better management of stock, bringing potential savings on overstock or out-of-date stock. • For a science simulation, it could be because it reinforces learning of certain concepts or simulates features that are difficult to create in a laboratory. • For computer games or utilities, explain the interest from the stakeholders in the game or the need for the utility. **Don't** simply state that you are going to create a program because it is needed. You must justify your decisions.
Research	**Do** provide detailed research into existing solutions to similar problems. **Do** show that the research identifies features that can be adapted for use in the proposed solution. **Do** show how the research provides insight into the proposed solution and how the features to be used are appropriate. **Don't** rely on your own input for the solution to a problem. **Don't** rely on an interview with an end user for all of your research into the problem.
Features of the proposed solution	**Do** identify the features of the proposed solution. **Do** identify any limitations on the proposed solution. • Some problems may be too large to complete in the time allowed. • It may be appropriate to identify desirable features that will not be included in the solution (these can be revisited in the evaluation). **Do** be realistic about what can be achieved in the time allowed. **Don't** attempt to solve problems that are too complex to complete in the time allowed
Software and hardware requirements	**Do** specify any hardware requirements for your solution. • If there are only limited requirements, specify the minimum hardware required to implement the solution. **Do** specify any software requirements for your solution. • If any additional software is required or if the solution only works with specific versions of software, identify this. **Do** identify any additional utilities that will be required to implement the solution. **Don't** list all the software available simply to justify a choice. **Don't** simply identify what software you are using.
Success criteria	Success criteria should link the stakeholder requirements to a test plan and will be used with evidence of testing to evaluate the final product. **Do** specify the success criteria for the proposed solution. • These must be measureable criteria based on the stakeholder requirements. **Do** specify success criteria that can be demonstrated through testing. **Don't** specify vague subjective criteria, such as a colourful interface or easy or quick to use.

Chapter 20

Design

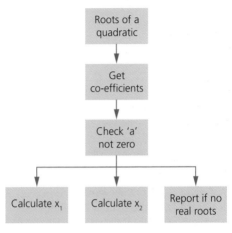

Figure 20.1 An example of top-down analysis of a problem

The problem identified will include some complexity and it will not be possible to code it as a simple linear program. It is important the problem be broken down into its component parts before attempting to create a design for a solution. Systematically decompose the problem until it is a series of solvable sub-problems suitable for a computational solution. Typically this will be a set of identified procedures needed to complete the solution.

These procedures will need to be completed in a specific order to solve the problem and this provides the detailed structure for the solution to be developed. These procedures and how they are linked must be fully described using suitable **algorithms**. The algorithms must be able to describe the solution in detail, showing how the program will solve each of the individual sub-problems and how these sub-problems are combined into a single solution for the whole problem. The algorithms should be detailed enough to hand on to another programmer to complete the project.

Example

An algorithm to calculate the roots of a quadratic equation of the form ax^2+bx+c

```
Input the coefficients a, b and c
Calculate d = sqrt(b²—4ac)
X₁ = —(b+d)/2a
X₂= —(b—d)/2a
```

Check:

For the quadratic x^2-3x+2, the coefficients are a=1. B=−3, c=2.

Variable(s)	a,b,c	d	X_1	X_2
Value	1, −3, 2	Sqrt(9−8)=1	−(−3+1)/2 =2/2 = 1	−(−3−1)/2 =4/2 = 2

$(x-1)(x-2) = x2-3x+2$

Programs create output from inputs by processing the data. Use the requirements for the program to identify the necessary outputs and consequently derive the necessary inputs and processing. Justifying the choices made and providing an outline demonstration of how these algorithms define a solution is important. Input and output is the means of communication with the end user of a program. These usability features should be chosen carefully and the choices justified in terms of

Including solutions to a quadratic equation

For a program that includes the solutions to a quadratic equation some decisions need to be made:

- Are non-integer coefficients allowed?
- Are we interested in non-real roots?
- Will we accept a=0; that is, a simple linear equation?
- If we are only accepting coefficients that are integers, some validation on the input values is required and this needs to be checked with real values to make sure they are rejected.
- For real roots only a check that b2>=4ac is required and values such as 1,2,4 should return an error message such as 'this equation has no real roots'.
- If we want to ignore linear equations then a=0 must be validated and rejected

the stakeholder requirements. For a simulation, for example, the user will need to set starting conditions. Will these be typed or selected from a list or set using an on-screen dial or slider? The decision will be the result of choices made for the user interface for the program.

The solution will be processing data and it is vitally important to select appropriate data types, suitable data structures, necessary validation and variable names that identify their purpose. These data items will need suitable test data to be used during the development process to ensure the processing produces the desired results and the validation rejects unacceptable values.

Evidence

This section of the report to the examiner should include the following:

Decompose the problem	**Do** provide evidence of decomposing the problem into smaller problems suitable for computational solution. **Do** provide evidence of a systematic approach, explaining and justifying each step in the process. • A table showing how each problem is broken down or a description of the process will be suitable. **Don't** simply state the problem as a single process.
Structure of the solution	**Do** provide a detailed overview of the structure of the solution.
Algorithms	**Do** provide a set of algorithms to describe each of the sub-problems. **Do** show how these algorithms fit together to form a complete solution to the problem. **Do** show how the algorithms have been tested to show that they work as required. **Don't** simply provide an outline data flow. **Don't** provide code or reverse engineered code as an algorithm.
Usability features	**Do** describe with justification the usability features of the proposed solution. **Do** explain and justify the design of any user interface or interface with another system. **Don't** spend ages creating colourful drawings of the user interface.
Key variables and structures	**Do** identify and justify the key variables. **Do** explain and justify the data structures that are to be used in the solution. **Do** describe and justify any validation required.
Test data for development	**Do** identify and justify any test data to be used during development. • Identify appropriate data that can be shown to test the functionality of the program for development testing purposes. **Don't** create a full test plan for this stage; this is data to be used at each stage of the development process.
Test data for beta testing	**Do** identify and justify test data to be used post-development to ensure the system meets the success criteria. **Do** identify data that is designed to test the robustness of the solution; good testing attempts to break the program. **Don't** create a test plan for this at this stage; the data will be used in a final test plan for the product at the post-development testing stage.

Development

Introduction

Developing a computer program is an iterative process. Each procedure should be developed and tested then modified as necessary before moving on to the next one, using an agile development process to create your solution. In real life this process would be completed in consultation with the client and stakeholders. The design should have included a description of the procedures and the order in which they should be developed. Follow this process through, providing evidence of the testing at each stage. However, as with all development exercises, results of testing may provide insights or highlight problems with the original plan. It is perfectly acceptable to modify this plan during development, as informed by the testing. The development should be a narrative on the process showing each stage of the development,

the testing carried out with results, any modifications to that section or procedure and any modifications to the overall plan.

Code should be modular in nature, with each section of the code explained and suitably annotated to explain its purpose. To aid future maintenance of the code, it is important this annotation is clear and the variables are suitably named to indicate their purpose, with suitable validation to ensure the program works under all foreseeable circumstances. Sensible and meaningful variable names are just one way to make a program maintainable. It is important the code is presented with full annotation, in modular form and with detailed annotation to ensure it can be maintained by another programmer.

Example

If you are writing a program that includes a function to return the real roots of a quadratic, write the function separately within a suitable structure to test that it works using designed test data.

```
import math
#Define the function to calculate the roots of the quadratic
def quad(a,b,c):
    d=math.sqrt(b**2-4*a*c)
    root1=(-b+d)/2*a
    root2=(-b-d)2*a
    return root1,root2
# check that the x squared coefficient is not zero
a=0
while a==0:
    a=int(input('Input the x squared coefficient'))
b=int(input('Input the x coefficient'))
c=int(input('Input the constant coefficient'))
#Check that there are real roots
if b**2-4*a**c<0:
    print('This equation has no real roots')
else:
    print('Roots are ' ,quad(a,b,c))
```

This segment of code includes the routine necessary to check for real roots and the function and that the *x* squared coefficient a is non-zero. These key points are identified using suitable annotation. In this case, the variables *a*, *b*, *c* and *d* are those used in mathematics and appropriately named. The variables used to return the values of the root could be called *x1* and *x2* but it is clearer here to use *root1* and *root2*.

This code segment should be tested with the data from the design section, including testing for a=0 and situations with no real roots, as well as with data that returns a known result.

Test for a=0

Test for 1,2,4, which has no real roots:

```
●  ○  ●                          Python Shell
Python 3.2.3 (v3.2.3:3d0686d90f55, Apr 10 2012, 11:25:50)
[GCC 4.2.1 (Apple Inc. build 5666) (dot 3)] on darwin
Type "copyright", "credits" or "license()" for more information.
>>> ============================== RESTART ==============================
>>>
Input the x squared coefficient1
Input the x coefficient2
Input the constant coefficient4
This equation has no real roots
>>>
```

Figure 21.1 Test 1

Entering 0 for a is ignored as expected and the set of data 1, 2, 4 returns the error message 'This equation has no real roots', as expected.

Test for typical value 1,−3,2 which should return 2 and 1

```
●  ○  ●                          Python Shell
Python 3.2.3 (v3.2.3:3d0686d90f55, Apr 10 2012, 11:25:50)
[GCC 4.2.1 (Apple Inc. build 5666) (dot 3)] on darwin
Type "copyright", "credits" or "license()" for more information.
>>> ============================== RESTART ==============================
>>>
Input the x squared coefficient1
Input the x coefficient-3
Input the constant coefficient2
Roots are  (2.0, 1.0)
>>> |
```

Figure 21.2 Test 2

This returns 2 and 1 as expected.

This function can now be used within the program.

Evidence

This section of the report to the examiner should include the following:

Iterative development	**Do** provide evidence of iterative development showing how the complete program was developed stage by stage. **Do** provide evidence showing how each section of the program was coded and tested. **Don't** simply supply completed code for the program as evidence.
Prototyping	**Do** provide prototype versions of the program at each stage of the process that show the annotated and explained code. **Do** provide evidence of testing at each stage using the test data identified in the design section.
Annotated modular code	**Do** annotate the code at each stage of the process. **Do** use meaningful names for all variables, structures and modules. **Do** provide code in a modular form; simple linear code is unlikely to be sufficient for this unit. **Do** provide the code as separate modules. **Don't** simply supply the complete code for the program as evidence; the code must be developed in suitable stages.
Validation	**Do** supply evidence of validation. **Do** supply evidence that the validation has been tested and works as expected. **Do** supply evidence that all testing covers a wide range of valid and invalid inputs and situations.
Reviews	**Do** review each stage of the process in the development phase, summarising what has been done and how it was tested. **Do** explain any changes required and any modifications to the design of the solution that result from the testing.

Chapter 22

Evaluation

Introduction

Once the development is complete, the program needs to be tested against the original success criteria using typical and atypical data. The program needs to be tested to ensure it fulfils the brief and that it is robust. Test using typical data, including extreme values to ensure the product works as expected and meets the success criteria established as part of the design. Use atypical data to ensure the program does not fall over easily. Good testing will attempt to break the program and conditions that cause the program to fail should be explored and reported, along with any suggestions for remedial action that might be taken, or even reported with the remedial action that has been taken.

Example

A program that includes the solution of a quadratic equation

Typical success criteria for a program that includes the solution of a quadratic equation might include:

- does not accept an x squared coefficient of 0
- returns a message if there are no real roots for the equation
- returns values for the roots of the equation.

The testing completed as part of the development demonstrates that this is the case and the evaluation should cross-reference these tests with the success criteria.

Success criteria	Met?	Evidence	Comment
Does not accept an x squared coefficient of 0	yes	Test 1	
Message if there are no real roots for the equation	yes	Test 1	
Returns values for the roots of the equation	yes	Test 2	

It is quite possible for the plans to have changed during development and these changes should be commented upon and any unmet criteria acknowledged and explained. Future maintenance of a program is an important issue and the evaluation should consider the limitations of the solution and potential developments, and indicate how these might be addressed.

Evidence

This section of the report to the examiner should include the follow:

Testing	**Do** provide evidence of testing on the completed solution. **Do** provide evidence that the system functions as designed. **Do** provide evidence that the system is robust and will not fall over easily. • Show that you have tried to break the program. **Do** cross-reference the test evidence against the success criteria from the analysis section to evaluate how well the solution meets these criteria.
Usability features	**Do** show how the usability features have been tested to make sure they meet the stakeholders' needs.
Evaluation	**Do** comment on how well the solution matches the requirements. **Do** comment on any changes that were made to the design during the development stage. **Do** comment on any unmet criteria or features and comment on how these might be achieved in future development. **Do** comment on any additional features that might be useful and how these might be approached. **Don't** comment on the development process and anything you learned or how much you enjoyed it.
Maintenance	**Do** discuss future maintenance of the program and any limitations in the current version. **Do** discuss how the program might be modified to meet any additional requirements or changing requirements. **Do** comment on the maintenance features included in the program and report.

Glossary

Algorithm   A step-by-step procedure for performing a calculation.   2, 9, 15, 21, 35, 37, 49, 99, 117, 133, 158, 187, 204, 226, 241, 255

Attribute   A column in a table, equivalent to a field, is an attribute of the entity.   156, 190

Bit rate   The space available for each sample measured in kilobits/s (128 kbits/s uses 128 kilobits for each second of sampled sound).   144

BRA   Branch always. This is a jump instruction that is always executed.   37, 86, 125

BRP   Branch if the value in the accumulator is positive.   37, 86, 125

Build   This term refers to all the actions that a programmer would take to produce a finished working program. It includes writing the source code, compiling it, linking it, testing it, packaging it for the target environment and producing correct and up-to-date documentation.   45, 116, 209

Colour depth   The number of bits used for each dot or pixel. The more bits, the greater the number of colours that can be represented.   143

Computational thinking   A problem-solving approach that borrows techniques from computer science, notably abstraction, problem decomposition and the development of algorithms. Computational thinking is applied to a wide variety of problem domains and not just to the development of computer systems.   13, 23, 35, 130, 251

Data corruption   The opposite of data integrity. Data corruption can be caused by various technically based events such as:
- hardware failure
- software error
- electrical glitches.

It can also result from operator error or malpractice.   195

Data dictionary   Metadata; that is, data about data. In a relational database, it is the sum total of information about the tables, the relationships and all the other components that make the database function.   194

Data integrity   The maintenance of a state of consistency in a data store. It broadly means that the data in a data store reflects the reality that it represents. It also means that the data is as intended and fit for purpose.   195

Data redundancy   An unnecessary repetition of data. This is avoided in databases because of the risk of inconsistencies between different copies of the same data. In relational databases, avoiding data redundancy is largely achieved through the process of *data normalisation*.   189

Data security   Keeping data safe. Database software is designed to have in-built data security to minimise the risk of malpractice, though errors can still occur.   195

Datagram   A self-contained, independent entity of data that carries sufficient information to be routed from the source to the destination computer without reliance on earlier exchanges between this source and destination computer and the transporting network.   212

Decomposition   The breaking down of a problem into smaller parts that are easier to solve. The smaller parts can sometimes be solved recursively; that is, they can be run again and again until that part of the problem is solved.   15, 35

Direct discrimination   Treating someone with a protected characteristic less favourably than others.   240

Dynamic typing   Most compiled languages such as C++ require variables to be declared before they are used. At the time of declaration, the data type is assigned, so that a statement such as `int i` in C sets up a variable *i* as an integer variable that can then accept integer values during the running of the program. The advantage of this is that silly mistakes such as assigning the wrong data to a variable can be picked up by the compiler.
A dynamically typed language such as JavaScript does not need a prior declaration of a variable and it will create one when needed during the running of the program, assigning a data type according to what value is passed to the variable. This allows faster writing of the program but it is easier to make errors.   226

Encryption   The transformation of a message so that it is unintelligible to those unauthorised to view it.   218, 233

Entity   A real-world *thing* that is modelled in a database. It might be a physical object such as a student or a stock item in a shop or it might be an event such as a sale.   187

Exponent   The power to which the number in the mantissa is to be raised.   148

Functional programming A function, in mathematics, takes in a value or values and returns a value, for example:
double(4) would return 8
highestCommonFactor(36,24) would return 12
In functional programming, a description of the solution to a problem is built up through a collection of functions. Examples include Haskell and ML.   84

Heuristic An approach to problem solving that makes use of experience. It is not guaranteed to produce the best solution but it generally will produce a 'good enough' result. Heuristic methods are sometimes referred to as a 'rule of thumb'.
It is important to realise when 'good enough is good enough' and when it isn't.   34, 71

Hexadecimal A number system with a base of 16.   140, 204, 225

Immutable This means unchangeable. It is applied to certain entities – in the case on page 47, a Python string – to indicate that it cannot be changed by the program. A new string has to be made with the desired features to replace the old unchangeable string.   47, 156

Indirect discrimination Putting rules or arrangements in place that apply to everyone, but that put someone with a protected characteristic at an unfair disadvantage.   240

Instruction set The collection of opcodes a processor is able to decode and execute.   24, 85, 106, 109, 131

Logic programming Rather than stating what the program should do, in logic programming a problem is expressed as a set of facts (things that are always true) and rules (things that are true if particular facts are true). These facts and rules are then used to find a given goal. The most commonly used logic language is Prolog.   84

Mantissa The part of the floating point number that represents the significant digits of that number.   148

Master file A principal file held by an organisation that stores basic details about some crucial aspect of the business. It is generally a large file that tends not to change very often.
For a supermarket, it could be a stock file; for a school it could be a file of student details.   185

Metadata The information about the image that allows the computer to interpret the stored binary accurately to reproduce the image. This must contain the width and height in pixels and the colour depth in bpp (bits per pixel).   143

Most significant bit (MSB) The bit in a multiple-bit binary number with the largest value.   139, 151

Object-oriented programming A program made up of objects (custom-made data structures to represent often-used real-world entities) that interact. Object-oriented languages include Java and C++. Object-oriented programming is covered in more detail at the end of Chapter 6.   17, 84

One's complement Changing 0s to 1s and 1s to 0s in a binary number.   147

Procedural programming A program where instructions are given in sequence; selection is used to decide what a program does and iteration dictates how many times it does it. In procedural programming, programs are broken down into key blocks called procedures and functions. Examples of procedural languages include BASIC, C and Pascal.   84

Protocols The rules and standards governing how networks should function and communicate. Protocols apply to most aspects of a network.   212

Record A single unit of information in a database. It is normally made up of *fields*. So a student file would be made up of many records. Each record is about one student and holds fields such as student number, surname, date of birth, gender, and so on.   184

Relation In relational database terminology, a table is called a relation.   187

Reserved word A word that has a special meaning in the programming language and as such cannot be used as a variable name. Examples in many languages include if, else, while and for.   112

Resolution The number of pixels or dots per unit, for example dpi (dots per inch).   143, 230

Sample rate The number of times the sound is sampled per second, measured in Hz (100 Hz is 100 samples per second).   144

Scripting language An interpreted programming language that is designed to work inside some run-time environments, rather than generating object code that can be run directly from the operating system.
Examples of scripting languages include JavaScript, which runs inside a browser, and the shells of operating systems such as BASH.   225

Source code This is the code written in a programming language. It can be read and edited by other programmers. This is where the term 'open source' comes from; that is to say, software where the source code is openly available.   45, 106, 109, 226

Transaction A change in the state of a database. It can be the addition, amendment or deletion of data.   184

Transaction file A file of events that occur as part of the business of an organisation. Its contents are to a large extent unpredictable although they are usually in chronological order.   184

Tuple A row in a table, equivalent to a record. A tuple is data about one instance of the entity.   187

Index

Photo credits